Co
Dan L

MW00618585

Saints of the States

"Too few of the faithful in our great country are aware of the lives and sacrifices of the American Saints. Thank you for your latest book, *Saints of the States*."

Most Reverend Robert J. Baker
Bishop of Charleston
Co-author, *Cacique, A Novel of Florida's Heroic Mission History*

"Thank you in a special way for having invited me to do the Foreword for such a truly wonderful book. May God bless you for promoting His glory by honoring His saints! May many people be spiritually inspired by it to become 'saints' in their own situations!"

Father Andrew Apostoli CFR

Our Lady of Guadalupe, Hope for the World

"This book will instruct, encourage and inspire a wide variety of people in the Church and outside the Church. You may be a pro-life activist looking for signs of progress. You may be a priest seeking new ways to call your people to deeper faith. You may be a son or daughter of the Virgin Mary eager to find new ways to honor her. You may be someone considering abortion or wounded by it, and looking for hope. You may be away from the Church looking for a way back, or someone without any background in Catholicism but interested in finding out more. Whoever you are, give this book some of your time, and it will repay you abundantly."

Fr. Frank Pavone,
National Director Priests for Life

Our Lady of Guadalupe, Mother of Hope Video

"Stirring, gripping, comprehensive with moving testimonies!"

Reviews by producers Ted Flynn,
Dr. Tom Petrisko, Drew Mariani and
Ignatius Press

i

SAINTS

of the

STATES

Dan Lynch

Published by:
JKMI Press
144 Sheldon Road
St. Albans, VT 05478
www.JKMI.com

ISBN 0-9647988-7-5

iv

Contents

Foreword

Over 50 years ago, Archbishop Fulton J. Sheen, presently a Servant of God being considered for canonization, wrote an editorial entitled, "America Needs a Saint." He believed that a canonized saint would show that the Catholic Church in the United States had reached a full level of maturity since from its spiritual soil as from a seedbed; a man or woman would emerge bearing the fruit of heroic virtue! Such a saint, living in the American culture, would serve as someone to inspire and guide us personally on the journey of holiness. As Pope John Paul II said, "In the saints we see in a concrete way the working of the Holy Spirit."

Dan Lynch, in his fine book, *Saints of the States*, demonstrates clearly that the United States can now boast of a growing number of saints and saints-to-be. His book is a wonderful contribution for Catholics and others to appreciate the rich spiritual heritage we now possess in the lives of so many heroic men and women who have either come to or grown up in our land.

Beginning with the rich deposit of the Catholic Faith brought by the initial discoverers of the "New World" and solidified by the powerful influence of the apparitions of Our Lady of Guadalupe, Queen of America, the author traces the historical development, both secular and religious, through the centuries. He reminds us of how later Catholic explorers and missionaries courageously spread the faith further, and how the soil for sanctity was enriched by the blood of martyrs, especially the Jesuit martyrs of North America.

This is followed by the accounts of individual saints who helped mold the Church in America, significantly influencing the beginnings of our nation. Saints Rose Philippine Duchesne, Theodore Guerin, John Neumann and Frances Xavier Cabrini all immigrated to the United States and by their deep personal religious spirit and witness left a lasting impact. Other saints were native-born, such as convert St. Elizabeth Ann Seton and the other cradle Catholics like St. Katherine Drexel who used their God-given gifts zealously to serve the Lord and His Church. Finally, the author presents hoped-for saints, like Dorothy Day, to show that the Church will continue to harvest rich fruits of sanctity far into the future.

Dan Lynch has produced a very enjoyable, enriching and inspiring book. It challenges us to do in our times what these holy men and women did in their own. Their witness of heroic faith, hope and love show us that the highest stages of sanctity are still possible within, despite the secularized culture of our day. Like Jesus, they were "signs of contradiction" to the distortions of their time as we must be in our own.

In a real sense, these saintly men and women can say to us what St. Paul wrote to his converts at Corinth, "I laid a foundation as a wise master-builder might do, and now someone else is building upon it." (1 Cor. 3:10). That "someone else" is you and me. Following the example of these saints who have gone before us and building on what they have laid as a spiritual foundation, we must work to complete here in the United States what Pope John Paul II called "the civilization of love."

I thank Dan Lynch for his wonderful contribution that reminds all of us of the rich spiritual legacy we possess in the Catholic Church in the United States.

Father Andrew Apostoli CFR

Preface

Short biographies of heroes have attracted humans ever since Plutarch's 46 *Parallel Lives* written in the second century. Pope John Paul II recognized this and said that what is needed today is "a collection of short biographies of the Saints and the Beatified of America, which can shed light on and stimulate the response to the universal call to holiness in America." (Pope John Paul II, *The Church in America*, No. 37).

I hope that this book fulfills that need. We need heroes to imitate and to give us hope. The saints do that for us. I have included short biographies of St. Juan Diego and all of the saints and blesseds of the United States of America. These saints are those who lived, died and were buried in the United States. St. Juan Diego is included because he was the first chronological saint in the New World through his service to Our Lady of Guadalupe, Queen and Mother of America. Native American Blessed Kateri Tekakwitha, who lived in the states but died in Canada, is included because she is a fruit of the United States martyrs.

When we think of the saints, we often think of miracles, signs, wonders and mystical writings. In the saints of the states we have none of this. We simply have holiness and the practice of the virtues in ordinary people in an extraordinary way. They came from all walks of life – men and women, single, married, priests and religious. Their fruits are the conversions of the Native Americans, the establishment of American Catholic religious orders, parishes, school systems, hospitals, orphanages and the welcoming, teaching and works of mercy for the marginalized – the Native Americans, the African-Americans, immigrants and lepers.

I have placed the saints and blesseds of the states in their chronological order and in their historical context in order to better understand them and the times in which they lived. For ease of understanding, I have designated places by their current names with the original names in parentheses. We gain the true meaning of history when we read it through the lives of the saints. It is in the saints that God raises up in any given time and place that we can see the sovereign Lord of history working quietly beneath the passing parade of earthly kings and kingdoms.

St. Isaac Jogues had a vision at Auriesville (Ossernenon), New York, when he was a captive of the Mohawk Indians. He later described the vision in a letter. He had the vision in the grove where he prayed and seemed to be in the city of his birth in France. Then he entered the shop of a bookseller and was given a book. He heard a voice saying, "This book contains the lives of men illustrious for their sanctity."

Like the book of St. Isaac Jogues' vision, this book too "contains the lives of men (and women) illustrious for their sanctity," including his own. May their lives be examples of holiness for you to follow.

Dan Lynch

Introduction

"Today the Church needs saints. This calls for our combating our attachment to comforts that lead us to choose a comfortable and insignificant mediocrity. Each one of us has the possibility to be a saint, and the way to holiness is prayer. Holiness is, for each of us, a simple duty." Blessed Mother Teresa

Heroes

Simon and Garfunkel sang *Mrs. Robinson*, the classic song from the movie *The Graduate*. They lamented the lack of American heroes and sang, "Where have you gone, Joe DiMaggio? A nation turns its lonely eyes to you."

However, the true American heroes are not sport figures, but Catholic saints. We should turn our "lonely eyes" to them and follow their good examples, virtues and works. They are our true friends and are alive in Heaven with God. They are models of holiness for us. They can help us just like friends on earth by their prayerful intercession on our behalf. They give us courage and hope.

Pope Paul VI said, "Being a saint means being perfect, with a perfection that attains the highest level that a human being can reach." He continued:

> This perfection is attained because a saint is a human creature fully conformed to the will of God. A saint is a person in whom all sin – the principle of death – is canceled out and replaced by the living splendor of divine grace.
>
> The analysis of the concept of sanctity brings us to recognize in a soul that mingling of two elements that are entirely different, but which come together to produce a single effect: sanctity. One of these elements is the human and moral element, raised to the degree of heroism; heroic virtues are always required by the Church for the recognition of a person's sanctity. The second element is the mystical element, which expresses the measure and form of divine action in the person chosen by God to realize in herself – always in an original way –

the coming of Christ. (Pope Paul VI, *Canonization Homily of St. Elizabeth Ann Seton*, September 14, 1975).

Canonizations are solemn proclamations by the Church that a saint practiced heroic virtue and lived in fidelity to God's grace so they are proposed to us as models and intercessors. (*Catechism of the Catholic Church, hereafter "CCC,"* 828). The reasons for the canonizations of saints are to know them, to imitate their heroic virtues, to invoke their intercession and protection and to praise God who is wonderful in His saints.

Models and Intercessors

"Being more closely united to Christ, those who dwell in Heaven fix the whole Church more firmly in holiness. They do not cease to intercede with the Father for us, as they proffer the merits which they acquired on earth through the one mediator between God and men, Christ Jesus. So by their fraternal concern is our weakness greatly helped." (*CCC* 956).

We learn from the saints as models of holiness, particularly from the all-holy Virgin Mary, whom the liturgy of the Church celebrates in the rhythms of the Feast Days of the saints. (*CCC* 2030). But it's not merely for their models of holiness that we honor them but rather to be in communion with them to join us to Christ, from whom as from its fountain and head issues all holiness. (*CCC* 957). All Christians in any state or walk of life are called to this holiness, the fullness of Christian life and to the perfection of charity through the practice of the virtues. (*CCC* 2013).

The Virtues

There are three theological virtues of faith, hope, and charity. These theological virtues are the foundation of Christian moral activity and they inform and give life to all the moral virtues. They are infused by God into our souls to make us holy and dispose us to live in a relationship with Him. They have God for their origin, their motive, and their object – God known by faith, God hoped in and God loved for His own sake. (*CCC* 813).

There are also four Cardinal virtues of prudence, justice, fortitude and temperance, around which all other human virtues are grouped. (*CCC*

1805). The human virtues are rooted in the theological virtues, which adapt our faculties for participation in the divine nature. They dispose us to live in a relationship with God. They have the One and Triune God for their origin, motive, and object. (*CCC* 1812).

Prudence is the virtue that disposes practical reason to discern our true good in every circumstance and to choose the right means of achieving it. Justice is the virtue that consists in the constant and firm will to give their due to God and neighbor. Fortitude is the moral virtue that ensures firmness in difficulties and constancy in the pursuit of the good. It strengthens the resolve to resist temptations and to overcome obstacles in the moral life. The virtue of fortitude enables one to conquer fear, even fear of death, and to face trials and persecutions. Temperance is the virtue that moderates the attraction of pleasures and provides balance in the use of created goods. (*CCC* 1806-1809).

Human virtues are firm attitudes, stable dispositions, and habitual perfections of intellect and will that govern our actions, order our passions, and guide our conduct according to reason and faith. They make possible ease, self-mastery and joy in leading a morally good life. The virtuous person is one who freely practices the good.

The moral virtues are acquired by human effort. They are the fruit and seed of morally good acts; they dispose all the powers of the human being for communion with divine love. (*CCC* 1804). Human virtues acquired by education, by deliberate acts and by a perseverance ever-renewed in repeated efforts are purified and elevated by divine grace. With God's help, they forge character and give facility in the practice of the good. The virtuous person is happy to practice them. (*CCC* 1810).

The practice of all the virtues is animated and inspired by charity, which binds everything together in perfect harmony; it is the form of the virtues; it articulates and orders them among themselves; it is the source and the goal of their Christian practice. Charity upholds and purifies our human ability to love and raises it to the supernatural perfection of divine love. (*CCC* 1827). The saints practiced all of the virtues to a heroic degree.

The saints of the states were not mystics or great wonder workers. They were active in the apostolates of evangelization, teaching, works of mercy and founding of orders. God is glorified in these saints because in His eyes He sees only Christ's life reproduced in them. They are examples of holiness for our encouragement, proposed to us as models to be imitated and lifted up for our veneration. Their lives are written so that we may see in them model examples of the practices of virtues to a heroic degree whom we may invoke for their intercession for our needs.

The Communion of Saints

Christians have professed their belief in the "communion of saints" ever since the formulation of the Nicene Creed in 325 A.D. Even though they are dead, the saints are still a part of our community of the living. They are our companions in prayer and examples of holiness.

In the Preface for the Mass for All Saints Day, Catholics pray this prayer to God about His saints, "Their glory fills us with joy, and their communion with us in your Church gives us inspiration and strength." At every Mass Catholics pray to be worthy to join the saints "on whose constant intercession we rely for help." They help us by interceding with God on our behalf. We ask for their help just as we might ask a friend on Earth to pray for us.

Catholics keep images and statues of the saints, as their ancestors in the faith, to remind them of the saints' friendships and to inspire them to holiness. These reminders are like photographs of our deceased relatives that are kept for the same purposes. But saints are not simply pious plaster statues standing on pedestals. Moreover, all of them do not come from the same mold. They were real unique human beings who suffered from the human condition and their own faults and failings. They had many of the same human problems as we do. We can learn a lot from reading about them.

The lives of the saints show us how we too can follow Jesus who said, "I am the Way, the Truth and the Life." (Jn. 14:6). We can learn how to live, how to love, how to suffer and how to discern God's specific will for us. Sainthood is not reserved for only a few. It excludes no one. It is not the privilege of a spiritual elite. We can all aspire to sainthood because it is a goal within our capacity aided by grace.

A saint is an authentic, concrete person. His or her testimony of life attracts, beseeches and draws, because it manifests a transparent human experience, full of the presence of Christ.

A saint is an ordinary person who knows, loves and serves God to the best of his or her ability in the here and now. The lives of the saints make good stories. They led real, believable, exciting and human lives. They are our models in holiness and each one of us is called to this same holiness.

The Vocation of Holiness

The beatification of Mother Teresa of Calcutta highlighted the fact that there is only one authentic greatness in the world – holiness. This was evident from the multitude that filled St. Peter's Square in Rome. What other person in the world has been so honored? Such a large crowd gathered out of admiration and love for a woman who was not noted for her beauty, career, family, wealth, genius, artistic or athletic achievement, but simply for her holiness. "One drop of holiness," said the musician Gounod, "is worth more than an ocean of genius." Holiness does not end with time, but lasts eternally.

Pope John Paul II asked, "What is the vocation of a Christian? The answer is demanding: The vocation of a Christian is holiness. It is a vocation which has its roots in Baptism and is proposed anew by the other sacraments, and principally by the Eucharist. You are called to holiness in every season of life . . . in the spring of youth, in the summer of maturity, then in the autumn and winter of old age and at last at the hour of death and even beyond death." (*Address*, Croatia, June 8, 2003).

To encourage us to respond to this vocation and simple duty of holiness, Pope John Paul II canonized more saints and proclaimed more blesseds than all of his predecessors together since 1588, when procedures for these causes were first instituted. He presided at 147 beatification ceremonies, proclaiming 1,338 blesseds, and 51 canonization ceremonies, canonizing 482 saints. He personally canonized St. Juan Diego and two of the saints of the United States, St. Rose Philippine Duchesne and St. Katharine Drexel. He also personally beatified *all* of the blesseds of the United States: Blessed Kateri Tekakwitha, Blessed Junipero Serra, (now Saint) Theodore Guerin, Blessed Francis Xavier Seelos, (now Saint) Damien De Veuster and Blessed Marianne Cope.

The Canonization Process

The Canonization process to declare a person a saint has only been used since the tenth century. Before then, saints were chosen by public acclaim, starting with the first martyrs of the early Church. Though this was a very democratic way to recognize saints, some saints' stories were distorted by legend. Gradually, the bishops and finally the Vatican took over authority for approving saints.

In 1983, Pope John Paul II made major changes in the canonization process. The process begins after the death of a Catholic whom people regard as holy. It requires the careful study of the life of a candidate, his or her writings, eyewitness testimony of those who knew the candidate and the examination of any miracles attributed to the candidate's intercession. Five years must pass since the death of the candidate before a cause can begin, unless the Pope waives this requirement. This is to allow greater balance and objectivity and to allow temporary emotions to dissipate.

The canonization process is stringent and usually lasts several years. The process begins with the Bishop of the diocese where the candidate for canonization died. The Bishop must first obtain permission from the Congregation for the Causes of Saints in Rome after submitting a documented biography of the candidate, letters requesting the introduction of the cause for sainthood and his statement that the cause is timely and spiritually advantageous for the faithful.

If permission is granted, the candidate is given the title "Servant of God." This title is a declaration that the candidate led a life of demonstrable holiness. Then the Bishop appoints a postulator or promoter of the cause and forms a diocesan tribunal to begin the investigation of the candidate's writings and Christian virtues and determine whether they were heroic or whether the candidate was a martyr. This is called the "diocesan phase."

When the diocesan phase is completed, all evidence is submitted by the postulator to the Congregation for the Causes of Saints in Rome. The postulator presents a document called a *Positio* that demonstrates the exercise of heroic virtues by the candidate. Except in the case of martyrdom, which usually requires proof that the person's death was primarily related to his or her Christian faith, it is necessary to determine that the candidate is a model of holiness in all aspects of life. He or she must have lived the theological virtues of faith, hope and charity as well as the Cardinal virtues of prudence, justice, fortitude and temperance to a heroic degree. Nine theologians then review the *Positio* and vote whether or not the cause should proceed. If the majority of them approve, the Cardinal and Bishop members of the Congregation examine the cause. If they also approve, the Prefect of the Congregation sends all materials related to the cause to the Pope. If he gives his approval, the Servant of God receives the title of "Venerable" and the cause proceeds.

If martyrdom or a miracle is attributed to the intercession of the Venerable after death and a thorough investigation, the Venerable may be beatified and receive the title of "Blessed" by the Pope. A miracle is an extraordinary event that can be witnessed by the senses but cannot be explained according to the laws of nature or human science. It is attributed to divine intervention through the mediation of the candidate whom the faithful invoked. Both religious and scientific authorities must scrutinize all alleged miracles. A board of five doctors must unequivocally determine that no other possible explanation for a cure exists for alleged medical miracles and all cures must be instantaneous and complete. A miracle is used as a proof that the Venerable can effectively intercede before God and obtain special graces.

A second miracle is required for canonization and also a miracle for a martyr. The miracle must occur after the Blessed's beatification. Once canonized, the Blessed receives the title of "Saint" from the Pope that certifies that the person lived a holy life, is in Heaven and is to be honored by the universal Church. Canonization does not "make" a person a saint; it only recognizes what God's grace has already done through the cooperation of the candidate.

The Saints of the States

The saints and blesseds of the United States have received their recognition through their canonizations and beatifications. They were both men and women, priests, nuns, virgins, religious brothers, (René Goupil) single, (Jean de la Lande) and married (Elizabeth Ann Seton and Pierre Toussaint). They represent all of the states of life recognized by the Church: single, married, religious and clergy. Four of them lived as recently as the 20th century. Jesus said, "You shall know them by their fruits . . . every good tree brings forth good fruit." (Mt. 7:16-17). We know the saints by their fruits and each saint's chapter is ended by setting forth the "good fruits" of that saint.

St. Juan Diego and the 10 saints and four blesseds of the United States are listed in order of their chronological births, with the dates of their deaths, their canonizations or beatifications and their Feast Days:

	Death	Date of Canonization or Beatification	Feast Day
St. Juan Diego	1548	July 30, 2002	December 9
St. René Goupil	1642	June 29, 1930	October 19
St. Isaac Jogues	October 18, 1646	June 29, 1930	October 19
St. Jean de la Lande	October 19, 1646	June 29, 1930	October 19
Blessed Kateri Tekakwitha	April 17, 1680	June 22, 1980	July 14
Blessed Junipero Serra	August 28, 1784	September 25, 1988	July 1
St. Elizabeth Ann Seton	January 4, 1821	September 14, 1975	January 4
St. Rose Philippine Duchesne	November 18, 1852	July 3, 1988	November 18
St. Theodore Guerin	May 14, 1856	October 15, 2006	October 3
St. John Neumann	January 5, 1860	June 19, 1977	January 5
Blessed Francis Xavier Seelos	October 4, 1867	April 9, 2000	October 5
Saint Damien de Veuster	April 15, 1889	October 11, 2009	May 10
St. Frances Xavier Cabrini	December 22, 1917	July 7, 1946	November 13
Blessed Marianne Cope	August 9, 1918	May 14, 2005	August 9
St. Katherine Drexel	March 3, 1955	October 1, 2000	March 3

Many people think that saints must perform great miracles during their lifetimes – healing the blind, the deaf and the lame, delivering demons, and raising the dead. None of the saints of the states performed any miracles like these during their lifetimes. They simply performed their apostolic work, did their daily duty, prayed, and practiced penance, chastity and a virtuous life. They were ordinary Americans, if not by birth, by adoption, they had the "can do" spirit of Americans and they accomplished typically American great works. When St. Katharine Drexel did the Grand Tour of Europe with her family, her governess wrote to her and expressed her hope that she would return as a loyal American. Katharine replied,

"Don't be worried on that score, Miss Cassidy, for I am *now* and will be more of an American than ever on my return. I love my country with all my heart, the people, the habits, the cities, everything!"
God is glorified in His saints. They are our models of holiness, our friends, our intercessors of strength and protection and they encourage us as pilgrims on our way to share eternal life with them as we praise God with them. This role of the saints is expressed in Preface 69 of the Mass for Holy Men and Women in which Catholics pray, "Father . . . you are glorified in your saints, for their glory is the crowning of your gifts. In their lives on earth, you give us an example. In our communion with them, you give us their friendship. In their prayer for the Church, you give us strength and protection. This great company of witnesses spurs us on to victory, to share their prize of everlasting glory, through Jesus Christ our Lord, with angels and archangels and the whole company of saints we sing our unending hymn of praise."

Pope John Paul II said, "The saints are the true expression and the finest fruits of America's Christian identity. In them, the encounter with the living Christ is so deep and demanding . . . that it becomes a fire which consumes them completely and impels them to build His kingdom. . . . Their example of boundless dedication to the cause of the Gospel must not only be saved from oblivion, but must become better and more widely known among the faithful of the continent."(Pope John Paul II, *The Church in America*, No. 15). My hope is that this book contributes to that knowledge.

Our Lady of Guadalupe, Queen and Mother of America

*"We are certain that as long as
Our Lady of Guadalupe is recognized as Queen and as Mother,
the Americas and Mexico will be safe."*
Pope Pius XII

Part One

The First Evangelization of America

1. The New World: Columbus Discovers America

"They shall proclaim my glory among the nations." (Is. 66:19).

"Tierra! Tierra!" ("Land! Land!"), shouted the lookout, Rodrigo de Triana, from the boat *Pinta* as his eyes gazed upon the white sand cliff that gleamed on the western horizon in the light of the full moon. It was October 12, 1492 when he saw the eastern coast of one of the islands of the Bahamas later named San Salvador (Holy Savior) by the leader of the expedition. His name was Christopher (Christ bearer) Columbus.

Ever since Marco Polo had discovered land trade routes to the Indies in the 13th century, Europeans were consumers of silk, spices, pearls and gold from China, India and Japan. The trade crossroads for the 10,000-mile overland caravan network from the Indies to the eastern Mediterranean Sea was the city of Constantinople. In 1453, the Ottoman Turks conquered Constantinople and the crossroads was closed to trade. The need arose for a water route to the Indies. Christopher Columbus was confident that he could find it. He spent seven years persistently following the Spanish Court from castle to castle to persuade them that he could do it.

Finally, Ferdinand and Isabella, the King and Queen of Spain, gave their backing for an exploratory voyage to discover a water route to the Indies. Later, in a codicil to her Last Will and Testament, Isabella declared that her principal intention in the discovery of the Indies was "the

1

evangelization and conversion of the natives of those places to the Catholic Faith." When many Europeans later debated whether indigenous peoples were full human beings, Isabella insisted that the Native Americans were her subjects and should be treated justly.

Columbus wanted to find the fabulous treasures that used to come over the land trade routes and to convert the natives to Catholicism. He believed that he had a divine mission to bring the natives to the knowledge of the one true God.

In his *Book of Prophecies*, Columbus wrote, "It was the Lord who put into my mind that it would be possible to sail from here to the Indies. All who heard of my project rejected it with laughter, ridiculing me. For the execution of the journey to the Indies, I did not make use of intelligence, mathematics or maps. It is simply the fulfillment of what Isaiah had prophesied, 'I will . . . send fugitives to the nations, to the distant coastlands that have never heard of my fame, or seen my glory; and they shall proclaim my glory among the nations'." (Is. 66:19).

Catholics had been finally united in Spain after the Reconquest in 1492. The Moslems had been there since the 8th century until the uniting of the kingdoms of Navarre and Aragon formed the country of Spain under King Ferdinand and Queen Isabella. They destroyed the Moslem kingdom of Granada, drove the Moslems out of Spain and ended seven centuries of their occupation. On January 2, 1492, their royal standards were placed on the towers of the Moslem citadel of Alhambra in Granada.

Columbus witnessed the Moslem surrender. He wrote in his Journal, "I saw the Moorish King come forth to the gates of the city and kiss the royal hands of Your Highnesses." They agreed to support his voyage of expedition, as Columbus recorded in his Journal, ". . . as Catholic Christians and Princes devoted to the Holy Christian Faith and the propagators thereof, and enemies of the sect of Mahomet and of all idolatries and heresies, [and they] resolved to send me Christopher Columbus to the said regions of India, to see the said princes and peoples and lands and [to observe] the disposition of them and of all, and the manner in which may be undertaken their conversion to our Holy Faith."

After receiving Holy Communion at St. George's Church, Columbus set sail from Palos "in the name of Jesus" on his flagship, the *Santa Maria* (Holy Mary), on August 3, 1492. Two months later on October 12, after the sailors said their evening prayers, sang the *Salve Regina* (The Hail Holy Queen, in honor of Mary) and went to bed, Rodrigo de

Triana sighted the island at two o'clock in the morning. Later as he landed on the shore, Columbus gave thanks to Our Lord, knelt on the ground, embraced it with tears of joy, arose and gave the island the name of San Salvador. He prayed, "O Lord, Almighty and everlasting God, by Thy holy Word Thou hast created the heavens, and the earth, and the sea; blessed and glorified be Thy Name, and praised be Thy Majesty, which hath deigned to use us, Thy humble servants, that Thy holy Name may be proclaimed in this second part of the earth."

Columbus planted the flag of Ferdinand and Isabella and claimed the islands for Spain. He said that the discovery was "not to be attributed to any merit of [his], but to the Holy Christian faith, and to the piety and religion of [his] Sovereigns." Since he believed that he had reached the Indies, he called the native Tainos "Indians."

When he returned to Spain, Columbus reported to Queen Isabella that there was not much promise of material wealth in the lands that he had discovered. She responded, "Although there would be nothing but stones, I would continue there while there may be souls to save." And so, she continued to send missionaries to save these souls. She and her husband also sent other explorers to the Indies besides Columbus. One of them was an Italian named Amerigo Vespucci. Later, Europeans read a book that told of his discoveries and they called all of the new lands "America."

Pope Alexander VI sent his congratulations to Ferdinand and Isabella on Columbus' discoveries. He wrote, "We heard . . . that Christopher Columbus . . . by divine aid, having used diligence, discovered while navigating in the Ocean, certain very remote islands and also mainland which had hitherto not been found by others; herein dwell multitudes of people living peaceably and . . . imbued with good morals; and the hope is entertained that if they were instructed, the name of Our Lord and Savior Jesus Christ might easily be introduced to the aforesaid lands and islands."

The evangelization of the Americas thus began with all of its successes, faults and failings. Sadly, many Native Americans died from smallpox and other diseases that the Europeans brought with them. Many Europeans respected the human dignity of the natives and desired their spiritual welfare through conversion by love to the one true God. Many others just wanted to use them through force for their own material gain. They were used in forced labor or enslaved. Many of them were tortured or killed.

On Christmas Day 1511 on the island of Hispaniola (Haiti and the Dominican Republic), Father Antonio de Montesimos preached against this to the settlers. He said, "By what right or justice do you keep these Indians in such horrible servitude? Are these not men? Have they not rational souls? Are you not bound to love them as you love yourselves?"

Eventually, gold and silver from the New World made Spain the wealthiest imperial power in the world. By 1519, approximately 10,000 Spaniards were living in the Caribbean. One of them was Hernan Cortes.

2. The Conquest of Cortes

"We must risk something for God!"
Hernan Cortes as he smote the eyes of the Aztec idol with a
metal bar at the top platform of their temple.

"I counted 100,000 skulls on one rack!" said Bernal Diaz referring to
the skulls of human sacrifice that he saw as he marched with Hernan
Cortes and his army. In 1519, they marched through the hot valleys and
the cold mountain passes of central Mexico upon the Aztec Indian capital
of Tenochtitlan with their native allies who had lived in long subjugation to
the Aztecs. Along the way, his soldiers witnessed bloodstained temples
of human sacrifice.

A horrified and outraged Cortes announced his army's mission. He
said, "We are obligated to exalt and increase our holy Catholic faith,
uproot idolatry and abolish sacrifices and the eating of human flesh, which
is so contrary to nature and so common here."

Ten years before, in 1509, the light of God pierced the darkness of
Aztec Mexico. An Indian princess had a mystical experience. While she
was in a coma, an angel with a black cross on his forehead led her to the
ocean shore. There he showed her ships with white sails emblazoned
with black crosses coming to the Aztec nation. The angel also told her
that strangers would conquer the Aztec nation and bring them to the
knowledge of the one true God. She came out of her coma and related
this strange experience to the Aztec rulers.

The princess' name was Papantzin, sister of the Aztec Emperor
Montezuma. His rule of the Aztec Empire over the subjugated and
oppressed Indian provinces of pre-Columbian Mexico was about to end.
He brooded over his sister's prophecy and awaited his fate. The prophecy
of Papantzin was soon to be realized.

Hernan Cortes was a Spanish soldier who was running a small plantation
in Cuba when the opportunity arose to lead a voyage of exploration to
Mexico. In 1519, he came to the Aztec nation on ships with white sails

emblazoned with black crosses just as Princess Papantzin had prophesied to Montezuma.

In that same year, the Aztecs also expected the fulfillment of a prophecy that Quetzalcoatl, a former king who was exiled in 890, would return from the East to rule them. Quetzalcoatl was exiled because he opposed human sacrifice, but he prophesied that he would return on April 22 to start a new era. This day was Good Friday in 1519 and providentially it happened to be the exact day that Cortes landed in Mexico. The coming of Cortes coincided with the fulfillment of Papantzin's prophecy and the prophecy of Quetzalcoatl's return. The Aztecs thought that Cortes was Quetzalcoatl and that the Spaniards might be gods. Montezuma was unsure as to how to react to them and he was hesitant to engage them in combat.

This superstition aided Cortes' conquest of Mexico. He landed near present day Vera Cruz at age 33 with only 500 men, two priests and 16 horses. He deliberately scuttled and sank his small fleet of 11 ships so that no one would desert him. This exhibited his great faith in God since he then had no means of retreat. With this motley army, led by the Sign of the Cross and sustained by his devotion to the Blessed Virgin Mary, he defeated the Aztec nation.

In their first major battle, 300 Spanish soldiers defeated 30,000 Indian warriors. Montezuma believed that an invincible godly force confronted him. In reality it was the invincible force of the one true God who led Cortes' army by the banner of the Cross emblazoned with Cortes' own words, "Brothers and Companions, let us follow the Sign of the Cross with true faith and in it we shall conquer."

As they approached Tenochtitlan, the Spaniards were amazed at what they saw. Bernal Diaz, the earliest Spanish eyewitness, said, "We beheld the great towers and temples which seemed to rise out of the water. Never yet did man see, hear, or dream of anything equal to the spectacle which appeared to our eyes on this day."

Later, Cortes was a guest in Mexico City during a truce. He saw the idol Huitzilopochtli at the top of the temple. This idol was fat with horrible eyes and snakes girded about its body. Around its neck hung Indian faces and hearts. This was the idol before which 80,000 people were sacrificed in a four-day orgy in 1487. Cortes demanded its removal. The idol's caretaker witch doctors refused.

Cortes cried to God, "Why do you permit the Devil to be so grossly honored in this land?" He marched up the temple steps to the top platform and pierced the veil covering the idol. He then grabbed a metal bar and, according to an eyewitness, he supernaturally leapt up into the air and smote the idol's eyes saying, "We must risk something for God!" He later stripped the temple pyramid of its two idols, cleansed the stone of its blood and erected a new altar. Cortes, his soldiers and Father Olmedo then ascended the stairs with the Holy Cross and images of the Blessed Virgin Mary and St. Christopher. Upon this new altar, Father Olmedo offered the Sacrifice of the Mass. Upon what had been the place of evil pagan human sacrifices, now the unbloody, eternal and true sacrifice of Jesus Christ was offered. This marked the beginning of the end of human sacrifice in Aztec Mexico.

Cortes asked Montezuma, "I ask you not to sacrifice any more souls to your gods, who are deceiving you. I beg you to allow us to remove them and put up Our Lady and a Cross." Montezuma answered Cortes and said, "How sorry I am about the answer we have had from our gods; it is that we are to make war on you and kill you."

The Aztecs, led by their chief witch doctor, the Hummingbird Wizard, refused all peace offers from Cortes. They believed that their false gods would bring them victory. In 1521, they fought to the death in a 93 day siege of Mexico City. It resulted in the wizard's dethronement, the annihilation of Mexico City and the conquest of Mexico.

Against overwhelming odds, the Conquistadors (Conquerors) had conquered Mexico in the name of the Spanish King Charles V who was soon thereafter elected as Holy Roman Emperor, the temporal guardian of all Christendom. Cortes said, "Our Lady was pleased to show His power and mercy, for with all our weakness we broke their arrogance and pride." This Conquest was an epochal achievement in helping to realize the claim of the Americas for God that had been made by Christopher Columbus.

However, the New Spain government created a new social system that oppressed the Indians through slavery. This was due to their human greed and lust for power and glory. Slavery was justified by the argument that the Indians had no souls. The Spanish government in Mexico did not follow the social justice teachings of the Church that the Indians were children of God with equal human dignity. The Indians lived under the oppression of the Spanish governor, Nuno de Guzman. He sold thousands of them into slavery in the West Indies, enslaved thousands of poor Indians in Mexico and extorted from the wealthier ones.

Cortes' hope for a new Spanish Christian civilization in Mexico was not immediately realized. The Indians of Mexico were divided by languages and by the rugged terrain that made evangelization difficult. They thought Christianity was a "white man's religion." Moreover, their pagan beliefs were deeply rooted in their souls. Cortes had eliminated much of human sacrifice, but many Indians still held its belief and practice and Baptisms were few.

Cortes wrote to King Charles and requested missionaries. In 1523, Franciscan priests came to Mexico and began to evangelize. The missionaries involved themselves in the lives of the Indians. They preached to them the Good News that the one true God was the Creator of all things. He was a God of goodness and love who became man in Jesus Christ and died for them, freeing them from the power of Satan and forgiving their sins of the worship of false gods, the practice of human sacrifice, polygamy and sodomy. King Charles V appointed Bishop Zumarraga as "Protector of the Indians."

However, the New Spain government under de Guzman enslaved the Indians and decreed that any Indian who appealed to Bishop Zumarraga for help would be punished by death. After two of his priests were kidnapped and tortured by government agents, Bishop Zumarraga placed the entire city of Mexico under an interdict and excommunicated the leaders. Finally, in 1530 the King established a new government, issued a decree that prohibited slavery and confirmed Bishop Zumarraga as Protector of the Indians. The King's decree said, "No person shall dare to make a single Indian a slave whether in war or in peace, whether by barter, by purchase, by trade, or on any other pretext or cause whatever." An era of peace was about to begin, 12 years after the landing of Cortes.

However, the Indians still practiced human sacrifice and they had no confidence in Spanish goodness. They saw the disunity of the Spaniards because of the difference between those who followed their religious teachings and those who practiced their irreligious politics. They saw this as the weakness of the Spaniards and were on the verge of a general insurrection. Bishop Zumarraga sensed this and prayed for peace. The stage was now set for the entrance of the Blessed Virgin Mary.

3. Saint Juan Diego and Aztec Native Americans

Born   1474 in Cuautitlan, Mexico
Died   1548 in Mexico City, Mexico
Canonized   July 30, 2002 by Pope John Paul II at Mexico City
Feast Day   December 9
                Protector and Advocate of the Indigenous Peoples
                First Native American saint

"He was an Indian who lived an honest and secluded life, and who was a very good Christian, fearful of God and his conscience, a man of very good habits and behavior."
Marcos Pacheco, Elder of the village of Cuautitlan, Juan Diego's birthplace, in Canonical Process 1666.

Ten years after the Conquest of Mexico, on Saturday, December 9, 1531, 57-year-old Juan Diego, a recent widower, began a 9 mile walk from his home in Tulpetlac to Tlaltelolco near Mexico City "in pursuit of God and His commandments", according to the *Nican Mopohua*, the earliest account written in 1545. Juan was walking to attend Mass and catechetical instructions.

As he walked near Tepeyac Hill, the former site of worship to the Aztec goddess Tonantzin, he heard the music of singing birds. He stopped to look and said to himself, *Am I worthy and deserving of what I am hearing? Where am I? Am I perhaps in the earthly paradise?* He was looking toward the crown of the hill where the music came from and where the sun rises. Suddenly, the music stopped and there was complete silence.

Then, from the top of the hill, he heard a sweet feminine voice affectionately call him by name, "Juan, dearest Juan Diego." He quickly climbed to the top of the hill to see who was there. He saw a beautiful young lady. Her dress shone like the sun and transformed the appearance of the rocks and plants on the barren cactus hill into glittering jewels. The ground glistened like the rays of a rainbow in a dense fog. She appeared as shown in the Miraculous Image on page xx.

She identified herself to him as "the perfect and perpetual Virgin Mary, Mother of the one true God for whom one lives." She entrusted a mission to him to request Bishop Zumarraga to build a church on the hill so that she could manifest her Son to all of the people.

Formation

Juan Diego was born in 1474, eighteen years before Columbus discovered America. He was born in the village of Cuautitlan, (Place of the Eagle) Mexico, located 14 miles north of Mexico City (Tenochtitlan). He was a Chichimeca of the Family of Texcoco. His Indian name was Cuauhtlatoatzin which means "He who speaks like an eagle."

Juan received an early education according to the pre-Hispanic traditions, even including the knowledge of "the one true God for whom one lives." Later, he married his wife, Malintzin, and they had children. He was a landowner, a small farmer and was involved in textile manufacturing. He had a good deal of property, some he inherited, and the rest came from his mat making business. He made mats from the reeds growing along the shores of Lake Texcoco.

Juan lived in Mexico before and after the Spanish Conquest of 1521 and before the establishment of Jamestown, Virginia, the first permanent English colony, in 1607. The Conquest was an apocalyptic event for the indigenous peoples. They lost their freedom, their land, their religion, their culture, their society and their great city of Tenochtitlan. Juan's life bridged two cultures from the pre-Conquest worship of false gods and the human sacrifices made to appease them to the post-Conquest worship of the one true God and the end of human sacrifice.

Before the Conquest, the Aztec natives practiced human sacrifice. In 1487, when Juan was just 13 years old, he may have witnessed the horrible human sacrifices of Tlacaellel, the 89-year old Aztec leader of human sacrifice. He dedicated a new temple pyramid in the center of Tenochtitlan.

The temple was dedicated to the two chief gods of the Aztec pantheon, Huitzilopochtli, called the "Lover of Hearts and Drinker of Blood," and Tezcatlipoca, "the god of Hell and Darkness." More than 80,000 men were sacrificed over a period of four days and four nights in a horrific satanic ritual with the copious flow of blood and piles of dead bodies.

Juan's tribal family of the Chicamecas was part of the Triple Alliance with the Aztecs (Mexicas) and the Tlacopans. However, the Aztec Emperor, Montezuma, assumed total control over these tribes and made enemies of them. They later allied with the Spanish in the Conquest.

After the Conquest, Juan converted to Christianity between 1524 and 1525. He was baptized, together with his wife by the Franciscan missionary, Fray Toribio de Benavente whom the Indians called "Motolina" or "the poor one." He was baptized as Juan Diego (John James) and she was baptized as Maria Lucia. In 1524, they celebrated the sacrament of Matrimony. Shortly later, they heard a sermon regarding how the virtue of chastity is pleasing to God. By mutual consent they decided to live their marriage thereafter as celibates. Maria Lucia died in 1529. After that, Juan lived in voluntary poverty with his uncle, Juan Bernardino, in the village of Tolpetlac, located 9 miles from Tlaltelolco where they attended Mass.

Bishop Zumarraga was a saintly man, very just and compassionate. He built the first hospital, library and university in the New World. He tried to protect the Indians but his efforts and those of the Spanish Franciscans were not very successful. Neither the Spanish civil rulers nor the natives were disposed to conversion.

The Apparitions and Mission

When the Blessed Virgin Mary appeared to Juan on December 9, 1531 she entrusted a mission to him to request Bishop Zumarraga to build a church on the hill so that she could manifest her Son to all of the people.

She said, "I ardently desire that a little sacred house be built here for me where I will manifest Him, I will exalt Him, I will give Him to the people through my personal love, through my compassionate gaze, through my help and through my protection. Because I am, in truth, your merciful Mother and the mother of all who live united in this land and of all mankind, of all those who love me, of those who cry to me, of those who have confidence in me. Here I will hear their weeping and their sadness and will remedy and alleviate their troubles, their miseries and their suffering."

Juan dutifully went to the Bishop and delivered the Virgin Mother's message and request. The Bishop prudently asked Juan to return another time. So he returned to the Virgin Mother at Tepeyac and told her the Bishop's response. Juan told her that he was not worthy of her mission and that she should find someone else. He said that he was a nobody. But she reassured him. She told him that she had many messengers who could carry her message but that it was "altogether necessary that you should be the one to undertake this mission and it will be through your mediation and assistance that my wish should be accomplished." She commanded him to return to the Bishop the next day.

So the next day Juan returned to the Bishop and tearfully begged him to respond to the Virgin Mother's request. The Bishop prudently requested a sign from the Virgin Mother so that he could believe her request for him to build the church. Once again, Juan returned to her and gave the Bishop's answer.

The Virgin Mother promised to give Juan the sign on the next day, December 11. However, when he got home he found that his uncle, Juan Bernardino, was dying from a disease. So he stayed home the next day and took care of him instead of going to receive the sign from the Virgin.

On the day after that, December 12, he left his home and his uncle to get a priest to give him the last rites. As he approached Tepeyac Hill, he decided to go around it another way so that the Virgin Mother would not see him and detain him from getting the priest for his uncle. But she spotted him, intercepted him and asked him what path he was taking.

Juan was bewildered, frightened and ashamed since he had failed to meet her on December 11. He told her that he was on the way to get a priest for his dying uncle but that he would go to the Bishop with her message as soon as he was finished. After listening to his excuses, she told him not to worry and said that his uncle was cured at that very moment.

She said, "Listen and let it penetrate your heart, my dear little son. Do not be troubled or weighed down with grief. Do not fear any illness or vexation, anxiety, or pain. Am I not here who am your Mother? Are you not under my shadow and protection? Am I not your fountain of life? Are you not in the folds of my mantle? Are you not in the crossing of my arms? What else do you need? Do not let the illness of your uncle worry you because he is not going to die of his sickness. At this very moment, he is cured."

Juan was greatly relieved and consoled. The Virgin Mother then asked him to go up to the top of the hill, cut and gather the flowers there and bring them back to her. This sounded strange to him since it was a barren desert hilltop in the middle of winter when no flowers grow. But he obediently climbed the hill and to his astonishment he found miraculous flowers in bloom. They included Castilian roses that were native to the Bishop's homeland in Castile, Spain.

Juan was wearing a tilma, a poncho-like cloak, woven from the native maguey cactus plant. He gathered the flowers, placed them in his tilma and returned to the Virgin Mother. He was about to go off to the Bishop but he hadn't done a good job of arranging the flowers in his tilma. The Virgin Mother helped him to place the flowers as a beautiful bouquet in his tilma. Then she said that the flowers were "the sign to take to the Bishop. Tell him, in my name, that in them he will recognize my will and that he must fulfill it. You will be my ambassador, fully worthy of my confidence."

Mission Accomplished

For the third time, Juan walked to the Bishop. But this time his heart was filled with joy because he had a sign for the Bishop by which the Virgin Mother assured him he would recognize her will. He was confident that the Bishop would finally believe him. He endured the derision of the Bishop's servants and waited patiently to see him. Again, he delivered to him the Virgin Mother's request for him to build the church and told him that she had given him flowers as a sign.

As he opened his tilma, he said, "Here are the flowers." The roses fell to the ground and the Bishop fell to his knees and stared at Juan's tilma. Juan was perplexed and followed the Bishop's eyes to his tilma. There he saw the image of the Virgin Mother miraculously appear on it, just as he had seen her on Tepeyac Hill. Now the Bishop believed him and with tears in his eyes he asked pardon for his disbelief. He approached Juan, removed his tilma and immediately placed it in his chapel.

The next day, they went to Tepeyac and Juan showed the Bishop where the Virgin Mother wanted the church to be built. Then he went home to see his uncle and found him in perfect health. Juan Bernardino said that the Virgin Mother had appeared to him and told him that she wished to be known as, "The Perfect Virgin, Holy Mary of Guadalupe." Guadalupe was the name of a Marian Shrine in Spain.

Two weeks later, they built the church that the Virgin Mary had requested. Then the miraculous image was transported from the Bishop's chapel to the new church in a great procession so that all the people could admire and venerate it. In the procession were the Bishop, all the priests, Spaniards and natives. Everyone processed in great jubilation. A native archer shot an arrow inadvertently and it struck another native in the throat and killed him. The faith-filled people laid his body before the miraculous image and prayed that Our Lady of Guadalupe would intercede to bring him back to life. They extracted the arrow and not only did he regain his life, but the wound was completely healed. Everyone was very moved at the sight and they praised Our Lady of Guadalupe who fulfilled her promise to help the natives and all who call upon her with confidence.

Epilogue

Our Lady was also true to her promise to manifest her Son to the people. Nine million natives converted to Catholicism in the next nine years. Thousands of Indians left their homes and walked in search of priests for Baptisms and Confessions. Many of them were pregnant women, some gave birth on the way and many carried their children on their backs. Even the elderly, lame and the blind walked in search of a priest. Others went from monastery to monastery. They walked up to 250 miles.

Bishop Zumarraga wrote, "The light of the Star of the Evangelization was revealed as a moment of intervention of God in human history. If human persons, in spite of the divine intervention, continued with their limitations, infidelities and betrayals; there is no doubt that immediately after the date of the apparitions a marvelous change in regard to the conversions of the indigenous and the change of attitude of the Spaniards took place. A change in the depth of being of the inhabitants of Mexico."

The Miraculous Image was displayed in the church at the base of Tepeyac Hill. Later, Juan Diego built a one-room hermitage addition onto the east wall of the church. He was the caretaker of this church and the Miraculous Image. Here he spent his days sweeping the church, praying, telling and retelling the story of Our Lady's apparitions and messages.

He lived there as a poor widower hermit for the last 17 years of his life. He practiced penance and mortification, prayed, received frequent Communion and carried out the simple tasks of caring for his little hermitage. He lived a life of poverty, chastity and obedience and was revered by all.

Since Juan was learned in the Nahuatl language and Christian doctrine, he was able to explain the Miraculous Image on the tilma. It spoke to the natives as a pictograph. He explained its significance and the story of the apparitions and messages over and over again.

The Indians had no written language. They could not read or write. So God wrote for them in Our Lady's image. The Indians communicated by painted images in pictographs or codices. The tilma "spoke" to them as a pictograph through its symbols. It was the Indian's catechism. It taught them by picture-symbols that they could understand when they saw it. They received Our Lady's message to them through these symbols and through the words of Juan Diego.

The Indians understood that Our Lady was pregnant in her image which was visually obvious and which was symbolized by the only four-petaled flower located over her womb. This flower, known as the *Nahui Ollin*, symbolizes the center of the universe; the one true God and Christ Himself who was born through Our Lady. It is the Flower of the Sun, a symbol of plenitude, representing the four compass directions of the world, with heaven and the underworld vertically encountering earth in the center. With its placement over Our Lady's womb, the natives understood that the son of Our Lady of Guadalupe would replace their false god of the sun.

The sash or "cingulum" that is wrapped around Our Lady's body and tied high above her protruding pregnant womb is a piece of clothing that signifies both perfect chastity and pregnancy. From this and her message, the natives understood that she was the Virgin Mother of the one true God.

From looking at the tilma and listening to Juan, the Indians understood that they were not adoring Our Lady but honoring her as the pregnant Virgin Mother of the one true God. They saw that she came from heaven because she was surrounded by clouds and escorted by an angel. They understood, however, that she was not God because her head was bowed in humility and her hands were joined in prayer, interceding for them to the one true God. They heard that this God loved the world so much that

He sent His only begotten Son, Jesus Christ, to die for them and that His death was sufficient for all mankind to be saved from hell so that human sacrifice was totally unnecessary and absolutely evil. Human sacrifice ended completely.

The Indians heard that Jesus died on the Cross, as shown on the brooch near Our Lady's neck, so that they might have eternal life. (See Jn 3:16). They saw that this was the same Cross that they had seen on the helmets of the Spanish Conquistadors and which they now embraced as their own.

They understood from the tilma that Our Lady, although not God, was very close to Him and was the vanquisher of the Aztec false gods of the sun, which she eclipsed and which radiated from behind her; the stars, which she wore on her mantle; and the moon, upon which she stood.

Juan was Our Lady's messenger, "The Talking Eagle" until the day he died. He died at the age of 74 in 1548, almost a century before the Mayflower landed at Plymouth Rock. He was probably buried in his hermitage next to the church that he had cared for so well. His tilma is still displayed today in the Basilica of Our Lady of Guadalupe near Tepeyac Hill.

Protector and Advocate of the Indigenous Peoples

During Juan's beatification ceremony, Pope John Paul II described Juan as an authentic apostle to his people. He said, "In the likeness of the ancient biblical figures, which were a collective representation of all their people, we could say that Juan Diego represents all the indigenous peoples who accepted the Gospel of Jesus, thanks to the maternal aid of Mary we can invoke him as the protector and the advocate of the indigenous peoples."

The Holy Father further remarked on this point during his homily at Juan's canonization Mass. He said, "'The Guadalupe Event,' as the Mexican Episcopate has pointed out, 'meant the beginning of evangelization with a vitality that surpassed all expectations. Christ's message, through His Mother, took up the central elements of the indigenous culture, purified them and gave them the definitive sense of salvation.' Consequently Guadalupe and Juan Diego have a deep ecclesial and missionary meaning and are a model of perfectly inculturated evangelization."

Virtues

Juan Diego is a saint not because Our Lady appeared to him, but because he exercised heroic virtues. In his beatification address, Pope John Paul II praised Juan's virtues, "his simple faith, nourished by catechesis and open to the mysteries; his hope and trust in God and in the Virgin; his love, his moral coherence, his unselfishness and evangelical poverty."

"Living the life of a hermit here near Tepeyac, he was a model of humility. The Virgin chose him from among the most humble as the one to receive that loving and gracious manifestation of hers which is the Guadalupe apparition. Her maternal face and her blessed image which she left us as a priceless gift is a permanent remembrance of this. In this manner she wanted to remain among you as a sign of the communion and unity of all those who were to live together in this land."

Juan exhibited the Marian virtues of humility, obedience, charity, trust, patience, poverty and chastity.

Like Mary, who saw herself as the lowly handmaid of the Lord, Juan saw himself as a nobody. Like Mary, who obeyed and accepted to be a mother to carry Christ, Juan obeyed and accepted to be carrier of the message of Mary. Like Mary, who in charity cared for her elderly pregnant cousin Elizabeth, Juan cared for his elderly dying uncle, Juan Bernardino. Like Mary, who "trusted that the Lord's promise to her would be fulfilled" (Lk. 1:45), Juan trusted Our Lady's promise that the Bishop would recognize her will and fulfill it through the sign of the roses. Like Mary, who patiently waited for nine months for the Lord's promise to be fulfilled, Juan patiently waited for days for Our Lady's promise to be fulfilled. Like Mary, who lived in poverty and chastity as a widow, Juan, the widower, gave up his possessions and lived in poverty and chastity until his death. Finally, like Mary, Juan didn't argue with God's will, he didn't complain and he didn't doubt. He simply did as he was asked, endured the derision of the Bishop's servants and persevered in fortitude, as did Mary who endured the derision of her detractors.

At Juan's canonization Mass, Pope John Paul II said, "With deep joy I have come on pilgrimage to this Basilica of Our Lady of Guadalupe, the Marian heart of Mexico and of America, to proclaim the holiness of Juan Diego Cuauhtlatoatzin, the simple, humble Indian who contemplated the sweet and serene face of Our Lady of Tepeyac . . . Blessed Juan Diego, a good, Christian Indian, whom simple people have always considered a saint! "

"In this new saint you have a marvelous example of a just and upright man, a loyal son of the Church, docile to his Pastors, who deeply loved the Virgin and was a faithful disciple of Jesus."

Before his final blessing, the Holy Father said, "You have now in your new saint a remarkable example of holiness. . . . May he be a model for you and others that you may also be holy."

Fruits

Juan's mission resulted in the largest mass evangelization in the history of the world. Nine million indigenous peoples of Mexico were converted to the one true God in nine years, the practice of human sacrifice ended in Mexico and the indigenous peoples were reconciled to their Spanish conquerors, intermarried with them and formed the new Mexican race.

During his homily at Juan's canonization Mass, Pope John Paul II remarked on the formation of the Mexican people and said, "In accepting the Christian message without forgoing his indigenous identity, Juan Diego discovered the profound truth of the new humanity, in which all are called to be children of God. Thus he facilitated the fruitful meeting of two worlds and became the catalyst for the new Mexican identity, closely united to Our Lady of Guadalupe, whose mestizo face expresses her spiritual motherhood that embraces all Mexicans."

Saint

On May 6, 1990, John Paul II was in Mexico City for the beatification of Juan Diego. At the very moment that the pope declared Juan Diego "Blessed," Juan José Barragán Silva, a drug addict in his twenties stabbed himself with a knife at home in Mexico City in his mother's presence and went to a balcony to jump from the window.

His mother, Esperanza, tried to hold him by the legs, but he freed himself and plunged head-first thirty feet to the ground. He then was rushed to the intensive care unit of Durango Hospital in Mexico City.

Esperanza said that when her son was falling she entrusted him to God and Our Lady of Guadalupe. She invoked Juan Diego and implored, "Give me a proof . . . save this son of mine! And you, my Mother, listen to Juan Diego." Suddenly and inexplicably, three days after the fall, her son was completely cured. Subsequent examinations confirmed that he had no neurological or psychic effects, and the doctors concluded that his cure was "scientifically inexplicable."

Medical experts said the youth should have died in the fall, or at least been left seriously handicapped. J.H. Hernández Illescas, regarded internationally as one of the best specialists in the field of neurology, and two other specialists, described the case as "unheard of, amazing, and inconceivable. . . ." Juan is an intercessor for all families broken by sin.

This miracle was the decisive factor in the recognition of Juan Diego's sainthood. Our Lady promised Juan that she would reward him for his efforts on her behalf. She told him, "Yes, I will enrich you, I will glorify you." Her promise is now fulfilled. Pope John Paul II canonized Juan on July 31, 2002 in Mexico City. He was the first canonized Native American. His Feast Day is December 9, the date of Our Lady's first apparition to him.

Opening Prayer for the Mass in Commemoration of Saint Juan Diego

Lord God,
Through Saint Juan Diego
you made known the love of Our Lady of Guadalupe
toward your people.
Grant by his intercession
that we who follow the counsel of Mary, our Mother,
may strive continually to do your will.
We ask this through our Lord Jesus Christ, your Son,
who lives and reigns with you and the Holy Spirit,
one God for ever and ever.

Shrine:

Basilica of Our Lady of Guadalupe
Atrio de America
Villa de Guadalupe
Mexico, D.F. 07050
Telephone: 01152555577-6022
Website: www.sancta.org/basilica.html

Part Two

The Development of the First Evangelization of America

4. New Spain

The land that was to become America was like a new Eden. It was a vast land of unimaginable beauty, with many natural resources, brimming with virgin forests, prairies and waterways that served as the first highways for travel. Fish and game were plentiful. There were seven and a half million square miles of land in North America alone.

The natives who inhabited the land were mistakenly called Indians (Indios in Spanish) because Columbus thought that he had discovered the Indies (India, China and Japan). These Indians were the descendants of Indians who had migrated from Siberia across a land bridge from Asia about 40,000 years before. At that time, the sea level was lower and a land bridge existed across the Bering Strait that connected Asia and North America. Asian hunters crossed this bridge from Asia in search of wild animals and settled on the North American side. Later the Indians traveled and settled throughout North America and were divided into various tribes.

The Spanish established their first settlements centered in the Caribbean islands, particularly Cuba. Cortes left from Cuba to conquer Mexico. After the Conquest, the Spanish named as New Spain the area of the Caribbean and Mexico. As governor of New Spain, Cortes rebuilt Mexico City (Tenochtitlan) with a new cathedral over the ruins of the Aztec temple. He built other beautiful public buildings to the extent that the city was as beautiful as any in Europe. Many Spaniards settled in Mexico and the Caribbean. Millions of Indians converted to Catholicism through the intercession of Our Lady of Guadalupe and the efforts of the Franciscan missionaries. Many Spaniards married Indians and formed a new race (La Raza), the new Mexican people.

From the Caribbean and Mexico, the Spaniards explored and established missions in the Southeast and the Southwest of the United States. These exploratory expeditions always included missionaries and adventurers. They came for God and for gold and for glory. They came to bring the one true faith to the Indians and claimed the land for the King. The missions were established for conversion of the Indians and for homes for them where they could live in peace. They received from the missionaries, protection, health care, education and training in agricultural development.

Tensions developed among the Spaniards who were committed to the conversion and spiritual welfare of the natives and those whose motives were political and economic. Many of them came to bring knowledge of the one true God to the Indians. Many came simply for gold and glory as Conquistadors (conquerors) and to use the Indians for their own personal gain. They even argued that the Indians were not human and had no souls. In response, Pope Paul III issued a papal decree in 1537 that "the Indians are truly men who are by no means to be deprived of their liberty or the possession of their property; even though they be outside the faith of Jesus Christ; and that they may and should freely and legitimately, enjoy their liberty and the possession of their property; nor should they be in any way enslaved." He also commanded that they "should be converted to the faith of Jesus Christ by preaching the Word of God and by the example of good and holy living."

Some of this living was neither good nor holy. Father Bartolome de Las Casas came to New Spain in 1502 as a landowner with Indian servants. He saw how some Indians were mistreated by some Spaniards who treated them like animals and didn't teach the faith, both of which were against the law of Spain. But the laws were often not enforced. Las Casas became a priest in 1510, freed his Indians and began a lifelong crusade to defend all Indians as children of God equal in dignity to the Spaniards. He said, "When we preach to the Indians about the humility and poverty of Jesus Christ, and how He suffered for us, and how God rejoices in the poor and in those the world despises, [the Indians] think we are lying to them." His voice for the Indians resulted in the prohibition by Spanish law of the slavery of Indians in 1573.

Ponce de León was a Spaniard who accompanied Christopher Columbus on his second voyage to the New World. He became the first Governor of Puerto Rico by appointment of the Spanish Crown. From there he equipped three ships and set out on a voyage of discovery in 1513. On April 2, he landed on the east coast of present day Florida, probably at the present site of St. Augustine. This was six years before Cortes landed in Mexico. It was the first landing by a European on what is now the United States.

Ponce de León claimed the land for Spain and named it *La Florida* (The Flowers) probably because of the beautiful flowers and foliage or because he landed during the Easter Season which for the Spanish was *Pascua de Florida* (The Feast of Flowers).

There is evidence at his probable landing site of the planting of a Cross by him in the ground. This would have been the first Cross planted in the United States. It consists of individual coquina stones which still lie there laid like slate. The Cross consists of 27 stones, 15 placed vertically and 13 placed horizontally, signifying the date of his landing in 1513.

When Pedro Menendez de Aviles later landed in St. Augustine in 1565, he also claimed the land for Spain with both a flag and a Cross. Seeing him and the rest of the Spaniards reverence the Cross, the native Timucuan Indians who had gathered at the site imitated them.

The first Mass in the United States was celebrated at St. Augustine by the priest who accompanied the expedition, Father Francisco Lopez de Mendoza Grajales, on September 8, 1565, the Feast of the Nativity of the Blessed Virgin Mary. Thereafter, the Franciscan church and friary was established in 1584 and dedicated to the Immaculate Conception. The first Catholic parish was established there and its baptismal records begin in 1594. St. Augustine is the oldest continuous settlement in the United States.

After the Mass, Menendez de Aviles invited the Timucuans to join him for the first communal meal of Europeans and natives together. This was the first communal act of thanksgiving in the first permanent European settlement of what is now the United States. It was nearly a century before the Pilgrims' first thanksgiving with the natives of Massachusetts in 1621.

Spanish missions were later established across the north border of Florida and up its east coast and continuing north as far as the Chesapeake Bay. At various times in their history, the missions spanned from present day Miami, north to the Chesapeake Bay and west to Pensacola. There were at least 124 missions during the first Spanish occupation of the southeastern United States between 1565 and 1763. Although Spain held St. Augustine until 1763, English advances and destruction of missions virtually ended all missionary activity in Florida by 1706.

In 1537, the first white man entered New Mexico and reported the distant sighting of a golden city. He was a Franciscan missionary named Father Marcos de Niza. However, he was afraid to enter the city because Indians killed his companion, a Moorish slave, near there. Father Niza thought that he had observed the main city of the legendary "Seven Cities of Cibola" (Gold) with buildings covered in gold. But, in fact, it was only an Indian pueblo (town). Father Niza returned to Mexico City and reported his findings.

The next year, the Spanish explorer Francisco Vasquez de Coronado went to New Mexico to discover the city and its gold. His expedition was composed of some 300 soldiers and five Franciscan friars, including Father Juan de Padilla. Coronado conquered what he thought was the first of the "Seven Cities of Gold." However, the legendary city of gold turned out to be nothing more than the dusty adobe Zuni Indian pueblo of Hawikuh. From there, Coronado's expedition explored to the north and discovered the Grand Canyon. They tramped through New Mexico, Oklahoma and Kansas but failed to find any gold, did not settle and returned to Mexico City in 1542.

Father Padilla stayed behind in New Mexico with some Indians, two other friars and some soldiers to evangelize the Indians. He marched into the plains of Kansas. One day in November 1542, a band of Indians attacked them. Father Padilla urged his companions to flee for safety while he stayed behind. The eyewitness accounts say that he knelt to receive the arrows that pierced him "like a pincushion" and killed him. He was the first martyr of today's United States. The first North American martyrs were three Indian children who were killed for their faith by their own people in Tlaxcala, Mexico in 1527 and 1529. They were Christopher (Cristobalito), John (Juan) and Anthony (Antonio) who were killed at he ages of 12 and 13. His own cruel father killed Christopher. Pope John Paul II beatified them on May 6, 1990.

Spanish missions were also established throughout Texas, Arizona, New Mexico and California. They were serviced from their base in Mexico City. The Spanish founded the city of Santa Fe (Holy Faith) in New

Mexico and the Franciscans established many missions there. Within 100 years of the martyrdom of Father Padilla, 60,000 Indians were baptized Catholics in New Mexico. In 1629, a group of Jumanos Indians came from Texas to Santa Fe, requested Baptism and told an amazing story.

The Jumanos told the priests that a lady dressed in blue had made many appearances among them since 1620, instructed them in the Catholic faith, prepared them to receive Baptism and urged them to travel to the Franciscan missionaries in Santa Fe. They called her the "Lady in Blue." Some Franciscans traveled the 200 miles from Santa Fe to baptize the Indians in Texas. In 1631, some of them returned to Spain and learned the amazing story of the Lady in Blue.

The Lady in Blue was a nun who lived in Agreda, Spain. Her name was Mother Mary of Jesus and she was the Abbess of the Conceptionist Poor Clare Convent of the Immaculate Conception. She said that when she was in prayer, she miraculously bi-located from Spain to the United States and visited various Southwest Indian tribes approximately 500 times. A priest spoke to some of these Indians who described her appearance. He later met Mother Agreda who matched their description and she told him that she had in fact bi-located to the Indians by the power of God who desired in His mercy to bring them His truth.

During this development of New Spain, many missionaries were martyred by Indians of the Southeast and the Southwest of the United States. In 1571, eight Jesuits including two priests, three lay brothers and three novices were martyred near Williamsburg, Virginia because of Catholic teachings on morals. In 1597, four Franciscan priests and a lay brother were martyred along the coast of Georgia mainly for preaching monogamy and denouncing polygamy. After killing Father Pedro de Corpa, the regional superior of the missions, Juanillo, the Indian leader boasted, "Now the friar is dead. He would not have been killed had he let us live as we did before we became Christians. They take away our women, leaving us only the one and perpetual, forbidding us to exchange her." In 1680, 21 Franciscan Friars were martyred near Santa Fe, New Mexico during the Pueblo Revolt.

As the Spanish colonized the Southeast and Southwest of the United States, the French explored and settled in Northeast Canada. Their development was aided by the waterways that crisscrossed northeast America.

5. New France

"Quebec!"("What a rock!") yelled the lookout in his Norman dialect aboard the ship captained by Jacques Cartier. He looked up at the great 300-foot cliffs of Quebec City, Canada (New France), from the St. Lawrence River below in September of 1535.

Like Columbus before him, Cartier hoped to discover a water route to the Indies. He explored the northern waters of the New World with the authority of King Francis I who empowered him to claim for France all of the New World that he could find.

In 1534, he sailed from France across the Atlantic to a peninsula that he named the Gaspé along the mid-eastern boundary of today's province of Quebec, Canada. There he planted a Cross on a hill and claimed the land in the name of God for France.

The next year, he returned and sailed around the peninsula into a gulf that he named after St. Lawrence and from there up the St. Lawrence River. It's called "up river," although it looks on a map like it's down (southwest) because it's against the current. He sailed about 100 miles to Quebec City and continued up the river another 150 miles until he reached a large island with a prominent mount. He named this Mont-Royal (Mount Royal). Later in 1642, a city was founded there and named Ville-Marie de Montreal ("Mary's City of Mount Royal"), now Montreal.

Cartier spent the winter in the New World and returned to France without a new water route to the Indies and without any precious goods. Six years later, he returned and tried to establish a colony in Quebec but it failed. The survivors returned to France in 1543. France lost interest in the New World and became preoccupied in foreign, civil and religious conflicts. Cartier's discoveries were not acted upon for the next 65 years.

In 1608, Samuel Champlain led a party from France that wintered at Cartier's old camp beneath the cliffs of Quebec City. It was the first permanent French settlement in New France. In July of the next year, he returned and captained a boat up river with 22 canoes containing two

Frenchmen and 60 Huron and Algonquin Indians. They paddled to its intersection with the Richelieu River (the River of the Iroquois) at Sorel, Quebec. He turned south and went up the river and entered a great lake that he named after himself. Lake Champlain is located between northern New York and Vermont.

A few days later, Champlain encountered a party of 200 Mohawk Indian warriors near Ticonderoga, New York, on the southwest shore of the lake. He said that he "saw them making a move to fire at us." So he fired his musket. "With the same shot, two fell to the ground; . . .When our side saw this shot so favorable for them, they began to raise such loud cries that one could not have heard it thunder." The Mohawks fled into the woods and this battle was the beginning of their hatred for the French.

In 1612, the King of France appointed Champlain as Lieutenant General of New France. In 1615, he invited Recollect missionaries to Canada. They came in response to Christ's command to "make disciples of all the nations." (Mt. 28:19). They labored for 10 years to evangelize the Indians, but their order was too few in number to accomplish this great task. They invited the Jesuits (Society of Jesus) to help them. In 1625, the first three Jesuit priests arrived at the small settlement of seven French families and less than 100 settlers. Many of these Jesuit missionaries were men of culture and learning and sacrificed important careers in the Church for the dangers and sufferings of the wilderness of New France.

France was divided between Catholics and Calvinist Protestants. Some of them went to England and obtained authorization to destroy New France. France didn't supply or protect the Quebec settlers who were starving and living on forage from the woods. When the British ships came, Champlain was forced to surrender Quebec on July 19, 1629 and the colonists and Jesuits were shipped back to France. Champlain was imprisoned for three years.

Champlain vowed to the Blessed Virgin Mary that he would build her a chapel and promote devotion to her if the land were restored to France. His prayers were answered in 1632 when a treaty returned New France to France. By 1633, some settlers and the Jesuits returned. Champlain fulfilled his vow and built a chapel dedicated to Our Lady of Recovery. He died in Quebec in 1635.

In 1634, the Jesuits established a residence about 150 miles up river at Three Rivers and dedicated it to the Immaculate Conception. On December 8, 1635, on the Feast of the Immaculate Conception, they dedicated their entire missionary apostolate to the Immaculate Conception. They wrote to their provincial in Paris, "We see clearly that it must necessarily be Heaven which shall convert New France. That is why we all desire to have recourse to Heaven and to the most Blessed Virgin, Mother of God, through whom God is wont to work when He wishes to do that which is impossible and to convert the hearts of the most abandoned."

The missionary efforts of the Spanish and the French differed. The Spanish missionary effort typically involved conquest, conversion, and a new European culture. The French missionary effort involved inculturation, conversion and maintenance of the native culture. French missionaries spent years learning the native language and culture before they baptized the converted. They were assimilated with the natives' way of life and explained Catholic beliefs in terms of the Indians' own language and understanding.

Three Rivers became the base from which the Jesuits began their mission of evangelization to the Huron Indians in present day Ontario, Canada. The Mohawk Indians had forced the Hurons into this corner of land east of Lake Huron. The Huron land measured approximately 50 miles long by 20 miles wide and was called "Huronia." It was separated from the Mohawk land 250 miles to the south by Lake Ontario.

The Mohawks lived in Auriesville (Ossernenon), New York, 40 miles west of Albany in the Mohawk River Valley. This was a fertile land in which the Mohawks raised their crops of beans, corn and squash.

The name "Mohawk" meant "man-eater" in the language of the Massachusetts, their Indian enemies. The Mohawks were one of the five nations of the Iroquois Confederacy that were historic enemies of the Huron and the Algonquins who allied with the French. The Iroquois and the Hurons each numbered about 30,000 people.

Europe was a great market for beaver pelts. The Iroquois had depleted the beavers in their territory of present-day western New York, so they invaded the Huron territory to obtain more beavers and killed many Hurons. The French traded with the Hurons at Three Rivers and allied with them against the Iroquois intruders.

The early history of the Indians and the Jesuits is told in the *Jesuit Relations*, a series of 73 volumes of reports of the Jesuits to their superiors in France. The missionaries sent these reports every summer for a period of 40 years. The Indians lived a primitive life-style. They lived in long multi-family bark huts called "Longhouses." They had no windows and their fires continually burned in the middle causing a smoky, smelly environment with no privacy for anyone. They ate what St. Isaac Jogues described as "the intestines of the deer, full of blood and half putrefied excrement, fungus growths boiled in water, decayed oysters, and frogs eaten whole, heads and feet, not even skinned or cleaned."

The Indian villages were walled in and protected from enemy attack by two rows of vertical pointed logs called palisades. Hunting and war were the main objects in life for the men. The women did the work in the houses and the fields. They were very stoic and endured great hardships of weather, shelter, lack of nutrition and warfare. They were also ferocious torturers of their enemies.

They practiced open fornication and adultery. They tortured, cannibalized and sacrificed their captives to their false gods. They brutally tortured them by beating and whipping them, burning them with firebrands, placing "necklaces" of red hot hatchets around their heads, eating their fingers off, amputating their hands, plucking out their eyes and replacing them with red hot coals in their sockets and by burning them alive. They ripped out and ate their hearts, chopped up their body parts and threw them into the "war kettle" from which they ate during their feasts in honor of their false gods.

They believed that a spirit named "Aronhia" presided over the earth and they offered human sacrifices to it to appease it. They believed that they were guided by dreams and followed them literally in strange quests of vigils and fasting. They also believed that demons had great power and had to be driven away by rituals of their sorcerers.

These Indians were not as progressive as the Aztecs in sciences, construction of cities and pictograph writing, but they were not as regressive as the Aztecs in the practice of human sacrifice which they practiced on a smaller scale. But they also had simple child-like hearts that were ripe for conversion to the one true God.

Into this primitive land the Jesuits paddled their canoes 1000 miles from Three Rivers southwest up the St. Lawrence River to Montreal, northwest up the Ottawa River and southwest down its tributaries to Ontario and the land of the Hurons (Huronia).

They paddled for 12 hours a day and covered many hundreds of miles in fragile bark canoes, through rapids and difficult portages, around waterfalls, through the forest amidst the scourge of mosquitoes. They ate sagamite, crushed corn boiled to the consistency of glue. Into the wilderness they carried their vestments, Mass kits, books and writing materials.

The Jesuit mission was located on the eastern shore of Lake Huron. It was named Sainte Marie and, like Three Rivers, it too was consecrated to the Immaculate Conception. When St. Jean de Brébeuf arrived there in 1634 he wrote, "Seeing them all together [the Hurons], we determined to preach publicly and make known to them the reason for coming to their country, not for their furs but to proclaim to them the true God and His Son, Jesus Christ, the one Savior of our souls." They learned the difficult Huron language, taught the Hurons how to write it and adopted their way of living and eating. They never tried to make the Hurons into French. They inculturated themselves with the Hurons to make them disciples of Christ.

Their lot was hardship, disease, solitude, torture and violent death. They endured the perils of the waterways and forests. They suffered from the intense cold and the wretched food and lodgings of the Indians. They were exposed to the sexual promiscuity of the Indians who called them "demons" because they were chaste and refused to accept any offers of sex. The missionaries begged the Indians to end their polygamy and promiscuity and to love their enemies. But this was contrary to Indian practices and thinking and their begging fell on deaf ears. Still, the missionaries labored on in faith.

St. Jean de Brébeuf spent 16 years laboring amongst the Hurons in a life of great suffering. The historian, Francis Parkman, wrote of him in *The Jesuits of North America,* "His was the ancient faith uncurtailed, redeemed from the decay of centuries, kindled with new life, and stimulated to a preternatural growth and fruitfulness."

The missionaries labored for almost six years before they baptized their first healthy adult. One of their first converts was Joseph Chiwatenhwa who was baptized on August 16, 1637 when he was about 35. He was the first Huron lay apostle. When his wife was baptized he declared, "My brothers, I am pleased to have you know that my wife is entirely resolved to believe in God and to serve Him, and that, from now on, she abandons forever all the superstitions of the country in order to be baptized."

The second Superior of Huronia was St. Gabriel Lalemant. He said that the reason for so few Christians in Huronia was because there were no martyrs. He later wrote that in fact they were living martyrs. Most would prefer to "be hit suddenly over the head by a hatchet blow than live through years of the life which we must lead here every day."

In 1636, St. Isaac Jogues arrived at Quebec from France. He too became a living martyr, but was also to "be hit suddenly over the head by a hatchet blow," as St. Lalemant preferred. Then the Dutch from Albany (Fort Orange), New York began trading firearms to the Mohawks for furs that gave them an advantage over the Hurons because the French would not trade firearms to them. The Mohawks were set to begin the genocide of the Huron nation. God raised up saints to meet them.

6. Saints Isaac Jogues, René Goupil and Jean de la Lande and Mohawk Native Americans

Saint Isaac Jogues

Born	January 10, 1607 in Orleans, France
Died	Martyred October 18, 1646 in Auriesville (Ossernenon), New York
Canonized	June 29, 1930 by Pope Pius XI
Feast Day	October 19
	Jesuit priest

Saint René Goupil

Born	May 13, 1608 in Anjou, France
Died	Martyred September 29, 1642 in Auriesville (Ossernenon), New York
Canonized	June 29, 1930 by Pope Pius XI
Feast Day	October 19
	Jesuit brother

Saint Jean de la Lande

Born	In Dieppe, France
Died	Martyred on October 19, 1646 in Auriesville (Ossernenon), New York
Canonized	June 29, 1930 by Pope Pius XI
Feast Day	October 19
	Lay missionary
	The United States' first and only canonized martyrs

"After they had seized me as being the most prominent and had cut off my thumb, they turned on him [René Goupil] and cut off his right thumb at the first joint, while he kept murmuring: 'Jesus, Mary and Joseph.' Picking up my severed thumb with my right hand, I offered it to You, my living and my true God."
Father Isaac Jogues, regarding the torture of him and René Goupil by the Mohawk Indians.

Twelve canoes paddled slowly and cautiously along the marshy shore of the St. Lawrence River on August 3, 1642. The eyes of the paddlers swept the waist-high marsh grass. They were Huron Indians led by their great Chief Eustace together with some Frenchmen including Father Isaac Jogues and his layman helper, René Goupil. They were on their way to bring missionaries and supplies to nourish the lives and Catholic faith of the Huron Mission in New France.

Suddenly, the quiet early morning air was pierced with wild war whoops as Mohawk warriors with grotesquely painted faces, and bodies streaked with blood-red paint stood above the grass and fired their muskets. The Hurons had no guns but they returned fire with a volley of arrows. Above the din of battle the voice of Eustace rose, "Great God, to you alone do I look for help."

Father Jogues made the Sign of the Cross and shouted the words of absolution over his companions. Then his canoe smashed against the shore and he was catapulted into the marsh grass that concealed him. He watched as his outnumbered companions were killed or captured. He could have escaped but, like Jesus in the Garden of Gethsemane, he surrendered himself.

Like the Good Shepherd, Father Jogues decided not to abandon his French and Indian companions. He stood up from the grass that concealed him and walked to the Mohawks with his arms stretched out in surrender. They sprang on him and beat him, stripped off his black robe and began to tie his ankles with leather thongs. He said, "No, no. You don't need to bind me. These French and Hurons whom you have taken, they are the bonds that will keep me captive. I won't leave them till death. I will follow them everywhere. You can be assured of my person as long as any one of them remains among you as a prisoner."

The Mohawks were so impressed with this eloquent statement that they left him untied. Father Jogues threw his arms around René Goupil and, like Job, whispered, "My dear brother, God has acted strangely toward us. But He is the Lord and Master. What is good in His eyes, that has He done. As it has pleased Him, so be it. Blessed be His Holy Name forever." "O my Father," replied René, "God indeed be blessed. He has permitted it. He has willed it. His holy will be done. I love it, I cherish it, and I embrace it with all the strength of my heart."

This ambush that God permitted seemed to the captives to signal the loss of hope for the Huron Mission. Father Jogues reflected about the loss of the Hurons at the beginning of his march into captivity and later lamented, "I was shaken by interior anguish when I saw this funereal procession of our Christians led before my very eyes, this cortege of death in which were the five tried Christians, the sustaining columns of the Church among the Hurons. Indeed, and I confess it honestly, time and time again I could not restrain my tears, grieving over the lot of these poor Hurons and of my French comrades, and worrying terribly about the things that might happen in the future. I had before my eyes continually the sight of the door of the Christian faith among the Hurons and other innumerable nations closed by these Iroquois, unless it might be opened by a most extraordinary dispensation of Divine Providence. This thought made me die every hour, in the depth of my soul. It is a hard thing, more, it is a cruel thing, to bear, that of seeing the triumph of the demons over whole nations redeemed with so much love, and paid for in the money of a Blood so adorable."

The martyrdoms of Father Jogues, René Goupil and Jean de la Lande remind us that this adorable Blood of Christ and theirs was shed not only for the Hurons but also to pay for the redemption of their Mohawk oppressors. Father Jogues later wrote in a letter to a friend, "In a word, this people [the Mohawks] are 'a bloody spouse' to me (Exodus 4: 25). May our good Master, who has purchased them in His blood, open to them the door of His Gospel, as well as to the four allied nations near them."

Formation

Isaac Jogues was born at Orleans, France on January 10, 1607. His father was a merchant. Isaac was the middle child in a good family of nine. He was a good student, gentle, affable, quiet but determined. He was very athletic, a strong swimmer and a fast runner. When he was 17, he left home and entered the Jesuit novitiate school at Rouen to begin his studies for the priesthood.

Later, he studied at the royal college of La Fleche where one of his teachers was Father Louis Lalemant. Father Louis had two brothers and a nephew serving as missionaries in Canada. In 1629, Canadians returned from Canada to France after the English captured Quebec. Isaac heard the tales of their missionary work with the Huron Indians and was inspired to follow in their footsteps.

He continued his education at the College of Clermont, University of Paris, and was grounded in theology, the classics and humanities. He was ordained in the Society of Jesus and was accepted for missionary service. On April 8, 1636, at the age of 29, he left his family, country and culture and embarked for the primitive wilderness in Canada (New France) with several other Jesuits, among them St. Charles Garnier.

Father Isaac wrote to his sorrowful mother, "If you accept this little sorrow as you should, it will be an act extremely pleasing to God; since, for the love of God, not only would it be right for you to give one son, but all the other sons, and even life itself, if that were necessary. For a little gain, some men traverse the seas and endure as much as we, at least; and we, for the love of God; we do not do as much as these men do for the affairs of this world. Adieu, Madame ma mère, I thank you for all the great love that you have always given me, and mostly for the love shown at our last meeting. May God reunite us in His holy Paradise if we do not ever see each other here on earth."

Journey to Canada

Sailing on the same ship with the young missionaries were adventurous tradesmen and Charles Huault de Montmagny. He was the new Governor-General of New France sent out to replace Champlain who had died a few months before. Eight weeks later they landed on the island of Miscou and two weeks later they sailed up the St. Lawrence River to Quebec City. Upon arrival, Father Jogues wrote to his mother, "I do not know what it is to enter Heaven, but this I know—that it would be difficult to experience in this world a joy more excessive and more overflowing than I felt in setting foot in the New World, and celebrating my first Mass on the day of the Visitation."

The Indians there named Father Jogues "Ondessonk" meaning "Bird of Prey" after his keen eyes and nervous gestures. Father was warned that the natives were proud, arrogant, vicious, treacherous, superstitious and without moral virtues but that they also had keen minds and some had converted to the one true God and became simple and docile.

Trade opened a path for the missionaries to visit the Huron nation in Ontario. Indians had no metals or woolen cloth. They wanted European clothing, iron pots, flint knives and iron and steel tools. The Europeans accepted furs in trade for them and the fur trade was born. The Hurons brought their furs from Ontario down to Three Rivers and traded. The missionaries there became familiar with them and soon received permission to visit their land.

Father Jean de Brébeuf wrote *Instructions for the Fathers of Our Society who shall be sent to the Hurons.* He counseled the Fathers to have sincere affection for the natives; to never make them wait in leaving in the canoes; to clean the sand from your feet; have a tinder box to light their pipes and fires for them; to eat their sagamite "although it may be dirty, half-cooked and very tasteless"; not to criticize; and to always be cheerful and help carry the baggage at the portages. "Leaving a highly civilized community," he wrote, "you fall into the hands of barbarous people who care nothing at all about your philosophy and your theology."

The Huron Mission

Father Jogues' companions were sent immediately far to the west to join Father de Brébeuf at the Huron mission at Sainte Marie, Ontario. Father Jogues went with them for about 50 miles to Three Rivers on the St. Lawrence River where he remained. A few weeks later, he saw a flotilla of canoes coming down the river from the west. Father Anthony Daniel, one of Father de Brébeuf's co-workers, led the flotilla. He arrived exhausted and emaciated with his cassock in tatters. He was bound for Quebec City to recuperate and Father Jogues was to replace him at Sainte Marie.

On August 24, 1636, Father Jogues with others began the 1000 mile journey over the waterways and through the forests to Sainte Marie. He paddled up the St. Lawrence River to Montreal and up the Ottawa River to Sainte Marie on Georgian Bay on the northern shore of Lake Huron. He endured long hours of crouching and paddling in his canoe. He made long portages carrying it around impassable rocks and waterfalls. He suffered from hunger pangs, the heat of the sun, the stings of the insects, the desolate loneliness, the profound silences and the terrible dark nights with its wails of wild beasts.

When he finally arrived at Sainte Marie on September 11, Father collapsed in the arms of Father de Brébeuf. The very next week, he and some others came down with influenza and were placed in the wretched smoke-filled lodgings to recover. Their food was poor and scanty and they slept on the bough-covered ground under animal skins for blankets. When they had recovered, an influenza epidemic broke out among the Hurons and they blamed the Jesuits whom they called "Blackrobes" because of the black cassocks that they wore.

Their lives were continually in danger. Father de Brébeuf wrote, "You must realize that our lives depend upon a single thread. Our cabin is only chaff, and it might be burned down at any moment, despite all our care to prevent accidents. The malice of the savages gives us special cause for almost perpetual fear; a malcontent may burn you down or may cleave your head open in some lonely spot."

They also faced continual spiritual dangers and occasions of sin. Father de Brébeuf wrote, "Here we have nothing which incites toward good. We are among a people who are astonished when you speak to them of God and who often have only horrible blasphemies in their mouths. I hardly dare to speak of the danger there is of ruining oneself among the impurities of these savages, in the case of one whose heart is not sufficiently full of God to resist firmly this poison."

As the influenza epidemic spread through the Huron lands, the Jesuits baptized those in danger of death. But the Huron sorcerers fanned hostility against them. The sorcerers boasted of their preternatural origins and their communications with demons. They said that the Blackrobes caused people to die by pouring water on their heads because many of them died soon thereafter. They performed ritual chants and dances to please the demons and to drive the disease away. But Father de Brébeuf insisted that they must believe in the one true God and keep His commandments. He proposed "that they give up their beliefs in dreams, that their marriages should be binding and for life that they observe conjugal chastity and refrain from vomiting feasts and the eating of human flesh."

By the following year, relations with the Hurons had so improved that Father de Brébeuf wrote, "We are gladly heard, and there is scarcely a village that has not invited us to go to it. And at last it is understood from our whole conduct that we have not come to buy skins or to carry on any traffic, but solely to teach them, and to procure for them their souls' health."

The mission eventually consisted of a church, living quarters, a cemetery, a hospital and a fort. The Jesuits' life of prayer and action, monastic and missionary, grew up in this remote land. The surrounding lands were cleared and cultivated, food was stored against famine, and the Hurons came to them in times of sickness and trouble, as well as on Sundays and feast days. In the lonely north woods the missionaries tried to create order and to be witnesses of the Gospel.

Father Jogues labored for six long years at Sainte Marie. He learned the language and ways of the Hurons, developed into a skilled woodsman with great physical stamina, and often went on missions. He and Father Garnier went on a missionary journey south to the Petun Indians. Like the Hurons, they too blamed these Blackrobes for their diseases and avoided them. Later he and Father Raymbault were sent to Indians further north where they traversed uncharted waterways and forests to Sault Sainte Marie at the juncture of Lake Huron and Lake Superior. They may have been the first white men to stand on the shore of Lake Superior. About 2,000 Ojibway Indians were gathered there to celebrate their Feast of the Dead. Father Jogues addressed them and erected a Cross facing west towards the Sioux country where they would later hear the Good News from other missionaries.

The total results from the missionary activity of the winter of 1640-1641 were the preaching of the Gospel to 17,000 Indians, 100 baptisms of the sick and a dozen in good health. The Huron church in its totality seven years after its inception and five years after Father Jogues' arrival consisted of only 60 dependable Catholics.

Father Jogues prayed. He spent long hours in adoration of the Blessed Sacrament. One day he was kneeling in adoration and felt an overwhelming desire to suffer for the glory of Jesus. He offered himself as a victim of Divine love. He offered himself, body, soul, will, mind and memory to God so that God might do with him as He pleased. Jesus then spoke to him in an interior locution and repeated it again and again, "Your prayer is heard. It will be done to you as you have asked. Be comforted, be of strong heart."

In 1642, the Hurons suffered from much sickness and a very poor harvest. Father Jogues led an expedition back to Quebec to get supplies and reinforcements. One of the reinforcements was René Goupil. He was a young French layman who was born in the village of Saint-Marin in 1608. He had to leave the Jesuit novitiate in Paris after a few months because of poor health. Nevertheless, he studied medicine and volunteered to come to Canada to help the missionaries as a layman.

These lay missionaries were called *donnés*. They vowed to work among the Indians as helpers of the missionaries, to be obedient to them, to live a life of celibacy and to receive no compensation except their perpetual support from the Society of Jesus. René arrived at Quebec in 1640 and spent the next two years in humble domestic work and in tending the sick. Father Vimont, the Jesuit Superior, referred to him as a gallant surgeon "who had dedicated his life, his heart, and his hand to the service of the poor Indians."

Father Jogues met René working in the Quebec hospital in June of 1642. He later wrote about him and his work in caring for the sick and wounded. He said that René had a "natural aptitude for surgery, that he rendered expertly as well as with loving care. For him it was a question of seeing Our Lord in each patient. And thus he left a sweet odor of his goodness and his other virtues in that place where his memory is still held in veneration."

Father Jogues begged Father Vimont to allow René to return with the expedition to Sainte Marie. The Hurons badly needed a surgeon. Father Vimont granted his request to the great joy of René. Father Jogues wrote, "One cannot imagine the joy of this young man when Father Vimont told him to prepare for the voyage. Nevertheless, he was fully aware of the dangers to be met along the St. Lawrence, and he knew too the great hatred of the Iroquois for the French. All this, however, once the will of God for him had been declared, could not dissuade him from setting out from Three Rivers."

The Iroquois Mohawks hated the Hurons and the French. They were envious of the Huron fur trade since they themselves had over hunted their own lands for them. They needed furs to trade for firearms that they obtained from the Dutch in Albany (Fort Orange), New York. They had the advantage over the Hurons because the Mohawks were the only Indians with firearms. So they wanted to annihilate the Hurons and obtain their fur supply. The Mohawks hatred of the French went back as far as

Champlain's first violent encounter with them that left several of them dead. To accomplish their goals, the Mohawks frequently ambushed Huron canoe flotillas that came from and to Sainte Marie and Three Rivers.

Mohawk Ambush

"We left Three Rivers on August 1st," wrote Father Jogues. "On the 2nd, we met the enemy. Split up into two bands, they were waiting for us possessed of all the advantages that a large cohesive group fighting on land had over a small non-descript group caught on the water in an array of bark canoes."

The group was ambushed and captured by the Mohawks on the St. Lawrence River. Most of the Hurons escaped. The captives included Father Jogues and René Goupil. While the Mohawks pursued the Hurons, Father heard René's confession and gave him absolution. Father wrote, "When the enemy returned from the hunt, they flung themselves upon us like wild dogs with gaping jaws, tearing out our finger nails and crushing our fingers. René bore all this with much patience and courage. His presence of mind amid such distress showed itself in the way he helped me, despite his painful wounds, instruct as best he could those Hurons who were Christians."

The ambush caused a terrible loss to the Huron Mission. They lost their Catholic leaders, their supplies of clothing, food and tools and their books and letters. Father Jogues later wrote about the trail of his captivity:

> Raising a joyful shout, which made the forest ring, "as conquerors who rejoice after taking a prey" (Isaiah 9:3), they bore us off, as captives towards their own land. We were twenty-two; three had been killed. By the favor of God our sufferings on that march, which lasted thirteen days, were indeed great; hunger and heat and menaces, the savage fury of the Indians, the intense pain of our untended and now putrefying wounds, which actually swarmed with worms. No trial, however, came harder upon me than to see them after five or six days approach us jaded with the march, and, in cold blood, with minds in nowise excited by passion, pluck out our hair and beard and drive their nails, which were always very sharp, deep

into parts most tender and sensitive to the slightest impression.

But this was outward; my internal sufferings affected me still more, when I beheld that funeral procession of doomed Christians pass before my eyes, among them five old converts, the main pillars of the infant Huron Church.

The captives were forced into the Mohawk canoe flotilla that paddled south from the St. Lawrence River up the Richelieu River (River of the Iroquois) and Lake Champlain. Along the route of captivity René Goupil helped to prepare the Hurons for Baptism. He expressed his willingness to die if God so willed it. Father Jogues wrote that he was "the soul of gentleness, for covered with wounds as he himself was, he dressed the wounds of others persons, of the enemies who had received some blows in the fight as well as those of the prisoners."

René and Father could have escaped during their march since they were often not bound. However, Father did not want to "forsake in death Frenchmen and Christian Hurons, depriving them of the consolation which a priest can afford" but he encouraged René to escape. René never accepted the offer and preferred to leave everything to the will of God.

René asked Father to accept him as a Jesuit brother and Father received his vows. As Father wrote, René said to him, "Father, God has always given me an intense desire of consecrating myself to His service by religious vows in the Society of Jesus. Heretofore my sins have always rendered me unworthy of this grace. Nevertheless I hope that Our Lord will find acceptable the offering which I wish to make to Him now by pronouncing, as best I can, the vows of the Society, in the presence of my God and before you." Father accepted Brother Goupil's vows in the name of the Society and blessed him, filled with joy.

On August 9th, the eighth day of their captivity, the captives were brought to a small island (now known as Jogues Island) located in Lake Champlain near Westport, New York, on the western shore of the Lake. There 200 Mohawk warriors waited for them to force them to "run the gauntlet" and be tortured. The Mohawks called these tortures "caresses."

Father wrote:

> On the eighth day we fell in with a troop of two hundred
> Indians going out to fight; and as it is the custom for
> savages when out on war parties to initiate themselves,
> as it were, by cruelty, under the belief that their success
> will be greater as they shall have been more cruel, they
> thus received us. First rendering thanks to the Sun, which
> they imagine presides over war, they congratulated their
> countrymen by a joyful volley of musketry. Each then
> cut some stout clubs in the neighboring wood in order to
> receive us. After we had landed from the canoes they
> fell upon us from both sides with their clubs in such fury,
> that I, who was the last and therefore most exposed to
> their blows, sank overcome by their number and severity,
> before I had accomplished half the rocky way that led to
> the hill on which a stage had been erected for us. I thought
> I should soon die there; and so, partly because I could
> not, partly because I cared not, I did not arise.
>
> How long they spent their fury on me He knows, for
> whose love and sake it is delightful and glorious thus to
> suffer. Moved at length by a cruel mercy, and wishing to
> carry me to their country alive, they ceased to strike.
> And thus half dead and drenched in blood, they bore me
> to the scaffold. Here I had scarce begun to breathe when
> they ordered me to come down to load me with scoffs
> and insults, and countless blows on my head and
> shoulders, and indeed on my whole body. I should be
> tedious were I to attempt to tell of all that the French
> prisoners suffered. They burnt one of my fingers, and
> crunched another with their teeth; others already thus
> mangled they so wrenched by the tattered nerves, that
> even now, though healed, they are frightfully deformed.
> Nor indeed was the lot of my fellow-sufferers much
> better.

The captives were led from Jogues Island southwest to the Mohawk
Village at Auriesville, New York (Ossernenon). It was located 40 miles

west of Albany (Fort Orange), New York on a bluff overlooking the Mohawk River. It housed about 600 Indians in multi-family Longhouses. The village was surrounded by "palisades" – tall double fences made of pointed logs that protected the village from attack. The palisades were about 100 yards parallel to the river by 115 yards deep.

First Mohawk Captivity

Father Jogues wrote of the arrival of the captives in Auriesville on August 12th, the 11th day of their captivity:

> Upon our arrival where we were treated with so much cruelty, René demonstrated patience and a gentleness simply extraordinary. Having fallen under a hailstorm of blows heaped upon us with clubs and iron rods and not being able to get up he was carried half-dead to the scaffold where we had been placed in the middle of the village. But he was in such a piteous state that he would have moved even cruelty itself to compassion. His body was livid with bruises so that one could see in his face only the white of his eyes.
>
> Scarcely had he, like us, got back his breath, when he was struck with three huge blows from a club, just as they had treated us earlier. For the six days we were exposed to all and sundry who wished to make sport of us, René showed forth an admirable gentleness. His chest was all burned by the hot coals and ashes which the young boys threw on our bodies during the night while we were fastened to the ground.

During these six days, the captives were tortured in the same way in all three of the Mohawk villages from village to village and from scaffold to scaffold. Father wrote, "We had become a spectacle to God and His angels, as we hope from His Divine Goodness, a scoff and jeer to the vilest savage." Then they were left with sleepless nights because, Father wrote, "of our wounds which remained raw and unhealed thus far. All of these sufferings were made more difficult to bear because of the clouds of fleas and lice and bugs which we could not ward off, except with difficulty, because of our wounded and maimed fingers. More than this, we suffered from a lack of food and we were brought to the verge of starvation. Patience was our physician."

About six weeks later, an old Indian observed René guide the hand of his four-year-old grandson in making the Sign of the Cross. Because of this, the grandfather ordered a young Indian to kill René. That afternoon as he and Father entered the village praying the Rosary, the Indian struck René on the head with his hatchet. He fell face down on the ground, uttering the holy name of Jesus. Father knelt in expectation of receiving a similar blow but it didn't come. So he got up and ran to the dying René and gave him absolution. René died at the age of 35 on September 29, 1642. The Indians ordered Father to return to his cabin where he thought he awaited his martyrdom. While he waited, he had the courage to go out and search for René's body to give it a Christian burial.

Father wrote, "After René had been killed, the children had stripped the body and dragged it by a cord attached to its neck to a stream which flows beside their village. The dogs had already gnawed a part of his sides. I could not hold back my tears at the sight of him. I took the body and placed it beneath the water and weighted it down with stones so as to conceal it. I planned to return the next day with a spade when there would be no one around so as to dig a trench and bury him."

However, when Father returned for the body, he found it gone. Some young Indians had pulled René's body out of the water and into the woods where it was ravaged by animals. Later in the spring, Father found René's head and some of his bones which he buried. He wrote, "I kissed these remains reverently several times since they were the bones of a martyr of Jesus Christ. I gave this title of martyr, not only because he had been killed by enemies of God and His Church, and also while engaged in obvious charity on behalf of his neighbor, placing himself in evident danger for the love of God; but, especially because he had been killed for his prayers and the Sign of the Cross."

Father Jogues' continued to live under constant threat of death. He wrote, "Every day I die, or rather live a life harder to bear than any death." It was a daily slavery and a living martyrdom. The Indians respected the bravery of their strange captive, naming him "the indomitable one." Later, Father Jogues reported to his spiritual director, "The only sin I can remember during my captivity is that I sometimes looked on the approach of death with complacency."

During Father's first winter with the Mohawks, he was forced to go as an equipment bearer on their winter hunt north in the snows of the Adirondack Mountains. For clothing he had only a thin shirt and torn breeches and a cloak. His stockings were shreds and his moccasins were worn into holes. His legs and feet were torn and bloodied by the stubble along the trail. He could scarcely walk from the pain after the first day but he stumbled along, day after day, climbing higher into the mountains and at night sleeping on the ground.

The Mohawks offered the meat from the hunts to Areskoui, their false god of the hunt. But Father refused to eat it because it had been sacrificed to a false god. He fasted and endured great hunger. Then the hunting got poorer and the Mohawks blamed this on Father's refusal to eat of their sacrifice. He wrote, "The savages interpreted my abstinence from meat and my contempt for the demon as the cause of their taking little game: 'the wicked have hated me without cause.' "

The Mohawks then sent Father back to Auriesville loaded with moose meat. He staggered under the tremendous burden and stumbled through the snow and underbrush with frostbitten arms and legs. Eight days later he arrived at the village.

Later, one of the young girls in his cabin practiced open fornication in Father's presence with a brave who frequently visited her. Father rebuked her and made her an enemy but he was not tempted. Father wrote, "Chastity, indeed, is not endangered here so much by delight; but it is endangered, nevertheless, by the promiscuous and intimate manner of living together of both sexes, in the free permission for anyone to dare to do anything whatsoever, and most of all in the complete nudity." His confessor, Father Buteux wrote, "Never once during all that time, and in such dangerous occasions of sin, did Father Jogues experience any emotion or any imagination or any thought against purity."

The historian Francis Parkman wrote, "He would sometimes escape and wander in the forest, telling his beads and repeating passages of Scripture. In a remote and lonely spot he cut the bark in the form of a Cross from the trunk of a great tree; and here he made his prayers. This living martyr, half clad in shaggy furs, kneeling in the snow among the icicled rocks and beneath the gloomy pines, bowing in adoration before the emblem of his faith in which was his only consolation and his only hope, is alike a theme for the pen and a subject for the pencil."

"How often," Father wrote, "on the stately trees of the forests did I carve the most Sacred Name of Jesus, so that, seeing it, the demons might take to flight, and hearing it, they might tremble with fear? How often did I strip off the bark from those trees, and fashion on them the most holy Cross of the Lord, so that, at its sight, the enemy might flee before it, and that through it, O Lord, My King, thou 'might rule in the midst of thy enemies,' the enemies of the Cross, the unbelievers, the pagans who dwell in these lands and the demons who rule far and wide through all these regions?"

By that spring, Father had at least one good friend among the Mohawks. She was an old woman whom he called "aunt." She tried to warn and protect him when danger threatened. His days were passed in menial work, learning the language, and comforting Huron prisoners who were sometimes brought in. He baptized children that he found dying. During the year he baptized some 70 persons. On July 31st, his "aunt" and some other Mohawks took Father Jogues down the Mohawk River to the Dutch settlement at Albany to trade.

Escape

After Father arrived at Albany, the Dutch leader, Arendt Van Corlaer, told him that it would be possible to escape to a boat lying off on the Hudson River. It was ready to sail for Bordeaux, France. Father and his Mohawk guards slept in a Dutch farmer's barn. Before dawn, Father picked his way over the Indians sleeping around him and got to the river. On his way the farmer's dog gave him a vicious bite. Father rowed out to the anchored vessel where he was taken on board and concealed. The enraged Mohawks were soon on his trail, threatening reprisals against the Dutch for their part in his attempted escape.

When Father learned of this, he insisted on going back to shore. "If this trouble has been caused by me," he said, "I am ready to appease it at the loss of my life. I have never wished to escape if it meant injury to the least man in the colony." So the Dutch took him back to shore and hid him in hopes that the Mohawks would eventually accept some presents from them and be satisfied.

For the next six weeks, Father hid and waited for another boat and was kept in close, uncomfortable confinement in a garret. He could stand up only in the center. There was only one tiny window for ventilation and the thatch roof leaked. He slept on the hard planked floor, drank putrid water that wracked him with cramps and suffered from his dog bite wound that had gangrened. Father Lalemant wrote, "Only God and His saints were his company."

Finally, in late September, Father was smuggled out of the garret to a ship and sailed south down the Hudson River to New York City (New Amsterdam). He was the first Catholic priest to visit the settlement. "No religion is publicly exercised here but the Calvinist," he noted, "and orders are to admit none but Calvinists; but this is not observed. There are in the colony Catholics, Puritans, Lutherans, Anabaptists, etc."

On November 5, 1643, Father sailed for Europe. He reached the coast of Cornwall, England towards the end of December. Then he was able to get aboard a boat bound for France and landed on the coast of Brittany on Christmas morning in a state of absolute destitution. He joyfully went to Confession and attended Christmas Mass. It had been 17 months since his last Confession, Mass and Communion.

Home Again

After his arrival in Brittany, kindly people helped him reach the town of Rennes. At the priest's house, Father sent word by a servant that he was the bearer of news from Canada. Unknown to him, his own fate was a matter of widespread concern in France since the latest volume of the *Jesuit Relations* had contained the news of his capture. When the priest came to the room, after an exchange of courtesies, he asked the shabbily-dressed man if he had known Father Jogues.

"Very well indeed," Father answered.

"Have those barbarians murdered him?" the priest asked.

Father answered, "He is at liberty. Reverend Father it is he who speaks to you."

Father Jogues tearfully fell on his knees, kissed the priest's hands and begged his blessing. The whole household was filled with awe and they celebrated Mass in thanksgiving for Father's return. This astonishing news spread quickly and Father Jogues soon reported to his superiors. He wrote to his Provincial, "After all, my sins have rendered me unworthy to die among the Iroquois. I still live, and God grant that it be to amend myself."

Father was so famous that ladies, courtiers, and even the Queen Regent wanted to meet him and do him honor. When Queen Anne, the mother of King Louis XIV, heard of his story she said, "They try to invent tragic stories, and use their imagination to concoct strange adventures to surprise one and to touch one's emotion. But here is a story of great adventures which have really happened; here is a recital of the most astounding deeds joined with the truest heroism."

The Queen received Father in an audience. After he told her his story, she took his mutilated hands into her own and her eyes filled with tears. Father received special permission to celebrate Mass with the stumps of these fingers. When Pope Urban VII granted this exceptional dispensation he said, "It would be shameful that a martyr of Christ be not allowed to drink the blood of Christ."

Father Jogues soon tired of the honors showered on him and longed to return to Canada. His heart still desired to serve God through the evangelization and salvation of the Indians.

Return to Canada

In late June of 1644, Father landed in Quebec City. The Mohawks were on the warpath and had decimated the Hurons and Algonquins. In July, Father was sent to Montreal (Ville Marie) to help maintain this haven for Christian Indians until the end of the Mohawk's warfare would allow him to return to the Hurons. He stayed there through May of 1646 in work and prayer.

On May 13, Governor Montmagny entertained an embassy of Mohawks at Three Rivers to discuss terms of a truce and the ransom of prisoners. Many fine speeches were made and gifts were exchanged. After the deliberations were concluded, the French thought it prudent to send a conciliatory deputation to meet with other Iroquois chieftains at Auriesville. The Governor chose Father Jogues and Jean Bourdon, an engineer, to be ambassadors of goodwill to the Mohawks. "Oh, how I should regret to lose so glorious an occasion," Father wrote to his Superior before starting, "when it may depend only on me that some souls be saved! I hope that His goodness, which has not abandoned me in the hour of trial, will aid me still."

Ambassador to the Mohawks

Father Jogues traveled back to Auriesville. The party traveled south and on May 30th they arrived at Lake George, New York. Father was the first White man to see it and he named it the Lake of the Blessed Sacrament. Next, he stopped at Albany, where he had a reunion with his Dutch rescuers.

On June 5, 1646, Father arrived at Auriesville after a three week journey. The Mohawks were impressed by his courage and disarmed by his gentleness. Father showed them no sign of ill-will for their previous mistreatment of him. He came as an ambassador of peace. His "aunt" greeted him warmly. Gifts were exchanged between Frenchmen and Indians and belts of wampum offered for the release of the Hurons held captive. The peace pact was confirmed and Father returned to Quebec. He left behind a locked black box that contained clothing, a cup and a prayer book. Father had showed some Mohawks its contents before he left, but he had locked it up for safekeeping and asked them to keep it. The Mohawks were suspicious of that black box.

Missionary to the Mohawks

Father Jogues arrived back in Three Rivers on July 3rd. Soon, he asked to be sent back to the Mohawks once again as a missionary. After much hesitation, his superiors agreed to his request. In a letter to a friend written shortly before his last mission to the Mohawks, Father wrote:

> The Iroquois have come to make some presents to our governor, ransom some prisoners he held, and treat of peace with him in the name of the whole country. It has been concluded, to the great joy of France. It will last as long as pleases the Almighty.
>
> To maintain, and see what can be done for the instruction of these tribes, it is here deemed expedient to send them some father. I have reason to think I shall be sent, since I have some knowledge of the language and country. You see what need I have of the powerful aid of prayers while amidst these savages. I will have to remain among them, almost without liberty to pray, without

Mass, without Sacraments, and be responsible for every accident among the Iroquois, French, Algonquins, and others. But what shall I say? My hope is in God, who needs not us to accomplish His designs. We must endeavor to be faithful to Him and not spoil His work by our shortcomings.

My heart tells me that if I have the happiness of being employed in this mission, *Ibo et non redibo* (I shall go and shall not return); but I shall be happy if our Lord will complete the sacrifice where He has begun it, and make the little blood I have shed in that land the earnest of what I would give from every vein of my body and my heart.

In a word, this people is "a bloody spouse" to me (Exodus 4: 25). May our good Master, who has purchased them in His blood, open to them the door of His Gospel, as well as to the four allied nations near them.

Adieu, dear Father. Pray Him to unite me inseparably to Him.

Father began his third and last journey to the Mohawks accompanied by a few Hurons and Jean de la Lande, a layman. Like René Goupil before be became a religious Brother, Jean was a *donné*. He was a lay missionary, who vowed to work among the Indians as a helper to the missionaries, to be obedient to them, to live a life of celibacy and to receive no compensation except his perpetual support from the Society of Jesus. Jean was born in the Norman seaport of Dieppe, France, and had been serving on the Jesuit staff in Three Rivers. Father Jogues warned Jean that it would be a hard and perhaps dangerous journey. But Jean was determined to go. He took Father's mutilated hands into his own and professed his desire to share his future with him even it meant martyrdom. Father Lalemant wrote about Jean's motivation. "Seeing the danger involved in this perilous journey, he protested at his departure that the desire of serving God was leading him into a country where he expected to meet certain death."

Jean and Father set out from Three Rivers for Auriesville on September 24, 1646. All but one of the Hurons soon abandoned them. They continued on, completely unaware of the mounting tension and antagonism in the

Mohawk village. The moderate Turtle and Wolf Clans could not persuade the Bear Clan to keep the peace truce. During Father's absence, the village had suffered from a sickness that killed many as it spread from Longhouse to Longhouse. Then, just before Father left Three Rivers to visit them, their crops failed. The Bear Clan blamed all of this on Father and called him an evil sorcerer who had left an evil spirit locked up in the black box that he had left behind in the village. They found the box and threw it into the river to trap the evil spirit. Then they decided to kill Father Jogues.

Soon after that, a war party of Mohawks met Father, Jean and their Huron guide on the trail near Lake George. They captured them, stripped them naked, slashed them with their knives, beat them and then led them on to their village at Auriesville.

Martyrdom

The captives were led into Auriesville on October 17, where they were threatened with death. Father protested his innocence and goodwill and his mission to confirm the peace and show them the way to Heaven. In the councils, the majority of the Mohawks were ready to give him his freedom, but the Bear Clan took matters into their own hands.

The next evening, a member of the Bear Clan invited Father to visit his lodging for dinner. As Father unsuspectingly bent his head and entered the Longhouse, he was brutally tomahawked by a Bear warrior hiding behind the entranceway. It was October 18, 1646. They dragged his body out into the lane and danced over it in triumph. Then they scalped him, cut his head from the neck and processed it through the lanes to the wall of the village where they impaled it on a pointed pole.

Then the mob searched for Jean who was protected in Father's "aunt's" Longhouse. She told Jean of Father's death and warned him not to leave the Longhouse. Jean waited and prayed. That day he had gone to Father for Confession and received his absolution. He was ready to die. He thought that Father's body was lying abandoned in the lane and wanted to rescue it and reverence it.

Jean waited for the silence of sleep in the village. Then, in the early morning, he left the Longhouse to retrieve Father's body. As he left, some Bear warriors leapt from their hiding by the walls and tomahawked him. Then they scalped him, cut his head from the neck and impaled it on a pointed pole next to Father's head as a warning to the French. Their bodies were thrown into the river. It was October 19, 1646.

A year later, Father Jogues' suspected murderer was captured and brought to Quebec. He converted, was baptized and received the name of his victim, Isaac Jogues. Father Lalemant wrote:

> It must be confessed that the spirit of Jesus Christ breathes where it pleases. This poor man astonished us all. He gave marked evidence of his belief, and asked pardon of God for his transgressions. "Yes, I believe," he said. "I wish to go to Heaven. But I am grieved to have offended Him who has made all. Jesus, pardon me! Jesus, pardon me!" he said in his own language. "Do not doubt," he added, "that I believe with all my heart what you teach me. And since we must all appear before God, according to your saying, at that time reproach me with treachery if my heart has not now the belief which my mouth declares to you." These excellent inclinations softened all who were near. He was baptized and was made to bear the name of Father Isaac Jogues – whom he himself had killed, as some said.

Once more, the Mohawks went on the warpath. They attacked and ambushed the French, Hurons and Algonquins. They attacked and plundered the Huron villages in Canada. They spared no one. Fathers Garnier, Daniel, Gabriel, Lalemant, and de Brébeuf were soon martyred in 1649.

Virtues

Father Jogues spiritual advisor, Father Buteux, wrote of his virtues:

> I can say in all truth, for I know it most certainly, having heard his general Confession, one of the most remarkable things I know of has been the purity in which he kept himself among so many various vicissitudes. One of his great faults was that of having quite often wished for

death in the midst of his long and continual exterior and interior sufferings.

His modesty kept secret from me the principal thing, that which adorns all else: I mean his interior virtues, his charity, his patience, his conformity to the will of God through which he suffered.

Father Buteux described Father Jogues' charity and patience with the Mohawks against whom he had no malice but only compassion like "a mother who was patient to her little son in a temper." He longed for their conversion and salvation and maintained his peace of soul in the sufferings that he received from them.

Father Jogues said, "I have always loved those who punished me, and even kissed the rods of my teachers. Especially was this the case with the Iroquois, after they had spared our lives. I did not cease, for many days in succession, from kissing the uprights of the platform on which we had suffered, and the sight of this place of exquisite torture was a source of consolation and an occasion of gratitude and thanksgiving for the favors that God had given me."

These virtues were the fruit of the extraordinary sacrifice that he made to God as a victim of Divine love which he repeated throughout his missionary years and his prayers before the Blessed Sacrament, to which Father Buteux said he was "glued." "It was before this hidden God that he performed all his spiritual exercises, his prayers, his examens, his breviary, and he did not mind the bitterness of the cold nor the annoyances of the insects."

Fruits

The blood of the martyrs is often the water that sprouts the seed of the Catholic faith. The blood of the only martyr saints of the United States, Isaac Jogues, René Goupil and Jean de la Lande, watered the seed of the faith in the Mohawk Village at Auriesville, New York. Blessed Kateri Tekakwitha was born there in 1656, ten years after the last of them were martyred there.

The example of Father Jogues' heroism had not been forgotten. The Mohawks remembered him for his bravery, the virtue the Indians admired most. Some years later, when there was peace, the three Jesuit priests sent from Canada to establish the Mission of the Martyrs were well received. Before long, Mohawk converts were traveling to the seminary in Quebec to be trained as Christian leaders.

Saints

Isaac Jogues was declared a martyr and canonized as a saint by Pope Pius XI on June 29, 1930 together with the seven other North American martyrs – René Goupil, Jean de la Lande and Fathers Jean de Brébeuf, Gabriel Lalemant, Charles Garnier, Antoine Daniel and Noël Chabanel. Their collective Feast Day is October 19.

**Opening Prayer for the Mass in Commemoration of
Saints Isaac Jogues, Jean de Brébeuf and Companions**

Father,
you consecrated the first beginnings
of the faith in North America
by the preaching and martyrdom
of Saints Jean and Isaac and their companions.
By the help of their prayers
may the Christian faith continue to grow
throughout the world.
We ask this through our Lord Jesus Christ, your Son,
who lives and reigns with you and the Holy Spirit,
one God, for ever and ever.

Shrine:

Shrine of Our Lady of Martyrs
136 Shrine Road
Auriesville, N.Y. 12016
Telephone: (518) 853-3033
Website: www.martyrshrine.org

7. Blessed Kateri Tekakwitha and Catholic Native Americans

Born 1656 in Auriesville (Ossernenon), New York

Died April 17, 1680 in Kahnawake (Sault Saint Louis), Quebec, Canada

Beatified June 22, 1980

Feast Day July 14

> *"The last months of her life are an even clearer manifestation of her solid faith, straight-forward humility, calm resignation and radiant joy, even in the midst of terrible sufferings. Her last words, simple and sublime, whispered at the moment of death, sum up, like a noble hymn, a life of purest charity: 'Jesus, I love you.'"*
> Pope John Paul II at the Beatification Mass for Kateri Tekakwitha, June 22, 1980

The young Mohawk Indian maiden hid in the woods from her uncle, Chief of the Turtle Clan. He was searching and hollering for her in anger to return home to her Mohawk village. He was humiliated that his adopted daughter had abandoned him and her tribe.

Kateri Tekakwitha had just escaped from the village in New York to travel to Canada to live the life of a Catholic Indian where she could practice her faith in peace.

Kateri's Baptism

Kateri lived in the Mohawk village at Auriesville (Ossernenon), New York with her Mohawk father and her Canadian Algonquin Catholic mother who had been captured in a Mohawk raid. When Kateri was four years

55

old, a smallpox plague broke out in the village that killed her parents and left Kateri disfigured with smallpox marks and with impaired vision. "Tekakwitha" in Mohawk means "one who stretches out her hands" or "one who feels her way," because Kateri had to feel her way as she walked because of her poor eyesight. She often stayed in the Longhouse because the sunlight hurt her eyes.

The orphaned Kateri was raised by her childless aunt and uncle, the Chief of the Turtle Clan. In 1666, the French attacked and burned down Kateri's village. The Mohawks built a new village on the north side of the Mohawk River at Fonda (Caughnawaga). Here Kateri heard of the Catholic faith from Father Jacques de Lamberville, a French Jesuit, who visited her village in September of 1667.

Kateri's adoptive parents wanted her to marry so that they would have grandchildren. But Kateri decided to remain a virgin. Virginity was unheard of amongst the Indians and they pressured her to marry which she refused. When they connived to have her lodge visited by a young warrior in the hopes of their union, she turned him out.

Father de Lamberville baptized Kateri on April 18, 1676, and she took the name "Kateri," which is Mohawk for "Catherine." After that, the Indians treated her as a slave and put her to work for the village. They persecuted her for her faith and mocked her devotion to the Blessed Virgin Mary and her recitation of the Rosary. Her family wouldn't feed her on Sunday because she refused to work on the Lord's day.

Kateri was not deterred but, in order to practice her faith freely, she escaped in 1677 with two Christian Indian visitors. They had come from the St. Francis Xavier Indian Mission in Canada. They avoided her searching uncle and trekked north through New York. They paddled down Lake Champlain and the Richelieu River and then walked to the Mission at Sault Saint-Louis, near Montreal on the St. Lawrence River. The journey took weeks, traveling by foot and canoe about 300 miles through woods, rivers, swamps and lakes.

Kateri had a note from Father de Lamberville to deliver to the Jesuits at the Mission. "Kateri Tekakwitha now comes to join your community. Granting her your spiritual guidance and direction, you will soon realize what a jewel we have sent you. Her soul is very close to the Lord."

The Lily of the Mohawks

At the Mission, Kateri lived with about 150 other Catholic Indian families from different tribes. Her life was dedicated to prayer, penitential practices and care for the poor, sick and aged. Her day at the Mission began at 5 a.m. each morning in church where she remained for several hours of prayer and Masses. She formed a group called the Slavery of the Blessed Virgin and they fasted and endured exposure to the cold in the woods as acts of penance. Kateri's spiritual director, Father Pierre Cholenec, prepared her for her First Communion. On March 25, 1679, he permitted her to make a public vow of perpetual virginity.

Kateri was a half-blind, pockmarked orphan Indian maiden. She was little more than a slave in her own clan but in God's eyes she was His pure daughter and a model for her race. Many Indians followed her good example and converted. Kateri received the Eucharist with the greatest devotion. Father Cholenec said, "Only God knows what passed between Himself and His dear Spouse."

Kateri attended daily Masses at 5 a.m. and 8 a.m. and visited the Blessed Sacrament five times daily, after her daily visitations to the sick and the poor. During her own last sickness, she dragged herself to Mass until she could no longer walk. She died at the age of 24 on April 17, 1680, in the presence of Father Cholenec. Suddenly, all of her smallpox marks disappeared. He said that Kateri's face, which was so dark and disfigured in life, "suddenly changed about a quarter of an hour after her death and became in a moment so beautiful, smiling and white, more beautiful than when she had been living. Kateri Tekakwitha had died as she lived, that is to say, as a saint."

Two hundred and ninety three years later, on the very same date, April 17, 1973, young Peter McCauley's hearing was spontaneously restored through Kateri's intercession. This was the miracle that led to her beatification by Pope John Paul II on June 22, 1980. Because of her purity, Kateri is known as the "Lily of the Mohawks." Her Feast Day is July 14.

Shrine:
The National Kateri Shrine
P.O. Box 627, Fonda, NY 12068 - Phone: (518) 853-3646
Website: www.katerishrine.com

8. New France and New Spain Expand

In 1673, Father Jacques Marquette and Louis Joliet canoed from St. Ignace in the Upper Peninsula of Michigan down Lake Michigan and other lakes and rivers to the mighty Mississippi River. They canoed down the Mississippi past the Missouri River and the Ohio River to where the Arkansas River flows into it. On their way down, they visited some Illinois Indians. Father Marquette told them that God sent him on a mission of peace because He "wished to make Himself known to all the peoples" and that they had "to acknowledge and obey Him." They learned that the Mississippi River divided the United States and ran south to the Gulf of Mexico.

In 1681, René de La Salle led an expedition to build forts and missions up and down the Mississippi River to protect New France from the Dutch and English. They traveled south all the way down the Mississippi River to its mouth in the Gulf of Mexico. He claimed the river and the land on both sides for King Louis XIV of France and named the lands in his honor as Louisiana. The French settlements were frontier regions much different than the established Spanish colonial towns.

New Spain also continued to develop in the 18th century. From the 1690s to the 1770s, Fathers Eusebio Kino in the Southwest and Father Junipero Serra in California established many Spanish missions. Jesuit Father Kino made 40 expeditions in 11 years through Arizona, New Mexico and California. He established over 20 missions and said that over a 21-year period "there have been brought to our friendship and to the desire of receiving our holy Catholic faith . . . more than thirty thousand souls, there being sixteen thousand of Pimas alone."

Father Kino gave an account of his evangelization efforts in Arizona with the Sobaipuri tribe in September of 1692:

> I went in, with fifty pack animals, my servants, and
> some native officials, to the Sobaipuris. I spoke to them

of the word of God, and on a map of the world showed them the lands, the rivers, and the seas over which we fathers had come from afar to bring them the saving knowledge of our holy faith. And I told them also how in ancient times the Spaniards were not Christian, how Santiago [St. James the Apostle] came to teach them the faith, and how for the first fourteen years he was able to baptize only a few, because of which the most holy apostle was discouraged, but that the most holy Virgin appeared to him and consoled him, telling him that the Spaniards would convert the rest of the peoples of the world.

And I showed them on the map of the world how the Spaniards and the faith had come by sea to Mexico and now to the land of the Pimas, where there were already many persons baptized, a house, church, bells, and images of saints, plentiful supplies, wheat, maize, and many cattle and horses. I told them that they could go and see it all, and even ask about it right away of the Indians who were with me. They listened with pleasure to these and other talks concerning God, Heaven, and Hell, and told me that they wished to be Christians, and gave me some infants to baptize.

Father Kino died on March 15, 1711. His successor, Padre Luis Velarde wrote, "His death bed, as his bed had always been, consisted of two calfskins for a mattress, two blankets such as the Indians use for covers, and a pack saddle for a pillow."

In 1750 at the age of 36, Franciscan Father Serra gave up his comfortable teaching services in Spain and volunteered to serve the Franciscan missions in the New World. He left Cadiz, Spain and sailed for Vera Cruz, Mexico. From there he walked for 24 days by foot to Mexico City and dedicated his mission vocation to Our Lady of Guadalupe at her shrine. He spent nine years preaching and ministering in Mexico.

England and Russia soon began to explore the Pacific coast from the north. Spain wanted to gain a foothold from the south in California. In 1769, a Spanish expedition was organized under Gaspar de Portola. At the age of 56, Father Serra accompanied the expedition to San Diego,

California, where he planted the Cross and established his first mission. From there he walked hundreds of miles while suffering from asthma and a chronically sore and painful leg. He established nine missions up and down the Pacific coast of California in 15 years between 1769 and his death in 1784. He established missions in San Diego, San Luis Obispo, Santa Clara, San Francisco and other places along the California coastline over a distance of 700 miles.

In April of 1770, at Monterey, he and Gaspar de Portola took possession of California for the king of Spain. In addition, Father Serra claimed Monterey for the King of Heaven. He rang a bell that he hung from a tree and shouted out to the Indians, "Come, Gentiles! Come to the Holy Church. Come and receive the faith of Jesus Christ!" He battled governors, bureaucrats and military commanders to secure a system of laws to protect the California Indians from injustices by the Spanish soldiers.

Father Serra had extraordinary administrative abilities. In four short years he settled and organized a functioning frontier through missions. He had to house and feed the residents of the missions. To do this he had to secure from the Spanish government food, grain and plant seeds, tools, supplies, horses, mules and wagons, cows and other animals. It was a huge task. The California missions were permanent structured communities where the Indians could live in peace. They were sheltered and protected from their enemies, taught the Catholic faith, techniques for farming and crafts and singing and the playing of musical instruments. Father Serra introduced agriculture and irrigation systems and created a network of roads. He helped the Indians to develop from hunters to farmers, from illiteracy to learning and from using primitive tools to the tools of the trade of carpenters and blacksmiths.

Father Serra baptized approximately 6,000 Indians who were about ten percent of the entire native population at the nine missions that he founded. He reported that "when we came not a Christian existed here. We regenerated all in Christ; and we have come and we are all here for their welfare and salvation. At all events, I believe it is well known that we love them."

Father Serra died from tuberculosis on August 28, 1784 at the age of 70. He had traveled a distance of over 5000 miles by land on foot or animal. Pope John Paul II beatified him on September 25, 1988. His Feast Day is July 1. In recognition of his achievements, Father Serra's likeness was placed in Statuary Hall in the foyer of the United States Capitol in Washington, D.C.

The English propagated the so-called "Black Legend" that the Spaniards were merciless persecutors of the Indians. In truth, many of them were, but many were also merciful to them and taught them the Catholic faith. They also intermarried with them. The English did none of this and simply killed by war or disease any Indians who got in the way of their colonies. By the 19th century, the Indian tribes of the Eastern woodlands no longer existed. It was now New England.

9. New England

A lack of national unification and interior political battles delayed the English explorations of the New World. Finally, when the nation consolidated in the 16th century under Queen Elizabeth I, it began to challenge Spanish and French rule in the New World. After the failure of the Roanoke Island colony in North Carolina in the 1580s, the English founded Jamestown, Virginia, in 1607. It was the first permanent English colony.

Later, the English Pilgrims sailed to join this colony, but they went off course and eventually landed at Plymouth, Massachusetts, where they established a colony in 1620. They drew up The Mayflower Compact, named after their ship, which established the government of their colony. This was the first document of self-government in the British colonies. The Pilgrims (who called themselves the Saints) came to freely practice their religion. They barely survived their first winter and lost one half of their numbers, but with the help of local Indians they endured as a colony.

In 1628, another group of English Christians settled to the north in Salem, Massachusetts. They called themselves "Puritans" and established their colony to "purify" the teachings and practices of the English faith of the Church of England (the Anglican Church) founded by King Henry the VIII in the 16th century. In 1629, another group of Puritans settled in Boston. These settlements and others in Massachusetts, Connecticut and Rhode Island became known as New England.

Eventually, New England consisted of all of the English colonies located in the northeast of the present United States. The Catholic population of these colonies was only about 25,000 out of a total population of 2.5 million or one percent of the total. Most of the colonists practiced the faith of the Episcopalian Church, the American name for the Church of England.

Many Catholics found a home in the colony of Maryland. Maryland was settled in 1634 by Lord Baltimore (Sir Cecil Calvert), the son of a prominent English convert to Catholicism. The first party settled at St. Mary's where they established the first Catholic place of worship in the English colonies. Over the next 10 years, the Catholics suffered from discrimination from the English Puritans. Priests were arrested and banished from the colony. This resulted in the Act of Religious Toleration in 1649 that foreshadowed the Bill of Rights of the United States Constitution more than 100 years later.

The Act established religious freedom in the colony and provided that "no person or persons whatsoever within this Province . . . professing to believe in Jesus Christ, shall from henceforth be anyways troubled, molested or discountenanced for or in respect of his or her religion nor in the free exercise thereof . . . nor anyway compelled to the belief or exercise of any other religion against his or her consent."

Unfortunately, the Puritans repealed the Act in 1654 and intolerance returned. In 1702, the official state religion of Maryland became the Episcopalian Church. However, the colony remained the most Catholic of all of the English colonies and the Mass continued in private chapels in spite of the governor's 1704 condemnation of it and the Church's teachings as "gawdy shows and serpentine policy."

On August 18, 1662, four English war ships sailed up the Hudson River to the Dutch city of New York (New Amsterdam) harbor on Manhattan Island. They demanded that the Governor, Peter Stuyvesant, surrender the colony to the king of England. The English took the colony and all the other Dutch American colonies without firing a shot. King Charles called his new colony New York, in honor of his brother James, the Duke of York. New York became an English colony with the Episcopalian Church as the predominant religion. It later became the home of the United States' first native-born saint, Elizabeth Ann Seton.

In 1755, the French and Indian War broke out between Great Britain and France. On September 13, 1759, the British, under General Wolfe, defeated the French, under General Montcalm, at the Battle of Quebec. The great fort and city were defeated and the British controlled the St. Lawrence River from Montreal to the Atlantic Ocean. Montreal fell a year later and the fighting ended with the Treaty of Paris in 1763. The treaty gave all of Canada to the British. Great Britain now ruled New France.

Part Three

The First Evangelization of the United States

10. New Nation

After the French and Indian War, the British decided that the colonists should help to pay for it since they had benefited from the English victory. England's Parliament passed many acts levying heavy taxes on the colonists. They had no representation in Parliament and resisted the idea of taxation without representation. In a move towards independence, they formed a Continental Congress and the Massachusetts colonists stored arms at Concord. The British troops left Boston to destroy these arms. They met the colonial Minutemen (militia who could be ready in a "minute") on Lexington Green. The British shot and killed some of them and marched on to Concord where they met another group of Minutemen. These fired on the British who then retreated to Boston. The Minutemen harassed them from the woods all along the way to Boston. This was the beginning of the American Revolution.

On July 4, 1776, the Continental Congress approved the Declaration of Independence declaring that the 13 American colonies were free and independent states. In spite of this Declaration, many colonists were loyal to the English King George III. They were called Loyalists (or Tories) because they had taken an oath of loyalty to the king. One of them was Richard Bayley, father of Elizabeth Ann Seton. The Treaty of Paris of 1783 ended the Revolutionary War in victory for the new nation of the United States of America. Great Britain gave the new nation all the lands between the Atlantic Ocean and the Mississippi River.

In 1789, the Constitution of the United Sates of America was adopted, General George Washington was inaugurated as its first President and the new nation received its first Catholic Bishop, John Carroll. He was born in Maryland in 1735 into a prominent, wealthy, Maryland Catholic family. His proposal led to the founding by the Jesuits of the first Catholic college in the new nation, Georgetown University in Washington D. C. His diocese included the entire new nation and he invited Sulpician priests from France to establish the first American seminary at St. Mary's in Baltimore.

In 1792, Bishop Carroll dedicated the new nation to the Blessed Virgin Mary. He wrote:

> I shall only add this, my earnest request, that to the exercise of the sublimest virtues, faith, hope and charity, you will join a fervent and well regulated devotion to the Holy Mother of Our Lord and Savior Jesus Christ; that you will place great confidence in Her intercession; and have recourse to Her in all your necessities. Having chosen Her the special patroness of this Diocese [that included the entire United States of America], you are placed, of course, under Her powerful protection; and it becomes your duty to be careful to deserve its continuance by a zealous imitation of Her virtues, and reliance on Her motherly superintendence.

Sixteen years later, a young widow sailed to Maryland from New York City "under Her powerful protection" in "a zealous imitation of Her virtues, and reliance on Her motherly superintendence." Her name was Elizabeth Ann Seton, Foundress of the first community of religious women in the United States.

11. Saint Elizabeth Ann Seton and Frontier Girls of Maryland

Born	August 28, 1774 in New York City, New York
Died	January 4, 1821 in Emmitsburg, Maryland
Canonized	September 14, 1975 by Pope Paul VI
Feast Day	January 4

Foundress of the Sisters of Charity of Saint Joseph's, the first community for religious women to be established in the United States.

First United States native born to be canonized.

"I would say from the bottom of my heart, out of conviction from long and intimate acquaintance, that I believe hers was one of those elite souls, with the like characteristics found in St. Teresa [of Avila] and St. Jane Frances de Chantal, just as capable of as unbelievable a holiness, it being impossible to find similar or greater elevation, purity and love of God, Heaven, supernatural and eternal things than were found in her."
Father Simon Brute, spiritual advisor of
Mother Elizabeth Ann Seton.

The young mother huddled on the cold, damp floor with her eight-year-old daughter and her dying husband in the lazaretto, a stone tower on the coast of Leghorn, Italy. Elizabeth, Anna and Will Seton had been quarantined there for a month after arriving from New York City. Their ship was suspected of carrying the dreaded yellow fever. They were bolted into to a small, cold room with a single window double-grated with iron, naked walls and a brick floor on which they slept on the ship-mattresses. Elizabeth wrote, "My eyes smart so much with crying, wind and fatigue, that I must close them and lift up my heart."

And so it continued with Elizabeth and Anna reading, praying, singing hymns, jumping rope to keep warm and nursing Will. He was crying, coughing blood, shivering and in patient agony until they were released on December 19. He often said that this was the period of his life in which he was most blessed. Elizabeth wrote that if she thought that this was caused by human providence rather than Divine Providence, "you would find me a lioness, willing to burn your lazaretto about your ears, if it was possible, that I might carry off my poor prisoner to breathe the air of Heaven in some more seasonable place."

Will was carried off from the lazaretto to lodgings in Pisa. There he resigned himself to a death that he eagerly awaited saying, "I want to be in Heaven. Pray, pray for my soul." He died on December 27 at the age of 35 saying, "My dear wife – and little ones – My Christ Jesus, have mercy and receive me." His Protestant wife and daughter joined his prayer.

"Oh! Oh! Oh! What a day," Elizabeth wrote. "Close his eyes, lay him out, ride a journey, be obliged to see a dozen people in my room till night – and at night crowded with the whole sense of my situation." Her steadfast love and care for Will in his agony and death led her Catholic Pisa neighbors to exclaim, "If she was not a heretic, she would be a saint."

Formation

Elizabeth Ann Bayley was born on August 28, 1774, in New York City. She was the second daughter of Richard and Catherine Bayley. Betty's childhood bridged from life in an English colony to life in a new nation. She was one week old when the First Continental Congress met in Philadelphia to form independence and she became a charter citizen of the new nation at the age of two.

Betty's father was a nominal Episcopalian who exhibited no faith but in later life practiced the corporal works of mercy to a heroic degree. He ministered to the sick and investigated a cure for yellow fever, the terror of New York.

He became New York City's first Health Officer in a very unhealthy city. He had a running battle with merchants and artisans to stop them from their many unsanitary work habits that included throwing slops in the streets that helped to create the conditions for yellow fever.

Betty loved her father very much, but he was frequently away from home. One time he left for England to study surgery and was gone for two long years. But, he learned his surgery and became the first doctor to successfully amputate an arm at the shoulder. He was gone again when the American Revolution broke out and again when the Patriots burned the city as they escaped from its occupation by British General William Howe in September of 1776. Mr. Bayley was a Loyalist (loyal to Great Britain) and was stationed at Newport, Rhode Island, serving as a surgeon in the British forces. His wife died on May 8, 1777. They had been married for eight years and he had been gone for four of them.

Betty's mother was the daughter of the Rev. Richard Charlton, an Episcopalian minister for 30 years on Staten Island, New York, and a pioneer teacher who taught integrated classes of whites and African-American slave children. Betty's mother planted the seeds of the faith in her even though she died when Betty was only three years old. Her father was left a widower with three little girls, Mary, Betty and Kitty. He soon remarried in June of 1778.

Betty's stepmother did not give her a mother's love. Her only memory of her step-mother's religious teaching was that she "learnt me the twenty-second Psalm: 'The Lord is my shepherd, the Lord ruleth me. Though I walk in the midst of the shadow of death, I will fear no evil, for thou art with me'; and all life through it has been the favorite Psalm." It guided her calmly through her own shadows of death.

Betty missed her real mother and lamented this after the death of her sister Kitty. She wrote, "I was sitting alone on a step of the door, looking at the clouds, while my little sister Catherine, two years old lay in her coffin; they asked me: Did I not cry when little Kitty was dead: No, because Kitty is gone up to Heaven. I wish I could go too, with Mama." She was only four years old. One evening at sunset, when she was six, she carried her half-sister Emma to a window, pointed out the setting sun to the baby and told her, "God lived up in Heaven, and good children would go up there."

Betty was educated at home and in a private school where she learned social manners, French and music in addition to reading, writing and arithmetic. When she was eight, she and her sister Mary were sent from home to live with their uncle on his farm in New Rochelle, New York about 14 miles to the north. They stayed there for four long years. She enjoyed horseback riding across the fields, sailing on Long Island Sound and walking the beaches.

Betty's loneliness continued throughout her childhood, but it made an opening for God. She had a great heart that only God could really fill. Her father and stepmother could not meet her needs for love. She loved greatly, but little was returned to her. In her loneliness, she turned to contemplation, "the long, long thoughts of youth," and drew closer to God who was always there for her. Nature led her to Him as she reflected on "every little leaf and flower, or animal, insect, shades of clouds, or waving trees" as she wrote years later, all of which were "objects of vacant unconnected thoughts of God and Heaven."

When Betty was 12, she and her sister returned to her father's home now filled with their half-siblings – six under the age of seven. Betty became their second mother and sang hymns and read prayers to them. At 13, her father once again left home for more studies in England and she and her sister left to stay once again with their uncle in New Rochelle. This time he was gone for a year and no one heard from him for the entire time.

Outwardly, she seemed to enjoy the social life of parties and dances with her refined manners and her social graces of French conversation and dancing. She looked like a porcelain doll on the dance floor – barely five feet tall with chestnut curls framing her oval face. However, on the inside, she felt abandoned and unloved by her father and stepmother. Her teenage emotions were shattered. But, in her sorrow, God never let her down.

One day, while her father was gone, she sat down in a meadow on "a sweet bed – the air still a clear blue vault above – the numberless sounds of spring melody and joy – the sweet clovers and wild flowers I had got by the way, and a heart as innocent as human heart could be, filled even with enthusiastic love to God and admiration of His works."

"God was my Father, my all. I prayed, sang hymns, cried, laughed, talking to myself of how far He could place me above all sorrow. Then I laid still to enjoy the heavenly peace that came over my soul; and I am sure, in the two hours so enjoyed, grew ten years in the spiritual life." She continued to be led in her spiritual darkness by the light of God.

At the age of 16, the darkness came closer with her father's separation from his wife and her own estrangement from her step-mother. It led to Betty's leaving home and living with relatives for the next four years at New Rochelle, at her sister Mary Post's home in Manhattan and the Long Island home of her Aunt Mary, sister of her deceased mother. Apparently, she was even tempted to suicide, but thankfully overcame it. She wrote, "the praise and thanks of excessive joy not to have done the horrid deed." This joy overflowed into her entry to the New York social life in her late teenage years. Ironically, she also came closer to her father and they began a familiar correspondence and relationship that lasted until his death. She also dreamed of "a little country home, to gather all the children around and teach them their prayers, and keep them clean and teach them to be good." God fulfilled this dream beyond her wildest hopes.

Marriage

On January 25, 1794, Betty married William Seton. She was 19 and he was 25. He was a wealthy socialite and a member of the firm of Seton, Maitland and Company, one of the largest shipping businesses in New York. He was handsome and she was pretty – a diminutive five foot, brown-haired, black-eyed beauty. She was a pianist, fluent in French and an accomplished horsewoman. Together they enjoyed the high society of New York, attending balls, the theater and parties. William was a co-host of a gala ball honoring President George Washington on his 65th birthday.

Their first home was on Wall Street near their neighbors, the Alexander Hamiltons. They summered on Long Island and Staten Island. On May 3, 1795, they welcomed their first child, daughter Anna, followed by son William in January of 1796. Her husband's poor health was a constant concern of Betty's and, to avert her sorrow, she wrote that she became a "looker-up" to God. Eventually, she bore three more children – one son and two more daughters.

In the fall of 1797, Betty and other prominent New York ladies formed the Widows' Society, a charitable organization for the aid of widows and orphans. She visited them and took them food and clothing that she had begged from door to door. The next spring, Will's father died leaving seven children at home from eight to eighteen. Will and Betty assumed their care in addition to that of her own two children while she was pregnant with Richard, her third child. Will and Betty moved from their Wall Street home into the larger Seton family home on Stone Street taking their own two young children and joining up with Betty's seven children-in-law. She wrote, "For me, who so dearly loves quiet and a small family, to become at once the mother of six children is a very great change." Betty home-schooled the younger children. Rebecca Seton was the oldest at 18 and she and Betty became life-long intimates. Betty called her sister-in-law Rebecca her "Soul's Sister."

Hard Times

In the fall of 1799, William's business fortunes began to decline due to raids at sea upon his ships from pirates. He was sickly and worried about how he would provide for all of his family and the children of his deceased father. The next spring, Betty was pregnant with her fourth child and she had to make and mend everyone's clothing, do her usual household chores and write business letters and keep her husband's books until two in the morning. She wrote that she had "pain in the back all day and in the side at night, neither of which I have been one hour without for the last two months. I trust in Heaven that the storm will go over, but, really, at present it is hard times."

Betty practiced a cafeteria-style spiritual life. She picked and chose whatever spiritual beliefs and practices that intuitively appealed to her. She wore a Catholic crucifix, admired the cloistered life, believed in angels, appreciated Protestant hymns and Quaker silence, practiced meditation and worshiped at the Episcopal Church. In the spring of 1801, she came under the influence of John Henry Hobart, an Episcopalian minister who began to give her spiritual life some structure. A little light was granted to her in the darkness of her hard times.

The Setons moved to the Battery at the extreme southwestern tip of Manhattan Island in May. Their house had a view of New York Harbor and the Quarantine Station where boatloads of immigrants were held. Many of them were sick with yellow fever and other diseases contracted on their long voyages in holds with poor food and without fresh air or light. Betty was moved to pity, but could do nothing for them because of the danger of infection. She wrote to Rebecca, "I cannot sleep. The dying and the dead possess my mind. Babies are perishing at the empty breast of the expiring mother. Father goes up early in the morning to procure all possible comforts for the sufferers." And he continued to do so daily, often from three in the morning until long after sunset all summer long until he too collapsed from yellow fever.

Day and night Betty sat by his deathbed as he cried out, "My Christ Jesus, have mercy on me." In a sacrifice reminiscent of Abraham's, Betty took her baby Kit in her arms, went out onto the piazza, looked up to Heaven and offered her daughter's life in exchange for her father's salvation. God did not accept Betty's sacrifice, but probably granted her prayer since her father died in peace holding her hand.

"Troubles always create a great exertion of my mind," she wrote, "and give it a force to which at other times it is incapable. I think the greatest happiness of this life is to be released from the cares of what is called the world."

Betty accepted her hard times as she accepted all of her sufferings – with trust in Divine Providence. She had suffered her mother's death as an infant; her father's absences from home as a child; her difficulties with her step-mother and separation from her family as a teenager; the deaths of her father-in-law and father and the sickness and business losses of her husband as an adult. Then, after all of that, the next winter she and her husband fed her sister-in-law Eliza's household of six after her husband went to jail. The next spring, a newly pregnant Betty wrote her remedy "of the blessing and practicability [to her soul] of an entire surrender of itself and all its faculties to God."

The Voyage to Italy

Will was far into the final stages of tuberculosis in the summer of 1803. He began to place his trust in God and he and Betty decided to make a voyage with their eight-year-old daughter Anna to Leghorn, Italy, to visit his business friends, the Filicchis. They hoped to find a warmer, healthier climate. There was little hope of Will's recovery, but Betty wrote that she was to "go fearless, for you know where, and how strong, is my trust." So with a heavy heart, she parceled out her four other children and her sisters-in-law to relatives and left waving good-bye to them with Will on October 2 to face the dangers of storms and pirates on their seven-week voyage. She wrote to a friend, "Take my darlings often in your arms."

They arrived in Leghorn Harbor on November 18 and learned that their ship was suspected of carrying yellow fever from New York. So,

Will and Betty and Anna were quarantined in the lazaretto, a cold and damp stone tower on the coast. There they were bolted into a small room, 20 steps up, where they suffered for a month awaiting their release. Will's sickness grew progressively worse. Betty wrote, "Will has had a violent fit of coughing so as to bring up blood, which agitates and distresses him through all his endeavors to hide it. What shall we say? This is the hour of trial. In permitting it Our Lord gives us support and strength. In looking around us we are only burdened with more anguish. Let us press forward towards the goal and the reward." Betty nursed him while Anna jumped rope to keep warm. They were released on December 19. Betty wrote, "Two men carried William to the Filicchis' carriage while I held his hand. A crowd was watching compassionately and kept repeating: 'Oh, the poor man!' " Will died only eight days later and Betty wrote, "His soul was released. I felt I had done all that the tenderest love and the duty of a wife could do."

Catholic Influences

Elizabeth was now a 29-year-old widow with five young children. She, who had helped establish the Widows' Society, was now one of them, away from her children in a foreign land with only her daughter Anna. Antonio Filicchi hosted them in his home. He and his brother Filippo provided everything for them. Anna was so moved that she said, "Oh, Mama, how many friends God has provided for us in this strange land! For they are our friends before they know us."

They visited Florence and Elizabeth admired the beautiful Catholic churches with their sacred art and music. She was impressed by the worshipers kneeling at Mass and joined them herself in prayer. When Antonio's wife, Amabilia, told her at Mass that Jesus was really and truly present on the altar, Elizabeth placed her face in her hands and cried. On another occasion, an English tourist mockingly told her at the Consecration, "This is what they call their Real Presence." Elizabeth was shocked and wrote, "My very heart trembled with shame and sorrow for his unfeeling interruption of their sacred adoration; for all around was dead silence, and many were prostrated. Involuntarily I bent from him to the pavement, and thought secretly on the words of St. Paul, with starting tears, 'They discern not the Lord's Body.' " She was on her way to becoming a Catholic.

Return to America

On February 18, 1804, the Filicchis wished Elizabeth and Anna safe passage as they left for home to America. However, before they even got out of the harbor, a severe storm smashed their ship into another and they had to return to shore for repairs. Then Anna came down with scarlet fever and they had to remain until she recovered. Elizabeth wrote, "The hand of God is all I must see but it pinches the soul." Anna recovered within three weeks, only to give the disease to her mother. The Filicchis works of mercy for them moved Elizabeth to write, "You would say it was Our Savior Himself they received in His poor and sick strangers."

Elizabeth was coming closer to belief in "Our Savior Himself" in the Blessed Sacrament. She wrote, "The other day, in a moment of excessive distress, I fell on my knees without thinking when the Blessed Sacrament passed by, and cried in agony to God to bless me, if He was there – that my whole soul desired only Him."

The Filicchis' teachings and witness brought Elizabeth closer to the Blessed Virgin Mary, sacramentals and expiatory penitential practices. Mrs. Filicchi's prayer book led Elizabeth to write of the Virgin Mary, "that I felt really I had a Mother – which you know my foolish heart so often lamented to have lost in early days." Antonio taught her the Sign of the Cross so that "deepest thoughts came with it of I know not what earnest desire to be closely united with Him who died on it." And "the dear Mrs. F., who I am with, never eats, this season of Lent, till after the clock strikes three. And she says she offers her weakness and pain of fasting for her sins, united with Our Savior's sufferings. I like that very much."

Elizabeth summed up her lessons of the suffering she endured in Italy and wrote to God. "I must always love to retrospect Thy wonderful dispensations: to be sent so many thousands of miles on so hopeless an errand; to be constantly supported and accompanied by Thy consoling mercy through scenes of trial which nature alone must have sunk under; to be brought to the light of Thy truth, notwithstanding every affection of my heart and power of my will was opposed to it."

Antonio decided to accompany Elizabeth and Anna on their return voyage as their chaperone and attend to some business in the States. Finally, on April 8, Elizabeth left Italy for good, leaving her deceased husband in its earth. It was difficult and tempting for both her and Antonio to keep their love for one another chaste on such a long voyage. But God preserved it. Holy men and women are not immune from their natural attraction to one another. Elizabeth wrote in her Journal, "Most dear Antonio, a thousand times endeared to me by the struggles of your soul, Our Lord is with us! If the Lord had not helped me, it had not failed that my soul had been put to silence. But when I said my foot had slipped, thy mercy, O Lord, held me up."

Yes, her foot slipped, but she caught her balance and didn't fall down. She spent the rest of the voyage as Antonio's spiritual friend as he taught her the Catholic faith and they prayed and fasted together.

Elizabeth anguished about how she should tell Reverend Hobart of her leaning towards conversion to the Catholic Church. Before she befriended Antonio, he was her best spiritual friend and advisor. She didn't want to lose his friendship, but was prepared to sacrifice it for the true faith. She wrote him from the ship to prepare him for her announcement:

> As I approach to you, I tremble; and while the dashing of the waves and their incessant motion picture to me the allotment which God has given me, the tears fall fast thro' my fingers at the insupportable thought of being separated from you.
>
> Still, if you will not be my brother, if your dear friendship and esteem must be the price of my fidelity to what I believe to be the truth, I cannot doubt the mercy of God who, by depriving me of my dearest tie on earth, will certainly draw me nearer to Him – and this I feel confidently from experience of the past and the truth of His promise, which can never fail.

On June 4, they landed in New York. Elizabeth received the welcome reunion of her four other children and the sad news that Rebecca, her sister-in -law and "Soul's Sister," lay dying. She went to her bedside for yet another death vigil and taught her what she had learned about the Catholic faith. Rebecca made an act of faith in the Catholic Church by telling Elizabeth on her deathbed in the words of Ruth of the Old Testament, "Your people will be my people and your God, my God." She died soon thereafter in July. Elizabeth wrote of her losses in hope, "My husband, my sisters, my home, my comforts – poverty and sorrow. Well, with God's blessing, you, too, shall be changed into dearest friends."

She tried to make friends of poverty and sorrow. She no longer had servants to keep the fire going, prepare the meals, dress the children, wash the dishes, wash and mend the clothes and care for the house. She had to do it all and rely on the charity of friends and relatives for food and lodging. Then her announcement of her Catholic leanings strained her relations with them. They were bigoted against those whom they called "shiftless, shabby and scrubby Catholics." All voices tried to dissuade Elizabeth and save her from what they thought were foolishness and disgrace to the family. Reverend Hobart told her that he thought that she would go to Hell.

The Cataclysmic Conversion

Elizabeth was bewildered and in spiritual and emotional anguish. She read and heard from Protestant and Catholic books and apologists and the Devil himself who, she said, "has taken his place so near my soul that nothing good can enter in it, without being mixed with his suggestions." She cried incessantly, slept little and lost so much weight that she appeared skeletal. As a mother, she was concerned for the salvation of her children. She begged the Blessed Mother "with the tenderness and confidence of her child to pity us and guide us to the true faith, if we are not in it, and if we are, to obtain peace for my poor soul, that I may be a good mother to my poor darlings."

One day she went to a Protestant church and sat in a pew facing a Catholic church in the next street. She found herself "twenty times speaking to the Blessed Sacrament *there*, instead of looking at the naked altar where I was." Later, she honestly attributed her conversion to "my hatred of opposition, troublesome inquiries, etc, [that] brought me in the Church more than conviction."

Filippo Filicchi had the best advice for her. "Sincerity, confidence and perseverance in prayer; calmness and tranquility of mind; courage and resolution in heart; a perfect resignation to Providence – you cannot fail to succeed. Avoid the labyrinth of controversies."

She followed his advice and in January 1805, "it finished calmly at last – abandoning all to God – and a renewed confidence in the Blessed Virgin. . . . I WILL GO PEACEABLY AND FIRMLY TO THE

CATHOLIC CHURCH; for if Faith is so important to our salvation, I will seek it where true Faith first began, seek it among those who received it from GOD HIMSELF."

She boldly wrote that God Himself had to answer for her decision for herself and her little ones:

> Come then, my little ones, we will go to judgment together, and present Our Lord His own words; and if He says, "You fools, I did not mean that." We will say, "Since You said You would always even to the end of ages, be with this Church you built with Your Blood – if You ever left it, it is Your word which misled us. Therefore, please to pardon Your poor fools for Your own word's sake.

And so on March 14, 1805, Elizabeth "professed to believe what the Council of Trent believes and teaches." After her first Confession she exclaimed, "It is done! Easy enough: the kindest, most respectable confessor is this Mr. O. with the compassion and yet firmness in this work of mercy which I would have expected from Our Lord Himself. I felt as if my chains fell, as those of St. Peter at the touch of the divine Messenger." And then, after her First Communion, "GOD IS MINE AND I AM HIS!"

Conversion Calamities

Elizabeth stopped worshipping with the establishment and the wealthy socialites at the Episcopalian church and started to worship at St. Peter's Catholic Church. It was filled with poor immigrants with poor manners who wore poor clothes. Elizabeth's sister-in-law, Mary Post, distastefully called them "Dirty, filthy, red-faced – the church a horrid place of spits and pushing." Indeed, Elizabeth admitted that she "found it all that indeed." But she came to honor God in the true faith and not to honor the congregation.

The conversion calamities began with estrangement from her relatives and friends. The hardest break for her was from her only Protestant spiritual advisor, Reverend Hobart. She reported that her last painful conversation with him "was repaid fully and a thousand times on Sunday morning by my dear master at Communion, and my Faith, if possible, more strengthened and decided than if it had not been attacked." It was so strengthened that "happen now what will, I rest with God. The tabernacle and Communion! So now I can pass the Valley of Death itself."

She tried to support herself and started a private school, but the rumors flew that she was going to try to convert the Protestant children. The school failed for lack of students and Elizabeth was humbly forced to move in with her sister and brother-in-law. Family relations were further strained when her teenage Seton sisters-in-law, Cecilia and Harriet, whom Elizabeth had raised as daughters and their cousin, also became interested in Catholicism. Elizabeth wrote Cecilia a beautiful teaching on prayer:

> We must pray literally without ceasing – without ceasing; in every occurrence and employment of our lives. You know I mean that prayer of the heart which is independent of place or situation, or which is, rather, a habit of lifting up the heart to God, as in a constant communication with Him.
>
> As, for instance, when you go to your studies, you look up to Him with sweet complacency, and think: O Lord! How worthless is this knowledge, if it were not for the enlightening my mind and improving it to Thy service; for being more useful to my fellow-creatures and enabled to fill the part Thy Providence may appoint me.

The family strain was somewhat eased by Elizabeth's attendance at the death beds of her half-sister Emma Craig and her estranged step-mother both of whom died in the summer of 1805. That fall, she was able to return to her home and take in Protestant students "to board, wash and mend for." But in the summer of 1806, the Seton family once again rose up against Elizabeth on account of 16-year old Cecilia Seton's conversion to Catholicism. They blamed Elizabeth, but Cecilia was a mature young lady with a mind of her own. Her family threatened to ship her out to the West Indies and to banish Elizabeth from New York. They locked Cecilia in her room for several days to consider these consequences.

Cecilia then courageously walked out for Elizabeth's home and left a note. "In consequence of a firm resolution to adhere to the Catholic Faith, I left your house this morning." Three days later, she made her act of faith in the Catholic Church. Her family ostracized her and her wealthy relatives disinherited Elizabeth. Her former friends warned everyone not to support her and to shun her. Anti-Catholic feelings rode so high that on Christmas Eve a crowd gathered outside of St. Peter's to heckle the worshipers, who may have included Elizabeth and Cecilia. They were dispersed, but the next day the Catholics formed a cordon to defend the church and a riot broke out in which one man was killed and several others wounded.

Elizabeth worried about bringing her children up in such a Protestant environment and worried further about their salvation if she were to die. She dreamed of a convent life in Montreal where she might teach her children or to go to "some corner of the earth and devote our whole time to God!" She was alarmed because of "the ridicule they are forced to hear of our holy religion and the mockery of the Church and ministers."

God provided some of the best of these ministers to Elizabeth as together they began to form the Catholic Church in the United States. She was advised by the best of the early Catholic clergy: Archbishop John Carroll; Father William Dubourg, president of St. Mary's College in Baltimore; Fathers John Dubois and Simon Brute; all of Maryland and Fathers Cheverus and Matignon of Boston. Fathers Dubourg, Dubois, Brute and Cheverus all later became Bishops.

Elizabeth met Father Dubourg after Mass at St. Peter's where she told him of her desire to teach children. He went on to Boston and met with Fathers Matignon and Cheverus. Then he returned to New York with an idea for Elizabeth to start a school for Catholic girls in Baltimore, Maryland. Father Matignon prophetically wrote her, "You are destined, I think, for some great good in the United States and here [Baltimore] you should remain in preference to any other location."

Then Elizabeth was again called on to give a final witness to her relatives of her works of mercy at deathbeds. Her half-sister Eliza Maitland called for her from her deathbed. Both Elizabeth and Cecilia ministered to her needs, night and day in turns. Finally, Elizabeth "closed her dying eyes." Then Elizabeth began to close her own eyes on New York and look towards Baltimore for her family's future. Her spiritual advisors were there and Catholics were welcome there. Cecilia was invited to live with the family of Will's brother James and help care for his five children. Elizabeth was free to go.

Elizabeth fixed her eyes upon Baltimore when her boarding establishment finally failed for lack of boarders in the spring of 1808. Father Dubourg providentially offered to give her a plot of land near St. Mary's, enroll six girls with her and take her sons in the College. She accepted and was on her way by ship to Baltimore within three weeks on June 8 with her daughters. She "saw once more the windows of State Street, passed the Quarantine, and so near the shore as to see every part of it. Oh, my Lord – in that hour! Can a heart swell so high and not burst? "

The Exodus to Maryland

They sailed for seven days over rough waters "with both little dear ones in my narrow berth, the hand held over to Ann who sleeps beneath me – praying every ten minutes." The seasick children hung their heads down low but "Mother's heart, in firm and steadfast confidence, [looked] straight upwards." What did she expect when she landed? Was she anxious or worried? "No. Can I be disappointed? No. Doubt and fear fly from the breast inhabited by Him. There can be no disappointment where the soul's only desire and expectation is to meet His Adored Will and fulfill it."

She met that Adored Will on June 15, 1808 and left for St. Mary's Chapel the next day to attend the Mass of its consecration. As she and her children entered, they were greeted by organ and the choir singing the *Kyrie*. She described it in a letter to Cecilia, who had remained in New York to care for her relative's children. "Your imagination can never conceive the splendor, the glory of the scene – all I have told you of Florence is a shadow." She had now experienced Catholicism in the United States and received a warm welcome.

The family moved into a modest home on Paca Street in Baltimore. Elizabeth had enough money from her frugal savings from the gifts that had been made to her by her friends. Her sons were now 12 and 10 and lived across the street at St. Mary's where they went to school. Thirteen-year-old Anna and her two younger sisters lived with Elizabeth. She started a little school with seven pupils consisting of her three girls and four other boarders. She followed a busy schedule of prayer and schooling that began at 5:30 a.m. She wrote that "from half-past five in the morning until nine at night every moment is full – no space even to be troubled." She dreamed of starting a larger Catholic school for girls and perhaps a religious order. This would be very unusual since she was still raising young children.

On December 7, 1808, Cecilia O'Conway arrived at Paca Street with her father who announced that he came "to offer her to God." She would help Elizabeth until her dream could be realized. Father Dubourg had a similar dream but they both faced the great obstacle of a lack of funds. They both prayed that the obstacle would be removed and the funds forthcoming.

Soon afterwards, Jesus spoke to Elizabeth in a locution after Communion, "Go, address yourself to Mr. Cooper; he will give you what is necessary to commence the establishment." She told this to Father Dubourg who knew Samuel Cooper, a wealthy man who had left the world to study for the priesthood. He advised Elizabeth to say nothing and let God work it out, if it was His will. She obeyed and on the evening of the very same day, Mr. Cooper visited Father Dubourg and lamented that nothing was being done for the education of girls. Father agreed and said he felt the same way but there were no funds. "Oh well," said Mr. Cooper, "I have ten thousand dollars which I can give you for this purpose." He later gave the money and made this prophecy, "Sir, this establishment will be made at Emmitsburg, a village eighteen leagues [about 50 miles] from Baltimore; and then it will extend throughout the United States."

On the Feast of the Annunciation, March 25, 1809, Elizabeth Seton made her vows of poverty, chastity and obedience in the presence of Archbishop Carroll. Now she became known as Mother Seton. By June, four more girls came to join Mother, including her sister-in-law Cecilia, "uniting under her banner, which is the Cross of Christ." On June 2, again the Feast of Corpus Christi in St. Mary's Chapel, one year after Mother's arrival in Baltimore, the five Sisters dressed in their religious habits, similar to Italian widows' clothing, and attended Mass for the first time as a religious society.

The Emmitsburg Community

On June 21, Mother led her daughter Anna, sisters-in-law Cecilia and Harriet, and another on their 40-mile journey to Emmitsburg. It took them four days of walking, more than half of which was next to their horse-drawn Conestoga wagon, over the fields and hills on the rough roads. Mother jokingly wrote, "The dogs and pigs came out to meet us, and the geese stretched their necks in mute demand to know if we were any of their sort, to which we gave assent."

Finally, they passed through the valley overlooked by St. Mary's Mountain and arrived at the crossroads village of Emmitsburg. Several hundred people lived there and about half of them worshiped at St. Josephs' Church built in 1793. Father John Dubois, its pastor, moved out of his house on St. Mary's Mountain so that the pioneers could stay there until their so-called Stone House was ready at the Fleming farm that Mr. Cooper had purchased for them. The Stone House was located about a half- mile from the village of Emmitsburg and two miles from St. Mary's Mountain and Mount St. Mary's College where her sons attended. Soon Mothers' daughters Catherine and Rebecca arrived and they all settled in for the next month. Mother said, "We are half in the sky, the height of our situation is almost incredible."

In July, Harriet converted to Catholicism with the exclamation to Mother, "It is done, my sister, I am a Catholic. The Cross of Our Dearest is the desire of my soul. I will never rest till He is mine." Then five more ladies joined them, including another widow with a boy, Mother's two sons and two other students. By July 31, they all moved to the Stone House and began to lead the religious life as the Sisters of Charity of St. Joseph. This was the first native Sisterhood in the United States.

Harriet's conversion had the same effect on the Seton family as had Elizabeth's and Cecilia's. They reviled her by mail including a letter from Gouverneur Ogden, an important member of the New York Legislature. He wrote what proved to be a great false prophecy, "that the establishments at Baltimore and St. Joseph's are novel things in the United States, and would not have been permitted by the populace in any other place than in the democratic, Frenchified State of Maryland. The religion they profess is uncongenial to the habits, manners and nature of Americans; and ere long I predict from many causes the demolition of every building in that state in any wise resembling a convent or Catholic hospital."

Harriet selected the site for the community's cemetery while walking the grounds. She came to a little grove of woods while eating an apple, threw the core against a tree, pointed to the ground where it landed and said that would be the place of her grave. She soon died on December 22 at the age of 22 after suffering for a month and was buried there. She was the first to die in the community. Harriet had been more like a child than a sister-in-law to Elizabeth since she had cared for her since the age of 10.

Soon more arrivals brought the group to 30 boarders crowding the Stone House with 40 day pupils. The House had only four rooms, two on the ground floor and two in the garret where the snow later blew in on the Sisters who slept on mattresses on the floor. There was only one fireplace for the whole house.

They patterned their religious life after the Daughters of Charity of St. Vincent de Paul in France. They rose at 5:00 for morning prayers and Mass followed by breakfast and chores until 11:45 when they had an examination of conscience, visited the Blessed Sacrament, and had lunch with Scripture readings. Recreation followed until 2:00 when they made another visit to the Blessed Sacrament, and did chores until five. Rosary, dinner, and recreation took place until 8:30 followed by night prayers and bed. The chores were manual labor, to which many of the ladies were not accustomed, but they adapted to them in the spirit of poverty. The chores consisted of cleaning, sewing, washing clothes in Tom's Creek and carrying them a few hundred yards to and from the House, tending the animals and cultivating the garden. Their life had order and regularity.

Father Dubourg, their spiritual director and Superior, suggested that they grow carrots to provide "carrot coffee" for themselves. This poverty coffee became their customary daily drink. Mother expressed her attitude towards poverty, "If you knew half the real good your friend possesses, while the world thinks she is deprived of everything worth having, you would allow that she has truly and really the best of it."

Mother's duties consisted of supervising and administering the convent and school and walking "about with my knitting in my hands (we supply or are to supply, by knitting and spinning, the college and two seminaries of Mr. Dubourg with stocks and cloth), give my opinion, see that everyone is in their place, write letters, read and give good advice."

Spiritual Clashes

In early August, Mother received a disturbing letter from Father Dubourg instructing the Sisters to disassociate themselves from their confessor, Father Pierre Babade. Apparently, Father Dubourg thought that Father Babade had too great an influence on them. Perhaps Father Dubourg may even have been a little jealous. His ruling upset the Sisters very much because they valued Father Babade's spiritual advice. He had instilled in them a spirit of enthusiasm in their pioneer venture. Mother didn't take this sitting down.

In defense of her Sisters, she wrote to Archbishop Carroll explaining, "I should have acquiesced quietly, tho' my heart was torn to pieces. But the others could not bear it in the same way." Father Dubourg then resigned as Superior in an apparent pique of sensitivity. Mother was deeply saddened and wrote him, "The Mother is worthless. Pity them, pity her; try her once more and if she ever even vexes you again, quit her and them forever." Unfortunately, Father Dubourg did not "try her once more" and he was succeeded as Superior by Father John David, a controlling person with whom Mother clashed from the very beginning.

Father David wanted to do and control everything his way, alone and without consulting the Sisters. He had great plans and schemes for how the new community of Sisters and their school should be run. He thought that Mother should be transferred to Baltimore and be replaced as Mother Superior. Then he planned that Mother would remain at Emmitsburg as school superintendent but be replaced as Mother Superior. Rumors of his plans were unsettling to the Sisters. They didn't know what was going on. Mother found herself unable to cooperate with Father David or to inform him of anything. She froze and wrote Archbishop Carroll, "I remain motionless and inactive. It is for you, my most revered Father, to decide if this is temptation, or what it is." He didn't answer her question, but advised her to sacrifice "yourself, notwithstanding all the uneasiness and disgust you may experience and continue in your place of Superior." So Mother remained in obedience and disgust under the direction of Father David for another year and a half.

St. Joseph's House

The Sisters soon outgrew the Stone House and moved into the new St. Joseph's House or the White House a couple of hundred yards away on February 20, 1810. Father Dubois led the procession from the Stone House with the Blessed Sacrament to St. Joseph's. It served as a combination convent and school and consisted of a schoolroom and 30 simple cells for the Sisters each with a bed, chair and table. Two days later, three parish children were admitted to the school. This was the first Catholic parish school in the United States.

They suffered from a plague of fleas that infested the construction materials and the Sisters' mattresses. They had to move from room to room to escape them. One escape that they all looked forward to was the Sunday excursion to St. Mary's Mountain for Mass. It was about a mile away over fields and streams without bridges or roads. Twenty Sisters and children waded over streams and climbed fences carrying their dinners in a sack. They ate on the mountain overlooking the valley near a stream at the base of a small grotto-like cliff and read the Divine Office.

In early spring, Cecilia's health began to fail and Mother prepared herself to accept her death which she expected within a few weeks. Mother wrote a friend and reminisced about her willingness to sacrifice a very happy life:

> I remember when Anna was six months old and everything smiled around me – venerating the virtues of my Seton and sincerely attached to him, accustomed to the daily visits and devoted love of my father, and possessed of all I estimate as essential to happiness – alone with this babe in the see-saw of motherly love, frequently the tears used to start and often overflow; and I would say to myself while retrospecting the favors of Heaven: "All these, these and Heaven, too?"
>
> Sometimes falling on my knees with the sleeping suckling in my arms, I would offer her and all my dear possessions – husband, father, home – and entreat the Bountiful Giver to separate me from all, if indeed I could not possess my portion here – and with Him, too.
>
> Nor do I remember any part of my life, after being settled in it, that I have not constantly been in the same sentiment, always looking beyond the bounds of time and desiring to quit the gift for the Giver.

God had accepted her sacrifice – the lives of her husband, father, and the loss of her home and possessions. She couldn't have "all these, these and Heaven, too." Now it was time to "quit the gift [of Cecilia] for the Giver." Mother continued in her letter, "We part, nature groans; for me it is an anguish that threatens dissolution – not in convulsive sighs, but the soul is aghast, petrified. After ten minutes it returns to its usual motion, and all goes on as if nothing had happened. This same effect has followed the death of all so dear. Why? Faith lifts the staggering soul on one side; Hope supports it on the other. Experience says it must be, and love says – let it be."

Cecilia died on April 29 at the age of 19. She was the first professed Sister to be buried in the Sisters' cemetery. Mother said, "I have seen more real affliction and sorrow here in the ten months since our removal than in all the thirty-five years of my past life, which was all marked by affliction."

In all of this time, she had not forgotten that her primary duty was to her children. Mother was in the very unusual and unprecedented position of being a natural mother in a family with minor children while at the same time being a Mother Superior of a religious community. She wrote, " the dear ones have their first claim, which must ever remain inviolate. Consequently, if at any time the duties I am engaged in should interfere with those I owe to them, I have solemnly engaged with our good Bishop Carroll, as well as my own conscience, to give the darlings their right, and to prefer their advantage in everything."

She was even prepared to leave her community and beloved Valley for their sake or accept if Father David succeeded in his plan to remove her. She wrote, "Everything here is again suspended and I am casting about to prepare for beginning the world again with my poor Annina, [Anna] Josephine [Catherine] and Rebecca; as our situation is more unsettled than ever." But she turned as always to Divine Providence and looked towards eternity. "His Adorable Will be done during the few remaining days of my tiresome journey which, being made with so many tears and sown so thick with crosses will certainly be concluded with joy and crowned with eternal rest. Look up! We are in the true and sure way of salvation for that long, long eternity before us; if only we keep courage we will go to Heaven on horseback instead of idling and creeping along."

Mother had remained obedient to Father David for a year and a half, but she firmly resisted his schemes. Thankfully for the good of the community, she wrote that she did not have a "pliancy of character I would for some reasons wish to possess, and may eventually be the fruit of divine grace, but as yet is far from being attained."

None of Father David's schemes were approved by Archbishop Carroll. He had allowed Mother to remain as Mother Superior and to keep her children in her care. On May 12, 1811, Father David was transferred to

Bardstown, Kentucky. Father Dubois replaced him as Superior and he remained as such for the rest of Mother's life.

The Sisters' Institute adapted the rule of St. Vincent de Paul's French Daughters of Charity to their own particular situation in their apostolate of education of young girls and works of mercy for the poor and sick. They also took in paying boarders to help to support their needs. Archbishop Carroll approved the permanent rules and constitutions of Mother Seton's Sisters of Charity on September 11, 1811. He hoped that this would bring peace to Mother and wrote, "It will be like freeing you from a state in which it was difficult to walk straight, as you had not certain way in which to proceed." There would be no more Father Davids because the Archbishop ruled that the Superior himself was not to be a ruler but an advisor to the Mother Superior who would be the ruler of the community under the Archbishop.

"The Old Knot of Oak"

Mother's husband used to call her "the old knot of oak." But the old knot was becoming severely tried through the sicknesses of her son William, daughter Anna and herself. William's illness was life threatening and both Anna and Mother contracted the dreaded "family enemy" of tuberculosis. On January 31, 1812, Anna became the first Sister to enter the community since the adoption of its rules and constitutions on January 17. The 16-year-old girl's lungs were devoured and her whole body was in pain. She offered it all to God and heroically said, "Let me pay my penance for so often drawing in my waist to look small and imitate the looks of my companions, let the ribs draw now with pain for having drawn with vanity."

Mother wrote about her deathwatch of Anna, "It appears to me I never saw or shall see anything to be compared to her. When in death's agony her quivering lips could with difficulty utter one word, feeling a tear fall on her face, she smiled and said with great effort: 'Laugh, Mother, Jesus!' "

On the eve of her death, Anna made a "Consecration at the Foot of the Cross" by which she consecrated herself to Jesus and offered Him all of her sufferings in union with His "in expiation of the offenses and grievous sins committed during my life. O my Jesus, pardon the impatiences, ill humors and numberless other faults." She died on March 12. Mother was desolated by the death of her life companion as never before since the death of her husband. "For three months after Nina [Anna] was taken I was so often expecting to lose my senses and my head was so disordered, that unless for the daily duties always before me, I did not know much what I did or what I left undone."

Anna was laid to rest in the cemetery. She was the third girl after Harriet and Cecilia, to be buried there. The school children decorated their graves with flowers. There were now 18 Sisters, 30 boarders and 20 day students in the White House that was surrounded by green fields, garden and a farmyard with cows, chickens and pigs. All were kept in good order according to Mother's principles of simplicity, discipline and order on the road to eternity in accordance with the Divine Will.

Mother had many financial difficulties in supporting the community. She was advised not to beg or write appeal letters as it would be fruitless in those times with little Catholic sympathy and the economic difficulties brought by the War of 1812 with England. Her friends and some of her family had always helped to support her. She was an able administrator and decided to pay the community's own way and support the school with tuition from the boarders of $100 per year while still offering free tuition to the poor. The school day was much the same for the students as it was for the Sisters. Rise at 5:45 a.m.; to chapel for prayers; breakfast; classes; Rosary; lunch; recreation; more classes; study; supper at 7:15 p.m.; reading and bed.

The purpose of the school was not to make nuns, but to prepare women for the world. As Mother said, "Your little Mother, my darlings, does not come to teach you how to be good nuns or Sisters of Charity, but rather I would wish to fit you for that world in which you are destined to live: to teach you how to be good mothers of families."

She taught them to be virtuous and warned them with a fable about the dangers of the world of theater and balls. She told them that the butterfly asked the owl how to avoid burning its wings when it approached a burning candle. "The owl," Mother said, "counseled her to abstain from looking even at the smoke of it. It is ever easier to abstain from such pleasures than to use them well." She spoke from the voice of her own experience with her early fascination of the theater and balls.

In 1814, the community branched out to Philadelphia where they assumed the administration of the debt-ridden first orphanage in the United States and made it solvent. In 1817 they opened a free school in New York City.

Soon after Anna's death, Mother's baby Rebecca began her march to the grave at the age of 10. She fell on the ice and injured her hip, but she hid her pain so as not to add to her mother's suffering. She suffered and continued walking on it until spring when Mother learned that she had aggravated her injury to such an extent that nothing could be done for it. A tumor developed in her hip and it broke in the spring of 1816. Rebecca could no longer walk or lie down and sat in agony on Mother's knee. She leaned against her to such an extent that Mother's left arm became atrophied.

Rebecca was not afraid to die. She said, "Dearest Mother, you think I am not willing to die, but I am. Indeed I am. All I fear is my sins." On November 2, she said, "I have just been handing Our Lord my little cup. It is now quite full. He will come for me." Our Lord accepted the cup and came for her the next day. Rebecca was only 14 years old. Mother buried her next to her sisters-in-law Harriet and Cecilia and her daughter Anna.

Her Sons

After the burial of two of her daughters and with Catherine, the third, in good health, Mother's anxieties turned towards her sons, William and Richard. Both of them were raised without a father in a female household. Later, during their schooling, their home was in a female convent. Neither of them was very brilliant or talented and their mother agonized over their future.

Nineteen-year-old Richard was trying to find his way in Baltimore. Mother wrote, "You would not guess half the trials we have had with him in Baltimore through his childish, thoughtless, disposition." William was having a hard time learning commercial business with the Filicchis in Italy. Mother wrote him:

> A mother's heart, I can truly say, has one continual agony. You have a hundred ways of forgetting me, but I not for one moment forget you. . . .
>
> You must take courage with me, and push on, and do not let your mind rest on the sad thought of future prospects, since the Providence of God turns out so often quite different from our calculations. You are but twenty,

my beloved, too young yet to begin the world if you even had means; so, be patient and trust.

Neither one of them succeeded in business and they both returned to Emmitsburg. Mother wrote to Father Brute, "My poor, poor, poor Richard, William – My God, oh if the bleeding of a mother's heart can obtain! Poor, poor, poor blind ones!" She got William an officer's position in the Navy through some influential friends, sent Richard off to Italy to try his hand with the Filicchis and sent Kit off to visit relatives. Her thankless sons begged her for money frequently and Mother always sent it. But, she never received a thank you or even an acknowledgement that the money was received. "DO, DO LET ME HEAR FROM YOU," she implored William.

Mother had a mysterious fiery love for her son William. She wrote him, "I often ask but what is this dear rover to me so much more than all the world? Why do the heart strings all wind round him so? That I cannot tell."

In September of 1818, William sailed from New York on a two-year voyage for the Pacific with Mother thinking that she would never see him again. However, his ship ran into storms off the coast of Virginia while he slept and dreamt of his mother. She wrote, that he was "dreaming that I stood by him, with all the agony of heart asking: 'Are you prepared, my William?' At that moment, they came to tell him the masts were going over and the gale tremendous, so that when he sprang from his hammock he was to the knees in water."

Providentially, the ship had to go to port for repairs and he got shore leave to visit his mother wrapped, as she wrote, in "old shawls and flannels." She had a happy visit of eight days when he left her for the last time.

Mother settled in to "pray and dote, dote and pray, [as] poor mother's all for her darlings." In fact, she had many more responsibilities with 20 Sisters and 100 students assigning chores, listening to their problems, disciplining them, encouraging them, limping from classroom to classroom making inspections and administering all of the works and business of the community. Only in her sleepless nights would she write by candlelight her long, loving letters to her distant children.

The Thief Approaches

Mother wrote, "I'll be wild Betsy to the last." She had a zeal to "shout like a madman alone to my God, and roar and groan and sigh and be silent all together until I had baptized a thousand [Indians] and snatched these poor victims from Hell." However, she was prevented from doing this by "rules, prudence, subjections, opinions, etc. – dreadful walls to a burning soul wild as mine. I am like a fiery horse I had when a girl, whom they tried to break by making him drag a heavy cart; and the poor beast was so humbled that he could never more be inspired by whips or caresses, and wasted to a skeleton until he died."

In the summer of 1818, Father Babade wrote her, "Ten years are passed; your work is consolidated. I desire nothing more for you but a happy death." When she was elected Superior for the third time in 1819, she protested that it was the election of the dead, but she lived on for another two years.

Mother wrote to Antonio Filicchi, "It is rather suspected that I, your poor little sister, am about to go and meet your Filippo [his pre-deceased brother], but nothing of health can be certain and calculated at my age, 45. I may recover and crack nuts yet with my nose and chin, as they say; I know not. All I know is, we must all be ready for this dear, dearest Thief who is to come when least expected." She wrote to Father Brute, "We talk now all day long of my death and how it will be just like the rest of the housework. What is it else? What came I in the world for? Why in it so long? But this last great eternal end."

Father Brute described this end:

> Her tranquility was perfect; she manifested it in her answers to the questions concerning her state, which she wished they should occupy themselves with as little as possible. She continued to follow as closely as possible the exercise and rules of the house, so calm, so recollected and so wholly united to her Blessed Lord. Her eyes so expressive, the look that pierces Heaven and the soul visible in it. I require her to renew her vows and she does, "with all my heart." To bless her Sisters as being the present Mother, and ask their prayers, and she does in the simple words, "Yes, I bless them and ask

their prayers." To bless her daughter Josephine (Kit), and her two sons, absent, and she does with such a look to Heaven.

When I approached, and as I placed the ciborium upon the little table, she burst into tears, and, sobbing aloud, covered her face with her two hands. I thought first it was some fear of sin and, approaching her, I asked,

"Be still, Mother! Peace, peace be to you! Here is the Lord of Peace! Have you any pain? Do you wish to confess?"

"No, no! Only give Him to me!" she said with an ardor, a kind of exclamation, and her whole face so inflamed that I was much affected.

Then Mother received a letter from Richard that he had returned from Italy and was in debt in Norfolk. Antonio Filicchi wrote that he had sent Richard home because he was of no use to him in his business and worse that he was unwilling to learn to be of use and was morally unsatisfactory. Of course, she tried to help by writing someone else to help him, "not dearest Antonio, for his relief, but for a mother's duty. For many years I have had no prayer for my children but that Our Blessed God would do everything to them and in them in the way of affliction and adversity, if only He will save their soul(s)!" Richard came to her in disgrace during her dying illness in December and left a few days later before Christmas.

On January 2, 1821, Mother lay on her deathbed and said to the gathered Sisters, "I am thankful Sisters, for your kindness to be present at this trial. Be children of the Church, be children of the Church." In the early morning hours of the 4th, she began to pray daily the prayer of Pope Pius VII, "May the most just, the most high and the most amiable Will of God be in all things fulfilled, praised and exalted above all forever." Finally, she stopped breathing "without convulsions nor extraordinary movement in the great silence." The next day, she was buried in the cemetery and joined 15 others, including her two daughters and two sisters-in-law. Fifty Sisters survived her.

Virtues

Mother Seton was a wife and mother, widow, educator, convert, religious sister and foundress who faced the crises of her life with courage, love and conformity to the will of God. She converted to Catholicism with total trust and abandonment to God and suffered the loss of family and friends.

Mother raised her five orphaned children as a widow and taught school to support them; fed and clothed many widows; nursed the sick and attended the dying.

Father Brute wrote of Mother's virtues:

> How profound her faith and how tender her piety! How sincere her humility, combined with so great intelligence! How great her goodness and kindness for all!
>
> Her distinguishing characteristic was compassion and indulgence for poor sinners. Her charity made her watchful never to speak evil of others, always to find excuses or to keep silence. Her other special virtues were her attachment to her friends and her gratitude; her religious respect for the ministers of the Lord and for everything pertaining to religion. Her heart was compassionate, religious, lavish of every good in her possession, disinterested in regard to all things.
>
> O Mother, excellent Mother, I trust you are now in the enjoyment of bliss!

Fruits

Mother Seton founded the Sisters of Charity of Saint Joseph's, the first community for religious women to be established in the United States. She also founded Saint Joseph's Academy and Free School, the first free Catholic School for girls staffed by nuns in the United States.

Mother was survived by three children, William, Richard and Catherine. William married and fathered nine children one of whom became a Bishop. He retired as a lieutenant after serving for 17 years in the United States Navy. Richard was only 25 when he died at sea from a fever contracted after nursing a sick Episcopalian minister. Catherine, whom Mother had offered to God as a baby in order to save her father's soul, became a Sister of Mercy and lived to the age of 91.

Mother Seton's religious Sisters grew into six communities with more than 5000 members operating hospitals, nursing schools, homes for the elderly, child-care centers, colleges and hundreds of grade schools and high schools.

She loved passionately with an affectionate heart, her husband, children, relatives, friends, Sisters and students. But her love of God always came first. She tried "rather to turn every affection to God, well knowing that there alone their utmost exercise cannot be misapplied, and most ardent hopes can never be disappointed." She was the Mother of the Catholic Church in the United States with its Father, Archbishop John Carroll. As a Roman Catholic convert from the Episcopal Church, she is an intercessor of Christian unity.

Saint

On December 18, 1959, Pope John XXIII gave Mother the title of Venerable. Within two years, two miracles were declared through her intercession. Sister Gertrude Korzendorfer, D.C. was cured of cancer of the pancreas and Anne Theresa O'Neill was cured of leukemia at the age of four. Pope John beatified Mother on Mach 17, 1963. He said, "In a house that was very small, but with ample space for charity, she sowed a seed in America which by Divine Grace grew into a large tree."

In October of 1963, Carl Kalin, a Protestant, was cured of a rare brain disease after his Catholic wife, along with many Sisters of Charity, invoked Mother Seton and fastened a first class relic of her to the wall above his head. He was cured on the last day of a novena to Mother. The cure was declared to be miraculous and Pope Paul VI dispensed with the need of a second miracle. On September 14, 1975, he declared, "Elizabeth Ann Seton is a Saint. She is the first daughter of the United States of America to be glorified with this incomparable attribute." Her Feast Day is January 4, the date of her death.

Opening Prayer for the Mass in Commemoration of Saint Elizabeth Ann Seton

Lord God,
you blessed Elizabeth Seton with gifts of grace
as wife and mother, educator and foundress,
so that she might spend her life in service to your people.
Through her example and prayers
May we learn to express our love for you
in love for others.
We ask this through our Lord Jesus Christ, your Son,
who lives and reigns with you and the Holy Spirit,
one God, for ever and ever.

Shrine:

Seton Shrine Center
333 South Seton Avenue
Emmitsburg, MD 21727
Telephone: 301-447-6606
Website: www.setonshrine.org

12. New Territory

At the same time that Mother Elizabeth Seton was ending her service in the rural East, nuns from France came to the United States to serve in the frontier West. The United States purchased the Louisiana Territory from France in 1803 and it instantly doubled the size of the country. Thirteen states or parts of states were eventually carved from the Territory. It was a vast geographic area with mostly French-speaking people and very few priests.

Napoleon Bonaparte ruled France which had owned the Louisiana Territory. He desperately needed money to build his army in pursuit of his dream of ruling a French Empire and ultimately a European Empire. So, he sold the Territory to the United States. President Thomas Jefferson said that there was enough land "for the thousandth and thousandth generation." For fifteen million dollars, the United States got over a million square miles, the port of New Orleans on the Mississippi River and control of the whole central river system of the continent. The Louisiana Purchase comprised 23.3 percent of the territory of the modern continental United States. Within four years, Robert Fulton invented the steamboat and the inland waterways could now be used easily and cheaply. Steamboats soon brought immigrants to settle on the land and furs, grain and many other products back to market.

The Louisiana Purchase sparked interest in expansion to the west coast. President Thomas Jefferson commissioned Meriwether Lewis and William Clark to lead a discovery expedition. In 1805, they set out to map the Louisiana Territory. After Louisiana became a state in 1812, the remaining Louisiana Territory was renamed the Missouri Territory.

On January 8, 1815, during the War of 1812 with England, British Major General Sir Edward Pakenham led his soldiers in an attack on the Americans at the Battle of New Orleans. New Orleans was an important port from which flowed over fifty percent of American shipping. It was important to defend it.

General Pakenham led his troops in well formed lines against the Americans led by General Andrew Jackson who hid behind barricades. As the British marched into the open, dressed in bright red uniforms, they made easy targets and were annihilated and driven out of Louisiana. General Jackson wrote to Secretary of War James Monroe, "Heaven to be sure has interposed most wonderfully on our behalf and I am filled with gratitude when I look back to what we escaped." He had escaped the gravest crisis to American independence. The war was over.

In 1817, Bishop William DuBourg came to France to beg the French nuns to establish schools for the French children and the Indians in his diocese. He was the Bishop of the New Orleans diocese in the Louisiana Territory. Coincidentally, he had once served as Mother Seton's spiritual advisor in Maryland. The next year, Mother Rose Philippine Duchesne answered his call and sailed to New Orleans with four other nuns.

13. Saint Rose Philippine Duchesne and Frontier Girls of Missouri

Born   August 29, 1769 in Grenoble, France
Died   November 18, 1852 in St. Charles, Missouri
Canonized   July 3, 1988 by Pope John Paul II
Feast Day   November 18
Foundress of the first Catholic school for girls west of the Mississippi.
Foundress of the Society of the Sacred Heart in the United States.

"You have come, you say, seeking the Cross. Well, you have taken exactly the right road to find it. A thousand unforeseen difficulties may arise. Your establishment may grow slowly at first. Physical privations may be added, and those more keenly felt such as lack of spiritual help under particular circumstances. Be ready for all.
You and I shall spend our lives in this thankless task; our successors will reap the harvest in this world, let us be content to reap it in the next."
Letter to Rose Philippine Duchesne from Louisiana Bishop William DuBourg, January 1817.

The tall, vigorous nun knelt down in the darkened chapel before the Blessed Sacrament in evening adoration. One of her mischievous students was so impressed by her reverence, stillness and lack of movement that she tested the nun's stamina. She cut tiny bits of paper and dropped them on the nun's habit as she was kneeling.

The next morning, she went to observe the nun to see if the pieces of paper had fallen from her habit revealing her movement during the night.

But the nun was found still kneeling in the same position with the papers undisturbed. It had been a motionless night of adoration for Sister Rose Philippine Duchesne.

Another student later wrote about Sister Rose:

> She gradually led us to devotion to the Sacred Heart. Her words had all the more influence with us because they were accompanied by such great virtue. An angel in adoration in the church would not have impressed us more, so reverent and recollected was she at prayer. Kneeling on the floor, upright and without support, hands clasped, she remained motionless for hours. One felt the presence of God in her.

Formation

"*This* is my pleasure," explained the young Rose Duchesne to her father. He was criticizing her for giving some of her toys and coins to poor children that he had given her for her own pleasure. The tension between Rose's vocation and her father's objections had begun.

Rose Philippine Duchesne was born on August 29, 1769, in Grenoble in southeastern France. She was named after St. Rose of Lima since she was born on the eve of her Feast Day. Her middle name was after St. Philip. She was the daughter of Pierre-François and Rose Duchesne, both of whom were from prominent families. She was the second of eight children. There were seven girls and one boy. Her older sister died when she was nine, her youngest became a Visitation nun. The rest of her siblings married.

Her family lived in adjoining apartments with her maternal uncle and aunt and their children. The two families had 20 children in 20 years. Rose's family lived a comfortable life while most of France suffered from want. Her father was a lawyer, a businessman and a prominent civic leader in Grenoble. However, he was a liberal who did not receive the sacraments. Her mother, however, raised her children to be faithful Catholics. Sometimes Rose accompanied her mother on visits to the sick and poor. When she was 11 she began to give her allowance to them for which her father criticized her.

Rose's home training gave her skills in cooking, candle making and clothes making. Her early education was at home by private tutors. From them she learned arithmetic, history, geography and literature and her mother taught her the fundamentals of the Catholic faith.

Rose loved nature, preferring to climb in the hills near her house than to play with dolls. She developed a capacity for solitude early in life, enjoying long walks while dreaming of traveling to far off lands. She had a strong personality and was a natural leader with the other children.

Rose also enjoyed reading the lives of saints and martyrs. Jesuit missionaries visited her town and told stories of their experiences with the American Indians. One of them lived in Grenoble. He had been a missionary in Louisiana to the French and the Indians and visited the trading post of St. Louis. His stories so intrigued Rose that she was determined to serve the Indians there someday. She later wrote, "I was just eight or ten years old, but already I considered it a great privilege to be a missionary. I envied their labors without being frightened by the dangers to which they were exposed, for I was at this time reading stories of the martyrs, in which I was keenly interested."

At the age of 12, Rose went with her sister to board in the convent of the Visitation nuns in Grenoble called Sainte Marie. There she began her life-long devotion to the Sacred Heart of Jesus. Two years later, she decided to become a Visitation nun and a missionary to the American Indians. When her father found out about this, he took her out of the convent and she continued her studies at home. To his surprise, Rose docilely obeyed and took up home life once again. For the next five years, she was allowed to study under tutors with her male cousins who were preparing for careers in business and politics. This was unusual for a young girl at the time and she became a highly educated woman.

Vocation

Rose took part in Grenoble's social events. She attended evening parties, concerts and dances. However, her sister later wrote, "When she took me into her confidence, she assured me that even in the midst of these amusements she was thinking with joy of the time when she would be a nun, but in the meantime she applied herself quite willingly to her dancing lessons."

When she was 18, Rose's father suggested a young man for her to marry. However, she felt called by God to the religious life so she refused to marry him. Determined to follow her calling, she began to live like a nun within the family home. She gave up her social life, refused to wear fancy clothing, performed the most unpleasant of the household chores and followed a routine of daily prayer.

A few months later in the spring, Rose went back to visit Sainte Marie's with her aunt. On an impulse, she suddenly announced her decision to stay there as a postulant. Her aunt could not persuade her otherwise and returned home alone. A few days later, her parents came and also tried to persuade her to return home, but she declined. Rose gave up her home and family for the convent.

Revolutionary Years

Rose's father championed social reform. He prepared a protest against the existing social injustices and called for reforms. But then the French Revolution broke out in the summer of 1788. The confiscation and sale of Church property soon began. In September of 1789, Rose was ready to make her religious profession but her father forbade it due to the threatening persecution. Rose wrote that this was "the severest trial God could have sent me." In September of 1792, when Rose was 23, the French revolutionary government suppressed the religious orders of women. Rose had to take off her religious habit and leave the convent where she had spent the last five years. She returned to her family in disappointment and lived as a laywoman for the next nine years. Her father had moved the family to a country home near the village of Grane. Here Rose and her nun cousin followed the monastic order of the day. They rose early and prayed the Divine Office.

Rose wrote the *Story of Sainte Marie* in 1805 in which she described these days:

> The decree which obliged all religious women [in France] to return to secular life obliged me to go back to my family. My heart was never attached to this sort of life and it was a land of exile for me, a foreign land, and Sion [the Promised Land of religious life], my true country, remained the goal of my desires and of my costliest endeavors. The dwelling for which I longed was the sanctuary of religious life. Although I was very lovingly

inclined toward the cloister in which I had received my vocation – and never for an instant did I feel a repugnance toward it – still, from the time of our dispersal several orders in different countries attracted my thoughts and became the object of my prayers, that I might know the will of God in my regard. Several times I changed my mind about the place and the order, but never did I lose sight of my high ambition.

In the Reign of Terror that followed the French Revolution between 1793 and 1794, Sainte Marie was turned into a prison for dissidents, priests were imprisoned and the guillotine decapitated many. The survivors went into hiding. Rose's family sheltered a fugitive priest for two years. He said Mass and provided Rose with spiritual direction.

Rose bravely returned to Grenoble and formed the Ladies of Mercy, an association that provided material and spiritual help to the priests. The ladies risked their own imprisonment and took priests to the dying, gave priests refuge, helped the sick and poor and performed the spiritual and corporal works of mercy. Rose also taught poor children, many of whom ran wild in the streets after the closing of the schools and orphanages. For nine years Rose continued this work, even after the government suppressed the Ladies of Mercy association. She did all of this while also nursing her mother during her last illness. An eyewitness wrote, "That daughter, who had formerly left her to follow God's call, was her most faithful nurse during her entire illness. Day and night she was at her bedside, caring for both body and soul; nor did she leave her until she had drawn her last breath."

Rose wondered about her vocation and whether she should remain in the world. She wrote:

> The time of trial, but not of indecision, seemed an eternity to me, and if, reflecting on its length, I wondered at times whether God meant me to remain in the world, He saw to it at once that some passage of the Gospel referring to detachment from one's family came to my attention and revived my courage. The separation from my father, who went to Paris, and the death of my mother, which occurred shortly after that, set me at liberty to

leave home and return to Grenoble in order to associate myself with some women who wished to live under a religious rule. One of the Jesuits whom I had known was still living. As soon as he learned of my decision, he wrote to me saying that *I had taken a step for which God would reward me.*

Rose lamented the destruction of religion by the Revolution and wrote in a letter, "Formerly I looked forward without imprudence to a life of security in religion. Now all is changed; my plans are no longer the same, for it seems impossible to follow my desires, as there is no religious order in existence in France."

Saint Madeleine Sophie Barat

In 1801, Pope Pius VII and the French Emperor Napoleon signed a concordat that restored some freedom to practice Catholicism in France. Rose began legal proceedings to rent Sainte Marie, the convent in Grenoble that had been turned into a prison during the Revolution. She succeeded and, with only a single companion, reopened the convent and went back to try to re-establish it as a convent for nuns. However, most of the nuns who had lived there were now dead or too old and she faced criticisms from those whom she thought would be thankful. They accused her of rashness in occupying a building that was falling in ruins and from which she might be expelled again.

She explained her problems to her sister in a letter to her in February 1802. "You are very kind to take an interest in the difficulties inseparable from an undertaking such as ours. What I feel most keenly is the opposition of some persons from whom I had expected gratitude. I have gotten myself talked about, both favorably and unfavorably; but as I did not act through worldly motives, I am not upset by blame nor elated by praise." Rose set to work on repairs, cooking meals and cleaning. Soon the community increased to four but it did not meet Rose's expectations of a religious community. There was no Rule, no silence and no habit. The others were just making a feeble attempt at religious life but not living it. They murmured against a discouraged Rose.

Finally in 1802, the former Superior of the community came back with a few nuns. They stayed until the end of August 1802 and then left Rose alone. It was too difficult to re-establish the convent. Rose was deeply saddened. She wrote, "I was crushed. I was the subject of scandal. Gossip had it that I had driven away the religious, that I would not yield in anything, that no one could bear to live with me."

Eventually, the little community of eight established a boarding school with 20 students and a free school for the poor but they were still not a religious community. Rose then heard of the Ladies of the Faith, later the Society of the Sacred Heart, a religious society founded in 1800 by St. Madeleine Sophie Barat under the direction of Father Joseph Varin. Rose was anxious to join them.

In 1804, Father Varin visited Rose and wrote to Mother Barat, "You will find someone in this house were she alone and at the remotest corner of the world, you should go after her." To insure the future of the convent, Mother Barat was invited to visit and become its Superior. When she arrived and entered the dimly lit hallway, Rose suddenly prostrated herself before her, kissed her feet and repeated the words of the psalmist, "How lovely on the mountain are the feet of those who bring the gospel of peace!" Mother Barat later said, "I let her do it through pure stupefaction." "I was utterly dumbfounded at the sight of such faith and humility, and I did not know what to say or do."

Rose resumed her novitiate that year. She had been an independent laywoman for nine years and for three years after that had tried to re-establish the convent unsuccessfully. Finally, in 1805, when Rose was 36, she made her first vows with six others. Rose was now under the direction of Mother Barat who was 10 years younger than she was. But Rose humbly accepted her superiority. She later wrote, "Humility is the virtue that requires the greatest amount of effort."

Sister Rose lived under the direction of Mother Barat for the next 11 years. Sister Rose was described as impatient, irritable and highly sensitive. Mother Barat tempered her impetuous nature and helped her to be more flexible in accepting the will of God. Both of them were strong willed and intellectually independent. They complemented each other and became life long friends. Mother Barat was Sister Rose's spiritual guide.

In 1806, Mother Barat wrote, "I realize my dear Rose, that for the moment Our Lord seems to leave you to yourself, and this makes virtue more difficult to practice." In November of the same year, she wrote to her again and said, "The thought that I might be able to lessen your interior sufferings by a little advice urges me to write today. The trial which your divine master is now putting you through is one that calls for some help."

In 1807, Mother Barat now called Rose by the name of "Philippine" and wrote her some spiritual advice regarding Lent:

> Take care of your health and do not weaken yourself by fasting. Endeavor to acquire the virtues so necessary for drawing hearts to Christ; meekness, humility, affability, evenness of manner, which is the fruit of patience, and above all that love of Jesus which I so desire to see in you. Oh, my dear Philippine, when will you be able to say and to experience the meaning of these sublime words of the great Apostle: "I live, no, not I, but Christ lives in me?" Try each day to die to self in order that Jesus Christ may live more fully in you. Meditate frequently on these words of the *Imitation*: My son, the more you renounce self, the more you shall find me. Again I recommend very specially to you a kind and gentle manner toward others, and I beg you to use it also in dealing with yourself. Be patient with yourself. Do not get downhearted about your faults, even if you commit a hundred a day. Draw from them, instead, an increase of humility and confidence.

A year later, Mother Barat wrote Sister Philippine words of encouragement during a dark period of her life:

> Grasp this fact clearly: Our Lord, in His goodness, wishes you to become a great saint. He brought you into this little Society just to give you the means of doing so. Oh, you can do all things now, if only you are faithful. Success depends on your willing it. Do not fear, I shall never lose patience with you. I know you cannot correct yourself suddenly. How could you become meek, stripped of all attachment to your own judgment, etc., when the contrary faults have been rooted in your character for so long?

Sister Philippine was very active in her early years in the Society. In

1806 she was secretary to the Superior, head of the boarding school, teacher of the older children, business manager for the school and the convent and nurse for the nuns and the students. What distressed her the most, however, was her lack of time for prayer and so she often gave up sleep in order to make time for prayer.

Sister Philippine was loved by her students at Sainte Marie. One of them who later became a nun in the Society wrote about Sister Philippine playing a game with them at the end of which she asked with enthusiasm, "Now, children, which of you wants to go with me to America to convert the Illinois [Indians]?" Every one of the students gave her their hand as a pledge.

The future nun also described Sister Philippine's work at Saint Marie's:

> It was not only in the development of our minds and the care of our bodies that she showed her motherly interest in us. Our souls were far more precious to her. Her corrections were often severe and often met with stubborn ill-humor on our part, but when we finally came around, she pointed out our faults and mistakes in such a kindly way that we gave in and made reparation, especially to God, by a sincere act of contrition.

Sister Philippine also nursed her father during his last illness in 1814. His agony was long and painful but he received the sacrament of Extreme Unction. Sister wrote, "I trust he is with God." In 1815, she was sent to found a new convent in Paris. She cleaned and organized the convent and joined the workmen in masonry and painting work. She was now known as "Mother" Philippine Duschesne. By the time the French Napoleonic Empire fell in 1815, there were eight Sacred Heart houses in existence.

The Mission to America

In her first year as a nun, Mother Philippine still had the desire to go to the American missions. In a letter she wrote to Mother Barat, she confided a spiritual experience she had had during a night of adoration before the Eucharist on Holy Thursday. "I spent the entire night in the new World carrying the Blessed Sacrament to all parts of the land. I had all my sacrifices to offer: a mother, sisters, family, my mountain! When you say to me 'now I send you,' I will respond quickly 'I go'."

However, she still had to wait for another 13 years to realize her dream. She renounced her own will and accepted the will of God. She bore her cross patiently. Later she wrote, "Let us bear our cross and leave it to God to determine the length and the weight."

Many times during the next 13 years, Mother Duchesne shared with Mother Barat her dream of becoming a missionary to the American Indians. The dream was ignited when Bishop William DuBourg visited the motherhouse in Paris in May of 1817. He was the Bishop of the New Orleans diocese in the Louisiana Territory.

This new vast geographic area contained mostly French-speaking people with very few priests. Bishop DuBourg asked Mother Barat for nuns to establish schools for the children in his diocese. Mother Duchesne pleaded with Mother Barat for permission to go but to no avail. Later, as the Bishop was about to leave the convent, Mother Duchesne suddenly appeared from a doorway, knelt with clasped hands on the threshold and pleaded with Mother Barat, "Your consent, Mother! Give your consent." Finally, she consented.

The Sisters' mission was to educate and form girls into Catholic women who could transform society through their daily actions and Catholic witness. Mother later stated her philosophy of Catholic education, "You may dazzle the mind with a thousand brilliant discoveries of natural science; you may open new worlds of knowledge which were never dreamed of before; yet, if you have not developed in the soul of the pupil strong habits of virtue which will sustain her in the struggle of life, you have not educated her, but only put in her hand a powerful instrument of self-destruction."

The Voyage to Missouri

A year later, in March 1818, Mother left Bordeaux at the age of 49 with four other nuns on the sailing vessel *Rebecca*. In Mother Duchesne's parting letter to her family she wrote, "In this hour when I am giving up everything almost as if I were going to die, since it is practically certain I shall never see you again, nor my many Mothers and Sisters in religion, my relatives and friends, I believe I have a right to ask great things of God, with the same confidence as St. Peter when he said to Jesus Christ,

'We have left all for you; what shall be our reward?' Oh, the reward I ask of Him is the great, the ineffable consolation of learning that you are all fervent in loving Him."

The Atlantic crossing was a stormy and hazardous journey that lasted 76 days. Mother compared the noise, confusion and terror on board to that of Judgment Day in a letter that she wrote to Mother Barat while at sea:

> A storm at sea is really a terrifying sight. The roaring of the deep mingled with the crash of the tempest would drown both thunder and the booming of cannon. Add to this ear-splitting din the rolling of the vessel in the midst of great waves. The shouting of the sailors as they encourage themselves at their work has a tragic, a lugubrious effect. But their silence is ever more dismal, and still worse is the sight of the captain pacing the deck in deep thought. A vessel tossed violently in an angry sea gives one some idea of the confusion of Judgment Day. The sky and the stars seem to disappear suddenly behind mountains of water. The sea nearly black during the storm, gapes wide, revealing its bottomless depths, then suddenly closes.
>
> The waves sweep over the deck and are hurled out to sea with a new rolling of the boat. Twice during the night the high waves burst open the portholes and flooded our berths. The bending masts, the sails furled or torn, the steering wheel abandoned lest the boat be too strained – all this is very terrifying unless one sees God in the storm. Seasickness is a wretched malady, affecting both stomach and head. One is utterly good for nothing: connected thought is impossible. One can scarcely drag from one's dull heart the least little prayer of love.

Finally on May 29, 1818, the Feast of the Sacred Heart, these nuns of the Sacred Heart sailed from the Gulf of Mexico into the Mississippi River and anchored near New Orleans. Only three years before, General Andrew Jackson and his American frontiersmen had defeated the British here in the Battle of New Orleans and ended the War of 1812. Mother knelt and kissed the marshy ground with tears in her eyes. She later wrote, "More fortunate than Moses, I had entered the Promised Land." Like many immigrants, Mother Duchesne had arrived too sick to travel any further. The Ursuline nuns hospitably welcomed the Sisters until they were able to travel upriver to St. Louis, Missouri.

On July 12, they boarded a steamboat and continued their journey north up the Mississippi River to St. Louis. The French explorers Father Jacques Marquette and Louis Joliet discovered the River in 1673. Father Marquette originally named it the River of the Immaculate Conception. The Sisters traveled on the boat for 1200 miles past plantations of corn and cane, flooded rice fields and green meadows.

It took them 40 days to get to St. Louis which at that time was only a frontier trading post. When they arrived, Bishop DuBourg informed them that he had not arranged an Indian mission for them as they had expected. Instead, he sent the disappointed Sisters 20 miles west up the Missouri River to primitive St. Charles to open a school for frontier girls. Once again, Mother had to postpone her dream to serve the American Indians. As she later wrote, "As for real Indians, we never see them because the Americans from the East are pushing them out and making war with them. They are withdrawing furtheraway."

The St. Charles Mission

Mother arrived at St. Charles which she called "the remotest village in the United States." St. Charles was a frontier settlement of a few hundred families. Mother established there the first convent of the Sacred Heart in America. On September 14, she opened a free day school for girls. It was the first of its kind west of the Mississippi River. In October she also opened a boarding school there with the hope that its revenues would support the day school. The Sisters taught catechism, reading, writing and arithmetic. The students shared the few books. Some spoke French, some spoke English. Mother spoke only French. She wrote to Mother Barat in France, "God has not bestowed on us the gift of tongues. Perhaps He wants His missionary nuns to sanctify themselves on failure." These proved to be prophetic words.

After Mother Duchesne settled in St. Charles, she received a letter from Mother Barat regarding the blessing of Pope Pius VII for the American mission. She wrote, "You see, our Holy Father the Pope has approved your mission; it was then, God's will and that is why all circumstances converged so remarkably to make it succeed."

An open fireplace heated the school. Both the Sisters and the students slept on mattresses on the floor of the main room which served as a dormitory by night, classroom by day and recreation room by evening. Mother understated the lodging when she characterized it as an inconvenient location in a letter that she wrote on October 8, 1818. "Our free school numbers twenty-one, which in proportion to the population equals a school of a hundred in France. The children have never heard of Our Lord, of His birth or His death, nor of Hell, and listen open-mouthed to our instructions. We are very inconveniently lodged and shall have to go elsewhere at the end of a year, for we are paying nearly 2000 francs in rent for a house consisting of six very small rooms badly in need of repairs. The large garden and orchard are uncultivated and we have no one to work them."

The Sisters lived an austere lifestyle. Their supplies were limited, money, food and water were scarce and living accommodations were uncomfortable. They cooked without pots or a kitchen stove. They endured cold and inclement weather, cramped living quarters with a lack of privacy and the crudeness of their frontier students. Mother wrote to her sister in France, "Neither doors nor windows close tight and no one here knows how to make a foot- warmer. We have logs but they are too large, and there is no one to chop them for us and no saw with which we might cut them ourselves."

The Sisters had to do the work normally done by men and still keep up with their spiritual program. It was a combination of grueling manual labor and a demanding spiritual regimen. When her brother offered to pay her way back to France, Mother wrote to her sister, "Tell him to use the money to pay the passage of two more nuns coming to America."

Enrollment in the free school increased, but not in the boarding school because the parents who lived in St. Louis were reluctant to send their daughters and pay for schooling in a remote settlement located across the often unnavigable Missouri River.

Mother Duchesne wrote to Mother Barat on February 15, 1819, "The experience of a winter here, and that a very mild one, has made us realize that at present we would only vegetate in this place, without accomplishing even the little good we might do elsewhere. But it is hard to abandon so many interesting children." It became increasingly obvious that the boarding school, the nun's only source of revenue, was a failure. After only 12 months, it was closed. This was a great disappointment that Mother docilely accepted.

Mother Duchesne took the closure of the St. Charles boarding school very hard and blamed it on herself. She had always thought that she was unfit to be Superior. She wrote, "The dear Lord has favored us with a share of His Cross. The greatest and undoubtedly the hardest to bear is the lack of success in our work here. If a saint had been in charge, all would have gone well. That thought makes the burden of my office all the heavier. Every day I see more clearly that I do not possess the qualities necessary in a Superior."

The Florissant Mission

After the closure of the St. Charles boarding school, Mother asked Bishop DuBourg to let her come closer to St. Louis to attract more girls from there to a new boarding school. The migration to Florissant began in September by taking the nun's baggage and furniture in carts down the steep road to the river where it was loaded onto rafts. Mother followed, leading the cows and chickens for 10 miles after which they crossed the Missouri opposite Florissant on a raft. Florissant was a farming community located about 10 miles northwest of St. Louis.

For the first three months, the Sisters and the five children who had accompanied them lived on the Bishop's farm in a log cabin that was even worse than their home in St. Charles. Mother described it as a "single room, which will serve as the children's dormitory, refectory, parlor and classroom. Above is a loft under a roof that is pierced by many holes. This will be our living quarters night and day. We are in a situation that calls for continual self-renunciation at times pestered by visitors, without a corner to which we can withdraw for prayer; now overcome by heat in such crowded quarters, and now racked by the cold and wind that come in on all sides." The nuns had no servants and had to gather their own wood from the forest and corn, apples and vegetables from the garden. Bishop Dubourg wrote to Mother Barat, "I cannot tell you how excellent an impression [the nuns] have made in this part of the world. Mother Duchesne is a saint."

The nuns remained in the Bishop's log cabin until their new home was ready. On Christmas Eve, 1820, Mother walked through a snowstorm guided by pig tracks while trying to lead her uncooperative cow that ran ahead of her. This caused Mother to run and fall through the snow and brambles, tearing her habit, getting lost, but finally arriving for supper and Midnight Mass. Mother established another boarding school and opened the Society's first novitiate at Florissant.

The new school's facilities were a big improvement over St. Charles. It had a classroom, reception room, kitchen and a dormitory upstairs where the students slept. Mother chose as her room a windowless closet-like space located under the stairway. It was stifling hot in the summer and very cold in the winter.

The school at Florissant also served as a novitiate for the Society of the Sacred Heart but it struggled to survive as a school on its low income from tuitions. Mother saw herself as a failure. She wrote, "I am the least useful in the community, but I am happy to share the hard work. I wish I were put in just that kind of employment; then I would be content. It is heart-breaking, after such ardent desire, to see our success hindered or slowed up and to realize that I am the obstacle." Later she wrote, "I think I heard in the depths of my soul, 'You are destined to please me, not so much by success as by bearing failure.' "

Later, Mother wrote to Mother Barat, "There is disillusionment in store for anyone who comes to this country in search of success, honor, pleasure. But those who desire only the good pleasure of God abide in peace even in the midst of failure, for God has not told us He requires us to be successful. Here all thought is but confusion when I want to do good, poor blockhead I am – old, without talents, without lovable qualities, without virtue. If I can be useful in the least little work for the glory of the Sacred Heart, I am willing to spend a long age here, without success, without friends, as my only means of imitating the Sacred Heart."

More Missions

In 1819, Missouri's application for admission to the Union as a slave state failed. This became a national controversy due to the delicate balance in numbers between free and slave states. In 1820, the Missouri Compromise cleared the way for Missouri's entry to the union as a slave state, along with Maine as a free state to preserve the balance. Additionally, the Missouri Compromise banned slavery north and west of Missouri forever. The following year, Missouri was admitted as the 24th state, with the state capital temporarily located in St. Charles until a permanent location could be selected. Still, there was not a single church nor priest from Missouri to Canada on the north and to the Pacific Ocean on the west.

In 1821, Mother Duchesne established her first convent after Florissant at the Grand Coteau in Opelousa, Louisiana. Soon more nuns were on their way from France and by 1824, within six years of the beginning of their mission, 22 young women had entered the Society of the Sacred Heart. With more nuns, more houses were established. In 1825 a house was established at St. Michael's; in 1827 another house and two schools in St. Louis and in 1828 St. Charles was re-opened. Mother Duchesne was pioneering the parochial school system in the United States.

It was necessary for Mother to visit these houses in her supervisory role. These visits were often difficult journeys up and down the Mississippi River. For example, in 1822 she left St. Louis to visit the house at Grand Coteau downriver in Louisiana. Her return trip lasted 80 days during which she traveled by riverboat, steamboat and a canoe in which she got lost in a swamp. She suffered from yellow fever and saw others dying of it like animals without any help; slept in bedding not washed since the sick-bed death of the prior user and sailed past her first steamboat and saw its burst boilers that had killed two men. She also waited five days until the water rose high enough to lift her grounded steamboat off a sandbank. In 1830, Mother visited the Louisiana houses once again and on her return upriver to St. Louis she only got as far as the Ohio River. From there she had to travel to St. Louis by oxcart.

Mother Duchesne traveled on the water over the Mississippi and Missouri Rivers by steamboats, raft sailboats and canoes. She journeyed overland over rough roads on foot or on horseback, in spring-less carriages or two-wheeled carts. She weathered flooded streams and extremes of heat and cold in drafty buildings without insulation and little heat.

Mother continually endured the frontier hardships that she described as "inconvenience in everything, especially our lodging, having no place even to put a sewing basket or writing pad, not a table for one's own use, food that is often disgusting, and very little variety in it, severe cold, prostrating heat. If some of those from Siberia are looking for a mission field with the same type of work and the same climate during a good part of the year, they might come to our section of the globe. It takes souls of that quality to persevere out here. Our lips froze together, and at night our breath froze on the pillows and sheets. There are advantages in the life of hardship and privation here. I must admit I fear for those who have had a life of ease and convenience."

In addition to the frontier's physical sufferings of poverty, hard labor, poor housing, clothing and diet, extremes of weather, floods that destroyed crops, cooking and cleaning in primitive conditions, there were spiritual sufferings. Mother suffered from the worldliness, lack of obedience and ingratitude of students; the complaints of postulants and other Sisters and calumnies circulated against her. But she didn't complain. She wrote, "Things will turn out as God wills. I hold to nothing and I know they can make complaints about me that are very true."

To all of her suffering she said, as did the Blessed Virgin Mary, "*Fiat!*" ("Let it be done!") She wrote, "An establishment in New Orleans would have supported this house [Florissant] but God does not will it, *Fiat*; for the money-shortage, *Fiat*; for the illness, *Fiat*. Here at Florissant we are no longer afraid of starving to death, and that is something. If God takes from us the means of doing good, we must accept His will. We wanted the Cross and not honor; poverty and not ease; the will of God and not our own."

In 1823, Jesuit missionaries came to Florissant and established their novitiate for a dozen of them, including the great missionary, Father Pierre De Smet. The Sisters had a convent and school in one corner of the Bishop's farm; the Jesuits had their house in the biggest section and the parish church of St. Ferdinand filled another part. Mother helped them to get established with their novitiate and in domestic work; cooking and sewing for them. Jesuit Father William Robinson said of her, "She saved the struggling Missouri mission and prevented it from failing through absolute lack of resources." Mother was very pleased that Pope Leo XII approved the Society of the Sacred Heart on the Feast of the Sacred Heart in 1826.

By 1830, twelve years after the beginning of their American Mission, the Society of the Sacred Heart had six convents in the Mississippi valley with 64 nuns and more than 350 students. In 1834, Mother moved from St. Louis and returned to Florissant where she remained for the next five years during which she was the Superior of the novitiate convent. She wrote Mother Barat, "I feel that I am a worn-out instrument, a useless walking stick that is fit only to be hidden in a dark corner." But her work continued. She wrote, "I have plenty to occupy me from four o'clock in the morning till eleven o'clock at night: treasury, pantry, sacristy, nuns' linen room, a class with the children of the free school, two hours a day with the orphans, surveillance of the workmen, visit, letters, etc."

In 1840, Mother Duchesne was replaced as Superior by Mother Elizabeth Galitzin. Mother Duchesne thanked Mother Barat "for having at last lifted the burden I have carried so inefficiently." In 1841, her spirits lifted when she learned that she might serve the Indians. Finally, 23 years after arriving for the American Mission, Mother was to realize her life-long dream of serving the American Indians.

The Sugar Creek Indian Mission

Father De Smet needed religious women for the Indian missions. When he was in St. Louis in 1841, he asked Mother Duchesne to establish a school for Potawatomi Indian girls in Kansas. The Potawatomis originated in the Great Lakes region. They had migrated to Kansas in 1835 because of the Government's policy of moving Indians west of the Mississippi. Later, when their Chief learned that there were Blackrobes he begged for them to visit his people.

At the same time, St. Louis Bishop Joseph Rosati visited Pope Gregory XVI and told him of Mother Duchesne's missionary desires for the Indians. The Holy Father supported her desires and the Bishop wrote to Mother:

> I am really surprised to learn that you are now pleading to leave Missouri in order to go among the savages. However, when one loves God, one never says "Enough." If I did not know you well, I might say it is too much for you. But knowing you as I do, I say: "Go! Follow your attraction, or rather the voice of God. He will be with you."

As the Sisters and Father Peter Verhaegen discussed plans for their trip to the Indians in the parlor in St. Louis, Mother prayed her Rosary. She wept in silence because her name was not mentioned as one of the missionaries. But Father turned toward her and said, "But she must come, too. Even if she can use only one leg, she will come. Why, if we have to carry her all the way on our shoulders, she is coming with us. She may not be able to do much work, but she will assure success to the mission by praying for us. Her very presence will draw down all manner of heavenly favors on the work."

However, Mother was in very poor health. One of the Sisters wrote, "The doctor thinks she is in continual danger of death, yet she wanted to fast and abstain all during Lent. Since then the swelling has increased, and it extends from her feet up to her chest, so that she is liable to be smothered at any moment. She feels that she is very near to death, yet once our Mother General gives her the permission, she will consider it an order and no one will be able to hold her back."

Mother Duchesne received her permission from Mother General, no one could hold her back and she left in June with three priests and four Sisters for the long and difficult journey of almost 200 miles west over the Missouri River into Indian Territory to the Sugar Creek Mission in what is now eastern Kansas. No white woman had ever gone to live with the Indians. Mother Philippine Duchesne was the first at the age of 72.

Some wondered about the wisdom of sending an elderly nun on such a difficult journey to a difficult mission. However, Mother Barat wrote to Mother Duchesne's Superior, "Remember that in leaving for America, good Mother Duchesne had only this work in view. It was for the sake of the Indians that she felt inspired to establish the order in America. I believe it enters into the designs of God that we should profit, if possible, by the opportunity offered us."

After four days on the river, the party got off the boat at present day Kansas City, Kansas, and traveled overland for four more days by wagon south to Sugar Creek. Two Indians on horses met the party at the Osage River when they were 18 miles from Sugar Creek. Every two miles for the rest of the way, a pair of mounted Indians met them and guided them on to their new mission. When they were a mile away, 500 braves in ceremonial dress of bright blankets, plumes and feathers met them, performed a series of circular horse maneuvers and then led them into their village. There another 700 Indians welcomed them.

One of the priests presented Mother to the assembled Potawatomi, "Here, my children, is the Sister who for 35 years has been asking God to let her come to you." The Indians then greeted each of the Sisters individually. However, the Indians had not completed their construction of a log house for the Sisters. So for the first four months their home was an Indian's small cabin in which they slept on the ground.

The Sisters opened a school for the Indian girls and their mothers came to learn domestic skills. All the Sisters except Mother learned the native language and the children learned hymns and prayers. One of the Sisters wrote, "As soon as we could, we taught our Indians the prayers of the Church, and especially the Litany of the Blessed Virgin, as it is sung on Sundays after Vespers. Soon our cabin could not hold all our scholars and we made a large room with green branches. Our children are intelligent and understand easily."

The Sisters suffered during the severe winter and Mother's infirmities became worse. She visited the sick and helped the Indian girls, but was not able to do much else. Worse, she was unable to learn the Potowatami language with its 10-syllable words. She could only communicate with them by signs. She lived a life of prayer and sacrifice. The Indians called her "Woman-Who-Prays-Always" because she spent so many hours in the church praying before the Blessed Sacrament. She prayed there all morning and four hours in the afternoon. Mother Galitzin, said, "If she cannot work at the mission, she will forward the success of the mission by her prayers." A Sister wrote, "Everyone admitted that a great number of Baptisms resulted from her prayers. Almost every Sunday afternoon three or four men or women and their families were baptized, and Mother Duchesne inscribed all their names in the register."

Mother Duchesne wrote to Mother Barat in France and told her about the 50 First Communicants, the 70 adult converts, the 200 who received the Brown Scapular, and how they gathered for morning and evening prayers, Mass and catechism. "They tell us there are many saints buried in the little cemetery," she wrote, "I beg God the favor of being buried beside them."

But her favor was not granted. Mother's health deteriorated during the winter due to the meager food and severe cold. A Sister wrote about her to Mother Galitzin, "She is here just to suffer, for she has aged much in this short time and is sometimes like a little child. She no longer has the fine mind of other days. She is feeble; her limbs are swollen; her digestion is poor; I fear she will have a stroke. All she can do at present is pray. That is all." Mother Galitzin arrived on Palm Sunday and decided that Mother should retire to the convent back in St. Charles, Missouri. Mother sadly resigned herself to God's will once more and left with Father Verhaegen on June 19.

"If Alexander the Great wept on the shores of the ocean because he could not carry his conquest further," she wrote, "I might weep also at the thought that my advanced age prevents me from saving so many poor people."

Rest

And so at age 73, Mother returned to the Sacred Heart Community at St. Charles. She arrived in St. Louis exactly one year after she had left for Sugar Creek. Her life-long ambition to serve the American Indians resulted in a stay of less than one year with them. Once again, she considered herself a failure. She wrote:

> I feel the same longing for the Rocky Mountain missions and any others like them that I experienced in France when I first begged to come to America. For thirty eight years my great desire was to work among the savages. Then after one year of uselessness at the Indian mission, I came back here by order of my Superior General, without accomplishing anything. As I live a very solitary life, I can employ all my time in making reparation for the past and in preparing for death. But I cannot put out of my mind the thought of the savages, and my ambition carries me even to the Rockies. I can only adore the designs of God, who has taken from me the thing I had so long desired. It seems to me that in leaving the Indians I left my real element, and now I can only yearn for that land from which there will be no departure. God knows why I was recalled, and that is enough.

Mother spent the last 10 years of her life in the convent at St. Charles in a tiny uncomfortable room. She had one window in which paper replaced the broken panes, a thin mattress laid out nightly on the floor for a bed and one old coarse blanket as a coverlet.

Her niece described her routine and her room, "now at prayer, now at manual labor. The furniture of her little room consisted of a low cot, a chair, a wooden box in which she kept her treasures – and what treasures they were! Some instruments of penance, some spiritual notebooks, some letters of our Mother General. There were two or three old pictures of pious subjects on the walls and some well worn prayerbooks on a little table."

Mother never complained about it, she praised it. In 1851 she wrote to Mother Barat, "If you could see the pretty place we have here, standing beside the church as it does, you would not have the courage to take it from us, even if there were only four of us to carry on the work."

As Mother prayed long hours before the Blessed Sacrament, "she saw nothing, heard nothing, knew nothing except that Jesus was there," said one of her companions. She spent hours writing and sewing in her small room. Her letters reveal a deep sense of personal failure, diminishing health and frequent loneliness. In 1846 she pleaded with Mother Barat that the Florissant Mission remain open. She wrote her, "If you refuse my petition, I shall submit, but I shall never be reconciled. The wound is too deep." Florissant was closed.

Mother had labored in the American missions for 35 years. She had patiently performed all of her duties, suffered many disappointments and failures and saw others reap the harvest that she had sown. Failure was her success. She wrote, "We cultivate a very small field for Christ but we love it, knowing that God does not require great achievements, but a heart that holds back nothing for self."

Such was her heart, that she was finally satisfied with what appeared to be failures. She learned the value of devotion to daily duty and doing her duties well. She learned that our standards of success are not important and that faithfulness is more important than fruitfulness.

A Sister wrote to Mother Barat in France, "I have seen a great saint and one who is nearing the end of her life. I found her very weak and her voice so feeble that it is hard to hear what she says."

In November of 1852, Mother Barat sent Sister Anna du Rousier from France to visit Mother Duchesne. Sister Anna's missionary vocation had come through Mother's inspiring words that she heard at her school shortly before Mother left for America many years before. Mother happily received her. Two days later, Mother died peacefully on November 18, 1852, at the age of 83. Her last words were, "I give you my heart, my soul, and my life – oh, yes – my life generously."

Father De Smet said, "No greater saint ever died in Missouri, or perhaps in the whole Union." Her whole life was a continuing living sacrificial death to herself as a victim soul offering herself to God. Mother expressed this in a prayer that she lived through 35 years on the American frontier:

O my God, I desire to live as a victim offered in a spirit of penance and love. Then let me prepare all that is needed for a sacrifice of love whose perfume will rise even to the Heart of Jesus. May my whole being be the victim, all that I am and all that I have. May my own heart be the altar, my separation from the world and all earthly pleasures the sacrificial knife. May my love be the one consuming fire, and my yearning desires the breeze that fans it. Let me pour on it the incense and perfume of all virtues, and to this mystical sacrifice let me bring all that I cling to that I may offer all, burn all, consume all, keeping back nothing for self. O Divine Love, my very God, accept this sacrifice which I desire to offer You at every instant of my life.

Father De Smet and Mother had made an agreement that the first to die should obtain for the other a particular favor. Immediately after her death, Father De Smet received his favor. As she lay dead in 1852, her nuns took a photograph of her. The community's annalist wrote in the convent's *Journal,* "We had her daguerreotype taken, in case she may one day be canonized."

Virtues

Mother Duchesne persevered through all the obstacles placed in the path of her vocation. She entered religious life despite her father's vehement objection and she returned to it after nine years of absence caused by the French Revolution. She courageously ministered to the needs of hunted priests during the Reign of Terror. She humbly accepted Mother Barat as her Superior even though Mother Duchesne was 10 years older than Mother Barat. She patiently waited for 12 years to leave France to realize her dream of serving the American Indians. She patiently waited another 23 years in America before it was realized. Then she obediently left the Indians after serving only one year with them. She docilely accepted the disappointments of the failure of the first mission at St. Charles and the order to leave her last mission with the Indians at Sugar Creek.

Mother Duchesne's whole American missionary experience was one great trial. She arrived in America when already 49 years old, a highly cultured French woman who never learned to speak English and found Americans hard to understand. Her fortitude was tested by many trials of weather, sickness, slanders and disappointments. However, she used these frustrations as means to achieve still greater detachment and docile acceptance of God's will.

In addition to teaching and administrative duties, Mother Duchesne undertook the hardest tasks that needed doing. She tended livestock, chopped wood, dug potatoes, and mended shoes and clothing and made soap and candles. She sat up at night and nursed the ill. A Sister wrote, "Just think of it – she has spent eleven successive nights at the bedside of one religious who was very ill, and she does not allow herself any respite from work. I cannot understand how she does it at her age. I think it is miraculous."

Mother survived loneliness, yellow fever and persistent feelings of failure. She interceded during her last 10 years for all of the needs of the missions that she had not been able to meet herself. After her funeral, Father Verhaegen wrote, "Eminent in all virtues of religious life, but especially in humility, she sweetly and calmly departed this life in the odor of sanctity."

But to attain to these virtues of religious life, Mother had to conquer herself and her faults. A Sister wrote, "She was her own heaviest Cross." She had a brusqueness of manner that showed in her tone of voice, her impetuosity and her impatience. She forgot promises, spoke hastily but was sorrowful for all of her faults and begged her community's forgiveness. Her faults were slowly transformed through prayer to sweetness, gentleness and patience.

Twenty years after her death, Father De Smet wrote, "On every return from my Indian missionary visits, I deemed it a most agreeable duty to pay my respects to good Mother Duchesne, and I never returned from one of these visits but with an increase of edification, with a full conviction that I had conversed with a truly living saint."

Mother practiced the virtues of religious life under the banner of the Sacred Heart of Jesus. She said, "On that banner one sees no other words but these: patience, simplicity, recollection, obedience, regularity, silence, sacrifice."

One of her former students wrote, "In my childhood I always looked on Mother Duchesne as a perfect model of all virtues. Never once did I see her lacking in poise and self-control; never did I notice in her the least movement of impatience in dealing with the group of children who were so difficult to handle. She showed the same gentle kindliness toward all. More than once I called the attention of my schoolmates to the heavenly radiance that shone on her countenance. One might have mistaken it for sunshine, but the light was softer than that. Then we would say, 'Mother Duchesne has just come from the chapel. She has had an ecstasy.' And we were sure she had a vision of our Blessed Lord. We certainly had a saint for a teacher."

Fruits

Father Varin wrote to Mother Duchesne from France, "What a consolation it will be for you, when the Divine Master calls you to Himself, to leave behind you a large community which will continue with living ardor, the work for which you sacrificed your liberty, your rest, your life!" In her 35 years on the American frontier, Mother founded schools and convents throughout Missouri and Louisiana but still considered herself a failure. She had prophesied, "You will see that when I am dead everything will prosper." Her prophecy was fulfilled. The Society of the Sacred Heart and its great missionary work spread throughout North and South America, New Zealand and Australia.

In 1841, after Mother's retirement, the Society began establishments in the eastern states and a convent was founded in New York City. In 1843, there were about 60 pupils in each of the Society's schools. The girls were taught elementary education as well as home skills including carding, spinning, sewing, knitting, embroidering and even artificial flower making. They learned to make clothes, to bake bread and to make butter.

By 1847 there were 1300 Christian Potawatomi coming to the Sugar Creek Mission. There were many confraternities and public devotions in the mission. The schools that she started in St. Louis became models for later educational institutions in the city. By the end of the century, more than 600 girls had been cared for and educated there.

Saint

Mother Duchesne was buried on the grounds of the Academy of the Sacred Heart at St. Charles. After three years, her body was exhumed, found to be miraculously incorrupt and reverently interred in a crypt within a simple octagonal shrine in the front yard of the Academy.

In 1949, Mother's remains were found to be no longer incorrupt and were removed from the little octagonal shrine and placed in a marble sarcophagus housed in an oratory.

In 1951, at the age of 60, a Sacred Heart Missionary named Mother Marie Bernard suffered from a malignant cancerous neck tumor. She was sent from Japan to St. Joseph's Hospital in San Francisco, California, for treatment. The tumor was too large to be surgically removed, so the doctors released her for radiation therapy with a prognosis of a life expectancy of six months to two years.

The Society prayed a novena for Mother's cure to Blessed Philippine Duchesne. The student body of the Society's school in San Francisco joined as well as Mother Marie herself. She wore a relic of Blessed Philippine around her neck. After Mother returned to Japan the tumor disappeared. She lived for another 10 years after that. In June of 1987 doctors reviewed her cure and stated that it was complete and scientifically inexplicable. The healing was approved for the cause of Blessed Philippine's canonization. She was canonized a saint on July 3, 1988 by Pope John Paul II. Her feast day is November 18.

The frontier post of St. Louis eventually became the Gateway to the West because the pioneers passed through it on their way to the West. There is a bronze plaque there called the Pioneer Roll of Fame. The plaque reads, "Some names must not wither." The name of Mother Rose Philippine Duchesne heads the list.

Opening Prayer for the Mass in Commemoration of Saint Rose Philippine Duchesne: Virgin, Religious and Missionary

Gracious God,
you filled the heart of Philippine Duchesne
with charity and missionary zeal,
and gave her the desire
to make you known among all peoples.

Fill us, who honor her memory today,
with that same love and zeal
to extend your kingdom to the ends of the earth.
We ask you this through our Lord Jesus Christ, your Son,
who lives and reigns with you and the Holy Spirit.
One God, for ever and ever.

Shrine:

Shrine of St. Philippine Duchesne
619 North Second Street
St. Charles, MO 63301
Telephone: 636-946-6127
Website: www.ash1818.org/shrine.htm
The Shrine of St. Rose Philippine Duchesne houses her tomb.

14. Saint Theodore Guerin and Frontier Girls of the Midwest

Born	October 2, 1798, Etables sur-Mer, Brittany, France
Died	May 14, 1856, Saint Mary-of-the-Woods, Indiana
Canonized	Pope Benedict XVI, October 15, 2006
Feast Day	October 3

Foundress of the Sisters of Providence of Saint Mary-of-the-Woods, Indiana.
Foundress of the first Catholic women's liberal-arts college in the United States.

"Put yourself gently into the hands of Providence.
And rest assured, my dear daughters, if you lean with all your
weight upon Providence, you will find yourselves well supported.
Our hope is in the Providence of God which has always protected
us until the present, and which will provide, somehow, for our
future needs."
Mother Guerin's counsel to her Sisters.

After three long months of travel by sailboat, trains, steamboats and stagecoaches, Mother Theodore Guerin along with two nuns and three novices arrived at Saint Mary-of-the-Woods, Indiana. "What was our astonishment," she wrote, "to find ourselves still in the midst of a forest, no village, not even a house in sight." They were led to a farmer's small house where they spent their first bitter winter in a land that she described as "wild, uncultivated, a world which seems to be in its cradle."

Formation

Anne-Therese Guerin was born in the village of Etables in Brittany, on the coast of France on October 2, 1798. It was during the French Revolution when her French contemporary, Saint Mother Duchesne, was 29 years old.

Anne-Therese's parents were Laurent and Isabelle Guerin. Her mother consecrated her to the Blessed Virgin Mary and she was home-schooled because the Revolution had closed the Catholic schools. Her father was an officer in the French Navy under Napoleon Bonaparte and was away from home for long periods of time.

One of her teachers was her cousin. He was so impressed by her learning ability that he obtained for her the privilege of making her First Communion at the then early age of ten. Young Anne-Therese confided to her confessor that she desired to belong to God alone. This consecration led to many sacrifices.

When she was 15, her youngest brother died and bandits robbed and killed her father as he traveled home after the French forces were demobilized following the defeat of Napoleon.

These tragedies left her mother completely distraught. Anne-Therese then had to interrupt her dream of becoming a nun and instead she became the caregiver for her mother and her younger sister. She nursed her mother and taught her sister until she thought that her mother's health was restored and that her sister was old enough to replace Anne-Therese.

Vocation

Anne-Therese now planned to enter the convent. However, her mother had grown to become dependent on her and objected to her leaving for the convent. She argued that Anne-Therese was already serving God in serving her mother and the poor. For five years her mother refused to consent to Anne-Therese's vocation but then she suddenly consented.

Her mother told her, "My daughter, you may leave now; you have your mother's consent and her blessing. I can no longer refuse God the sacrifice that he asks of me." Anne-Therese attributed this to the work of her Guardian Angel.

On August 18, 1823, when she was almost 25, Anne-Therese entered the novitiate of the Sisters of Providence at Ruillé and took the name of

Sister St. Theodore. This newly formed congregation served as teachers and cared for the sick and the poor.

Her time at Ruillé was difficult because she became extremely sick and nearly died. She took some medicine that saved her life but ruined her digestive system. She was never able to eat solid foods again and for the rest of her life she lived only on soft foods and liquids. Recurring illnesses from this malady plagued her for the rest of her life .On September 8, 1825, Sister St. Theodore made her first vows.

The Apostolate

In 1826, Sister was sent as Superior to the most abandoned district in Rennes at St. Aubin Parish. This district was filled with devastatingly poor and unchurched people. They were the aftermath of the French Revolution. Through Sister St. Theodore's loving and patient efforts, the children gradually became disciplined and learned the faith. This change in the children also had good effects on the adults of the parish.

A chronicler wrote, "This quarter which had been so long the abode of ignorance and all its regrettable consequences, was not long in becoming the pride of the inhabitants."

Sister St. Theodore credited this remarkable improvement to the Guardian Angels of her students and her concern for their welfare. She later told her community, "You must love the children if you wish to win them for God. To win children to virtue the road of precept is long, but the way of example is short." She continued:

> You must try to invent a means of correcting your children, but remember that the most powerful are rewards; a kind word, an approving glance, a little gesture is sometimes sufficient to correct what the harshest punishments would not have eradicated. It is necessary to be just, that is to say, to have no preference for any child. . . . But if it is necessary to be just, it is especially necessary to be kind; we must be the mother of our children, have for them maternal attentions and feelings. God confides these young girls to us so that we may form them to virtues. . . . Speak to them respectfully, and they will respect both you and themselves. Remember

that you are the visible Angels to the children and that
you ought to conduct yourself toward them as would
their holy Guardian Angels. . . .

Sister St. Theodore taught in Rennes for eight years but then her
relationship with the priest-Founder of her community was misunderstood
by her superiors. Sister favored him in the contentious separation of her
order from a congregation of brothers that he also founded. Her superiors
mis-judged her filial charity and sympathy toward him in his difficulties
and assigned her to another mission. Sister sorrowfully obeyed.

In 1834, Sister St. Theodore was named the Superior of Soulaines in
the Diocese of Angers. In this small parish, Sister St. Theodore continued
teaching and visiting the sick. She was an excellent teacher and received
a medal from the Academy of Angers for her skills. She learned the
basics of medicine and pharmacy from a local doctor so that she could
better serve the sick and poor of the region. She remained at Soulaines
until 1840.

The Call to America

Also in the year 1834, Father Simon Gabriel Brute, Mother Seton's
spiritual advisor, was consecrated as Bishop of the Diocese of Vincennes.
It consisted of the state of Indiana and the eastern part of Illinois. This
territory was vast with no schools and few churches. With only a few
priests and a great influx of Catholic immigrants of French, Irish and
German descent, the diocese was in great need.

In 1838, Bishop Brute sent Father Celestine de la Hailandiere, a Brittany
native, to Ruillé on a mission to recruit nuns to serve in his diocese. While
he was in France, Bishop Brute died and he was ordained to replace him.
Bishop de la Hailandiere asked the Sisters of Providence of Ruillé for
sisters for his young diocese. The Mother Superior asked Sister St.
Theodore to lead the missionaries. She considered herself incapable but
reluctantly consented, being mindful of the Rule of the Congregation,
"The Sisters will be disposed to go to any part of the world obedience
calls them."

Sister St. Theodore was sent by her Mother Superior to Indiana to
serve under the new Bishop as "Superior of the Mother house and
Superior-General of all the other houses that shall be established from

it." Sister and her five companions left France on July 27, 1840. Leaving home was very painful for her.

She wrote in her *Journal*, "The moment of separation and of death had come at last. We had to leave all. After having made the most painful sacrifices, which had cost our hearts so much, we had to break the last ties by tearing ourselves away from our dear home so tenderly loved by all the Sisters of Providence. . . . It would be difficult to describe what passed in my soul when I felt the vessel beginning to move and I realized that I was no longer in France. It seemed as if my soul were being torn from my body."

The boat sailed through a frightening hurricane. Sister wrote, "The sea lashed our poor ship fearfully; at every instant we thought it would sink. It is a horrible thing to pass the night in the bottom of a vessel, hearing continually the dreadful creaking which makes one fear that it will slit open, and that those whose only hope is in it will be engulfed forever. . . . Five days later I was better, though I was not well a single hour at sea."

The Sisters made a six-week voyage to New York City. Sister wrote that upon their arrival, "We threw ourselves on our knees, and with hearts full of gratitude we offered our thanks to God for all the benefits he had bestowed upon us. We prayed to him also for our future; we could not but feel some anxiety about it."

From New York, the nuns traveled by train, stagecoach and steamboat through Pennsylvania, Maryland and Virginia to Madison, Indiana. The journey unveiled the beauty of the mountains which Sister wrote "elevate the soul toward the Author of all things." It also unveiled a terrible roadway where "on one side, vast, jutting rocks would overhang, upon which were giant trees apparently uprooted and ready to fall at any moment; on the other hand, frightful precipices, whose depths one cannot fathom, were ready to swallow us up if our horse made the least false step. This was not the only danger. Bandits, infested the mountains, and we had to travel both day and night. But the protecting hand of the Lord, which guarded us on the deep, preserved us from accident and harm on the land."

They met the new Bishop at Madison, Indiana and from there they traveled by stagecoach and ferry boat to their destination at Saint Mary-of-the-Woods, Indiana, 73 miles north of Vincennes.

Arrival at the House

Father Stanislaus Buteux, one of the three diocesan priests, escorted the Sisters by ferry over the flooded Wabash River and by wagon to a remote wooded site. On October 22, they arrived at their destination, three months after they had left France. They found themselves in the middle of the forest without even a house in sight. Mother Theodore was a frail 42 years old.

She described their arrival in her *Journal*. "We continued to advance into the thick woods till suddenly Father Buteux stopped the carriage and said, 'Come down, Sisters, we have arrived.' What was our astonishment to find ourselves still in the midst of the forest, no village, not even a house in sight. Our guide having given orders to the driver, led us down into a ravine, whence we beheld through the trees on the other side a frame house with a stable and some sheds. 'There,' he said, 'is the house where the postulants have a room, and where you will lodge until your house is ready.' "

The six Sisters and four postulants shared this small farmer's house with his family and had the use of one room and one-half of the garret for the next month until the diocese purchased the house. They slept on straw mattresses on the floor under a poor roof which let in the wind and the rain. They cooked in an outside kitchen open to the weather. Every year several persons from the region froze to death.

Father Buteux led them to the church. Mother described it in her *Journal*:

> The church! I send you the picture. Yes, dear friends, that is the dwelling of the God of the Universe, in comparison with which the stables wherein you shelter your cattle are palaces. There it is that every day the Lamb of God is offered up, a sacrifice for the living and the dead. There He reposes night and day in a small pix in which the priest can scarcely put his two fingers. No tabernacle, no altar, for can the name of altar be given to three planks forming a table forty inches long, supported by two stakes driven into the ground? . . . A cotton cloth is spread over these planks; there is a small altar stone; and now you have the whole altar. . . . This then, is the

church of this place, which is also our chapel. It serves moreover as the dwelling of the priest, and still it is only about thirteen feet wide and fifteen feet long.

Mother noted, "It is astonishing that this remote solitude has been chosen for a novitiate and especially for an academy. All appearances are against it."

The Mission

The Sisters spent their first winter isolated in the forest where they studied English and Mother began their religious formation with her teaching conferences. There was a great need for religious instruction and education for children. So, in the Spring, the Sisters hastened to finish construction of a convent that could also serve as a boarding school. The tuition from boarders would help to support the community and enable the poor to attend school free.

"We must make a beginning," Mother wrote, "and trust in Providence. If it is God's work, it will not fail, for we shall leave it in the hands of our Blessed Mother." This entrustment was a consequence of her own mother's consecration of her to the Blessed Mother to whom Mother Guerin always gave the credit for all good things. She often said, "All the good that has come to us has come through Mary!"

The Sisters opened St. Mary's Academy, a school for girls, on July 4, 1841 at Saint Mary-of-the-Woods, Indiana. Her motto for the school was, "Knowledge and Virtue United." Mother's newspaper advertisement read:

> St. Mary's Academy for Young Ladies will open the second of July. Branches taught are as follows: Reading, Writing, Arithmetic, Geography and History, both Ancient and Modern, English Composition, Natural Philosophy, Chemistry, Botany, Mythology, Biography, Astronomy, Rhetoric, Plain and Fancy Needlework, Bead Work Tapestry and Lace Work.
>
> Terms – Boarding, including the above branches, per annum $100.

Mother continued to spiritually form her community through religious conferences. She urged the Sisters, "Always be children of the Church!" She reminded them of the dignity of their vocation. "God in calling us to the religious life had not wished only to sanctify us," she told them, "but He has called us to work with Him for the salvation of our brother. O, what a beautiful vocation is ours! Have you sometimes thought, my dear Sisters, that you have been called to do on earth what Our Lord Himself did? He instructed, and you instruct. He was surrounded by little children, and you – you pass your life among them."

Within a year, ten Americans joined the community. Mother urged them to "possess all the virtues in order to be able to teach them to our pupils." By 1842, Sisters of Providence schools were established in Jasper, Indiana and St. Francisville, Illinois. St. Mary's School grew and in 1846 it received a charter from the Indiana legislature. Its reputation also grew.

Author Booth Tarkington's mother attended St. Mary's. He wrote, "I think my mother's days at 'Old Saint Mary's' were the happiest of her life. The recollection of them was bright and vivid sixty years afterward. Something rare and fine was brought from France to Saint Mary-of-the-Woods, and none of those who were students there remained unaffected by it."

For more than a decade, from 1841 to 1852, the Academy at Saint Mary-of-the-Woods was the only Catholic boarding school for girls in Indiana. From Saint Mary-of-the-Woods the community and schools expanded. Mother accompanied each group of Sisters as they opened other schools in the diocese.

From the time of her arrival at Saint Mary-of-the-Woods in 1840 to January 1849, Mother established parish schools at Jasper, St. Peter's, Vincennes, Madison, Fort Wayne and Terre Haute, all in Indiana, and at St. Francisville in Illinois. In 1853, she opened Indiana establishments in Evansville and North Madison, Lanesville in 1854 and Columbus in 1855.

Mother's apostolate to the frontier girls of the mid-West was contemporary with Mother Duchesne's apostolate to the frontier girls of the West. Like Mother Duchesne's Sisters, Mother Guerin's Sisters suffered from inadequate housing and diets, extremes of heat and cold and storms. She wrote, "Our life is hard; obliged to have business relations with a people noted for its skill in and inclination toward sharp dealing; having in our own house Americans . . . certainly is like killing us, so to speak, with pinpricks."

On October 2, 1842, a devastating fire, probably set by a bigoted arsonist, destroyed the Sisters' barn and food harvest. They had no food for the next three days. Mother wrote, "If ever this poor little community becomes settled, it will be established on the Cross; and that is what gives me confidence and makes me hope, sometimes even against hope."

The Cross

Mother wrote, "Our congregation has grown in the shadow of the Cross. I hope that our heavenly Father will never deprive us of the precious mark which distinguishes His children." Like Mother Seton's Father John David, Mother Guerin's Father Buteux, tried to control the new order. He had his own ideas as to how it should be run, contrary to Mother's wishes. Mother wrote, "He had dreams of a religious house according to his own ideas . . . and he would change all our Rules . . . [and he] tried to convince [the Bishop] that I was not suitable for the position in which I was placed." Even though the Bishop removed him as her chaplain, he continued to contact Mother's Sisters in his efforts to found his own community.

However, Mother's greatest cross was her relationship with her Bishop, Celestine de la Hailandiere. She said that he "has one of those temperaments which makes martyrs of their possessors and still more of those who must put up with them from time to time . . . He is jealous of his authority and wishes to do everything himself. . . . It would be better not to have the congregation at all than to have one that would have no other rule than the caprices of a disordered imagination, which will condemn tomorrow what it commands today. . . . Here superiors have the title of 'Mother' and nothing more. One does not see a woman in this country involved in the smallest business affairs, the religious any more than the others. They stare at me in Terre Haute and elsewhere when they see me doing business, paying, purchasing. . . ."

On another occasion she wrote, "Woman in this country is only yet one fourth of the family. I hope that, through the influence of religion and education, she will eventually become at least one half – the better half."

Bishop de la Hailandiere was temperamentally unsuited to be a pastoral Bishop. He had an autocratic, controlling, suspicious temperament that pained both himself and others who were close to him. He was insecure and felt threatened by those with more talents.

The Bishop recognized his own shortcomings and wrote to Rome in

1842 offering his resignation. He wrote, "In the midst of so many difficulties, and being of so great an incapacity, I fear to lose my soul. That is why I beg his Eminence to examine before the good God whether it would not be expedient that I cease to occupy the See of Vincennes." His offer was not accepted.

In 1843, after the devastating fire, the Bishop urged Mother to return to France to beg money for repairs. While she was gone for eleven months, he assumed control of the community. He exercised his authority imperiously without regard for Mother's Rule or the desires of the Sisters. He admitted novices to vows, closed a school and moved the Sisters.

The Bishop continued to recognize his unsuitability and personally repeated his offer of resignation to Pope Gregory XVI in January of 1845 while visiting in Rome. His offer was refused. The next year, he wrote, "The mission confided to me has always seemed a charge much beyond my strength."

Mother returned from France after a hazardous voyage and a long illness and convalescence in New Orleans. From that Spring of 1844 until 1847, Mother endured with humility and tact the Bishop's obstacles, suspicions, accusations, broken promises, banishment from her community and the threat of excommunication of her Sisters.

Mother's relationship suffered its cruelest blow on May 20, 1847 when she visited the Bishop at his home. He made false accusations against her and insisted that she remain in the house until she agreed to all of his unreasonable demands. Mother could not agree to any demands that were against the community's Rule. The Bishop then locked Mother in the reception room while he went out for dinner.

When her Sisters later came to the Bishop's home and inquired of Mother's whereabouts, he went and opened the locked door. As he did so, Mother humbly fell to her knees and asked for his blessing. He gave it and motioned for her to leave.

Later that evening, the Bishop went to the convent and informed Mother that she was no longer Mother Superior and not even a Sister of Providence since he released her from her vows, that she had to leave the diocese immediately and that any Sister who left with her would be excommunicated.

In spite of all of these threats, all of the Sisters and even the workmen agreed to follow Mother. The Sisters said, "We will no longer have anything. We will be considered by [the Bishop] as the reproach of the world, but we shall have done our duty." However, before any of the Bishop's threats were carried out, a letter arrived from Rome accepting his resignation.

Mother returned to Saint Mary-of-the-Woods on June 10, 1847 by steamboat up the Wabash River to Terre Haute to the sound of the city's cannon fire and to Saint Mary's to the sound of the workmen's gunshots and a welcoming procession of Sisters. It was a happy reunion.

Mother had always obeyed the Bishop until he tried to unjustifiably run the Congregation contrary to its Rule. Her new Bishop Bazin assured her that he would ask nothing of the Sisters except that they follow their Rule. He wrote to Mother, "Bury the past in oblivion or think of it only to bless the Providence of God who sent you crosses because He loves you; for God never fails to try His true children. . . . The future is yours. I shall judge you only by the future and according to your Constitutions."

Mother charitably wrote Mother Mary in France, "We pray for Bishop de la Hailandiere daily, and I beg you, my dear Mother, not to forget him. He will be much higher in heaven, I am convinced, than if he had remained Bishop."

Know-Nothings

As the number of Catholic immigrants increased, many Protestants feared their influence and that of the Pope and the Bishops. Some of these Protestants formed an association called the "Know-Nothings" because when they were asked about its purposes or members, a member would reply, "I know nothing." Mother described them in a letter in 1855:

> They organized against the Catholics an infernal association which, in a month or two, covered the face of America like a flock of sparrows. They call themselves Know-Nothings, a name which they took in order to envelop their abominable designs in mystery. They swear by the most frightful oaths to destroy all that pertains to the Catholic religion. Murder, deceit and all the horrors at which an honest soul trembles are the means they promise to employ and which they swear to practice at the peril of their lives. In one of the Indiana newspapers,

they wrote that I am a tyrant, an abominable monster who keeps young girls against their will in our house, which they call a tavern or haunt of brigands. . . . For several days we thought they were going to come to burn us alive. Well, we are still living, but we do not know for how long. May the will of God be done!"

Mother survived these threats and within months most Protestant parents who had removed their children from her schools returned them. The public schools could not compete with her schools either in curriculum or in the dedication of the teachers which was a total self-giving for the sake of their students.

Spirituality

Mother trusted all to Divine Providence. She told her Sisters to ". . . rest assured, my dear daughters, if you lean with all your weight upon Providence, you will find yourselves well supported."

She found solace in prayer and wrote, "What strength the soul draws from prayer! In the midst of a storm, how sweet is the calm it finds in the heart of Jesus." She was consoled by the Eucharist and said, "If we truly knew how to appreciate it, it alone would suffice to fortify and sustain us." She encouraged her sisters to "send your heart a thousand times a day to adore our Lord really and truly present in the Holy Sacrament."

She entrusted the mission of the Sisters of Providence to the Blessed Virgin Mary and wrote, "We have promised to belong entirely to God. We have made vows, but especially we have invoked Mary and St. Anne, her august mother. It is to them that we owe our preservation."

In 1849, Mother wrote, "There are always from six to seven hundred pupils in our schools. . . . Several who have been educated in our houses, and are now married and in society, are advocates of our holy religion. We begin to see the good which our Congregation is doing in this country."

In 1853, a larger, permanent Motherhouse was opened and began to fill with vocations from former students who joined their teachers in the Congregation.

Thereafter, Mother Guerin's health soon began to fail, her intestinal ailments worsened and she was worn out from her many labors and visits to the missions. In 1855, she wrote to her other Superior in France,

137

"I neither die nor live. One week I am a little better and the next I relapse."

She regained enough strength to accomplish a long-held desire to build a chapel in honor of the Blessed Virgin Mary. She wrote in her diary on the anniversary of the founding of the Congregation, "Today, fifteen years ago, she brought us to our woods and has ever since protected us. What joy to erect a monument to her!"

When her Sisters lamented the length of her illness, Mother said, "O my poor daughters, it is very short compared to eternity." She made her last diary entry on Monday of Holy Week, March 17, 1856, "I am obliged to keep my bed. What a beautiful week to be upon the Cross! O good Cross! I will love you with all my heart!"

Mother died on May 14, 1856 at the age of 58. Her chaplain who administered the last rites at her deathbed wrote, "The extraordinary beauty which shone on the countenance of that good Mother proclaimed clearly that already God had glorified His servant. A reflection of that glory, I am sure, lighted her face, which became for a moment luminous and shining with purity and happiness. I had never seen her so beautiful and in the midst of my sorrow and of that desolating scene, I could not cease to contemplate her with a secret consolation. She did not seem to me to be dead, but to be sleeping in the sweetest and most peaceful sleep. It is thus that the saints die, or rather, that they sleep in the Lord at the end of their beautiful lives filled with good works and virtues."

Virtues

The *Catholic Telegraph and Advocat* in Cincinnati, Ohio, published the following notice about Mother Theodore after her death:

> This woman, distinguished by her eminent virtues, governed the community of which she was the Superior from its commencement, to the time of her death, a period of nearly sixteen years. Being a perfect religious herself, and endowed with mental qualities of a high order, she was peculiarly fitted to fill the duties which Providence assigned her.
>
> Not only her Sisters are bereaved by her death, but all those who knew her excellence and the amount of good she did, join in lamenting that she should have been

removed from the sphere of her usefulness. To judge from the celestial expression of her countenance as she lay in death, there is every reason to believe that she has already taken her abode among the Saints in Heaven, enjoying the munificence of God, who rewards His servants "according to their works."

Sister Mary Cecilia, Mother's assistant, wrote in the Letter Circular summarizing her life:

> She possessed to an eminent degree all the virtues of Christian perfection, though charity did seem to transcend them all; it was her favorite virtue. . . . Her instructions and recommendations breathed charity, unbounded charity, a charity involving all the other virtues. She blended the tenderness of a mother with the firmness of a superior so perfectly that her government, as you well know, was the most happy and effectual. . . . She has left us a legacy far more precious and valuable than can be bequeathed by the most opulent; it is the example of her virtues, which I hope shall ever dwell in our remembrance, to admonish us if necessary, but always to invite and urge us to a like perfection.

A shrine honoring Mother Guerin is located at the entrance to the Church of the Immaculate Conception at Saint Mary-of-the-Woods, Indiana. Her tomb is located near the altar. The base of a Celtic Cross memorial marks Mother's former burial site. It is inscribed, "I sleep, but my heart watches over this house which I have built."

Fruits

Mother Guerin once told her sisters, "Well, my daughters, ours is a preparation for the generation that will succeed us, and eminent good will be done this way by us. You may not live to see it, but you will have sown the seed, and your sisters will come to reap what will have been sown."

She wrote a summary of her mission for her Sisters:

Yes, my dear daughters, hope in God, and you will not be confounded. See what he has already done for you.

Fifteen years ago today, October 22, 1840, six Sisters arrived in this forest, at that time so savage; they were strangers to the country, to the manners and customs, to the ways of America; they did not know one word of English. Now we are a community composed of sixty; here at Saint Mary's we are eighteen Sisters wearing the religious habit, and twenty postulants ardently desiring to be clothed in it.

More than twelve hundred children receive religious instruction in our twelve houses of education which already bear abundant fruit. What good is being done by the Sisters of Saint Mary's!

At the time of Mother's death, she had founded the Sisters of Providence of Saint Mary-of-the-Woods, Indiana, who administered schools at Saint Mary-of-the-Woods and 10 other schools in Indiana. She also opened two orphanages in Vincennes, one for girls and one for boys.

Mother Theodore opened pharmacies where free remedies were dispensed to the poor at Vincennes and Saint Mary-of-the-Woods. She also oversaw the construction of a new motherhouse for the Sisters of Providence and several additions to the Academy, both at Saint Mary-of-the-Woods.

The Congregation that she founded grew from six Sisters and four postulants to 67 professed members, nine novices and seven postulants at the time of her death. Today, there are about 450 women in the Congregation serving in 20 states, China and Taiwan.

Saint

In 1908, Mother Theodore's intercession healed her biographer, Sister Mary Theodosia Mug, from breast cancer. Sister Mug underwent a mastectomy in 1906 that was made more radical by the crude state of medicine at that time. Her left arm was left crippled and her abdomen was swollen with cancer.

On the night of October 30, 1908, she prayed before Mother Guerin's crypt for a sick Sister. But, while standing there, the thought came into her mind, *I wonder if Mother Theodore has any power with Almighty God.*

She later wrote, "Instantly I heard in my soul the word, 'Yes, she has.' " Sister Mug went up to her room, did some work and went to bed. Three hours later, she awoke to find her once-rigid arm useful again. Her swollen abdomen had shrunk so much that she had to take in the waist of her clothes by four inches, her sight improved and her poor appetite and digestion returned to normal. She wrote, "Blessed be God in His saints. To Mother Theodore I owe all this." This miracle led to Pope John Paul II's beatification of Mother Guerin on October 25, 1998.

In 2001, Phil McCord entered the chapel on the campus of St. Mary-of-the-Woods College, founded by Mother Guerin. He was the director of facilities management for the Mother House of Mother Guerin's Sisters of Providence. He prayed for his sight.

Mr. McCord at the age of 59 was advised to have a corneal transplant because surgery to remove a cataract from his right eye in 2000 had resulted in a damaged cornea. His right eye was swollen dramatically. His vision was reduced to formless shadows and globs of light. But the thought of having his cornea cut out and replaced by a cadaver's cornea made him uneasy to consent to the operation. While he pondered whether to have the transplant, he entered the chapel and prayed. He decided to ask God to help him overcome his fear.

"I try to do things for myself," he prayed. "But that's not going to happen this time. I'm not going to be able to do this. Can you help me deal with this problem? Can you give me some strength?"

Mr. McCord felt ashamed of what had humbled him. For some reason, he then thought of Mother Guerin. He wondered whether she might be looking in and whether she could put in a good word for him with "the big guy", as he called God.

"This is your house, Mother Theodore," he prayed, silently, "and I am your servant."

But then he stopped, questioning what he'd said. After all, as director of facilities management, he was a paid employee. "Am I your employee or am I your servant?" he wondered.

Then he decided to drop the flowery language and to pray from his heart. "Mother Theodore, if you have any influence with God, I would appreciate it if you would exercise it on my behalf and kind of help look out for me."

Then he sat quietly for a moment, wondering whether he had done it right. He felt better about his situation, a little calmer, even though his eye was still a mess.

"Maybe there is something to this prayer thing," he thought. "Maybe I can do this. Thank you, God." Then he stood up and went back to work.

The following morning, Mr. McCord's vision remained obscured. But a lingering heaviness in his eye and cheek were gone. He felt different. A subsequent trip to his eye specialist showed that the swelling was gone and there was no need for the surgery. After scar tissue was removed from the cataract, Mr. McCord had 20/20 vision.

His eye specialist and a second doctor confirmed that there was no medical explanation for the sudden improvement. These two were among eight witnesses whose evidence supported the finding of a miracle.

Though grateful, Mr. McCord, a non-Catholic, still didn't go to church or pray regularly. He wondered why he found such favor, but one of the Sisters said that he was looking at it all wrong.

"It is an act of love," she told him. "Just accept it. There is no quid pro quo. There are no expectations. It is what it is. Just accept it."

Mr. McCord said, "I'm not a theologian. I don't understand all of the implications of what happened to me or how they determine it to be a miracle. I just leave it to those who are more learned in that area. All I know is that it's my story. I'm sticking to it."

The Church adjudged this healing to be a miracle. As a result, Mother Guerin was canonized a saint by Pope Benedict XVI on October 15, 2006. He quoted Mother Guerin and said, "How much good has been accomplished by the Sisters of Saint Mary-of-the-Woods! How much more good they will be able to do if they remain faithful to their holy vocation!"

At the end of the canonization, when reciting the Angelus, the Holy Father prayed that St. Mother Guerin will encourage "us to live the faith and to witness before our contemporaries, paying ever more attention to little ones and to the most abandoned in society." Her Feast Day is October 3.

Opening Prayer for the Mass in Commemoration of Saint Theodore Guerin

Loving God, in Saint Theodore Guerin, you have given us the example of a woman religious who trusted deeply in Providence. Through her intercession, inspire us to dedicate our lives to proclaiming the Gospel through works of love, mercy and justice. We ask this through our Lord Jesus Christ, your Son who lives and reigns with you and the Holy Spirit, one God for ever and ever.

Shrine:

Church of the Immaculate Conception
Saint Mary-of-the-Woods, IN 47876
Website: http://www.spsmw.org/cgi-bin/
site.pl?3208&dwContent_contentID=274

15. New Immigrants

The original Catholic immigrants to the United States before the American Revolution were mostly English or Irish. They were generally economically equal to the Protestants. America's first Bishop, aristocratic John Carroll of Irish descent, came from these immigrants. However, after the Revolution, the immigration pattern dramatically changed.

As Mother Duchesne labored in the frontier of the Mississippi Valley from 1818 to 1852, America experienced a flood of new immigrants. Waves of immigrants left Europe for America because of severe weather, famine, high taxes, social upheaval, political and religious persecution and unemployment. America offered mild weather, fruitful agricultural land, low taxes, political and religious freedom and employment. These new immigrants were not like the aristocratic Carrolls. They were poor. In the 1820s there were only about 150,000 immigrants. In the 1830s there was an increase to 600,000 and in the 1840s an increase to almost 2 million.

Like Mother Duchesne's "Judgment Day" voyage, the immigrants' voyages to America were often very perilous. Most of them sailed for over one month in "steerage," the lowest, darkest and most uncomfortable part of the boat. They ate poor food and had no privacy.

One woman who arrived in 1828 wrote home, "While we were passing over the water our sufferings were great. I will not grieve your hearts with all our sufferings, for my paper will not hold it. Little Mary was very ill with the fever that so many died with – seven children and one woman; to hear their cries and moans, it was very bad. We were shut down in darkness for a fortnight, till so many died, then the hatch was opened."

Most of these new immigrants were Irish and German who were poor, unskilled and uneducated Catholics. Many of them did not speak English. They became the foundation of the "immigrant Catholic Church" and they settled in the cities, primarily New York and Philadelphia. There they were met with discrimination because of their Catholic religion.

Most Americans were descended from English Protestants. England had a long history of Anti-Catholicism beginning in the 16th century with

King Henry VIII. In 1532, Henry wanted an annulment of his marriage to Catherine of Aragon. Pope Clement VII refused to annul his legitimate marriage. Henry defied the Pope and was excommunicated, but he soon persuaded Parliament to pass the Act of Supremacy making him "Supreme Head of the Church in England." During Henry's reign, many of the Catholic monasteries and convents were seized and many Catholics were martyred including Saint Thomas More and Bishop John Fischer. This anti-Catholicism continued with the conquest of Ireland and the English suppression of the Catholic religion there.

The English persecutions and martyrdoms continued through the reign of Queen Elizabeth and others until 1681. Thereafter, the penal laws inhibited the practice of the Catholic faith until the passing of the Catholic Emancipation Act in 1829.

Since the foundation of Maryland in 1632, there was only a small Catholic presence in America. Baltimore Bishop John Carroll died in 1815 with authority over the 40,000 Catholics then in the United States. After his death, this Catholic presence was augmented by the European immigrants. By 1826 there were approximately 250,000 Catholics out of a total population of more than 11 million. Over the next 30 years, the Catholic population rose to more than three million. This was a threat to the "Nativists."

"Nativists" were native-born American Protestants who wanted to preserve their heritage. They did this by discriminating against Catholics. As early as 1826, Bishop John England of Charleston, South Carolina, wrote, "I found [as an immigrant] what I was altogether unprepared for; that, in many of our States, a Roman Catholic, though legally and politically upon a level with his fellow citizens, was however to be looked upon, by reason of his religion, as in some degree morally degraded."

Nativist Samuel Morse, inventor of the telegraph, wrote about supposed Vatican conspiracies plotted against Americans. Protestant ministers preached inflammatory sermons against what they called the dangers of Catholicism. By the 1840s, this discrimination turned to outright hostility and violence. Catholic churches and convents were burned by Navitists with riots in Boston, Philadelphia, St. Louis, Louisville and Detroit.

Most of the public schools were in fact Protestant schools. They taught the Protestant faith. Catholic schools were started in the greater Maryland area by Mother Seton and in the Mississippi Valley frontier by Mother Duchesne. But the Catholics in the eastern cities needed them as well. In

1844, Philadelphia Bishop Francis Patrick Kenrick proposed that Catholic children in public schools read the Catholic bible instead of the Protestant one. This precipitated a riot that resulted in the burning of three Catholic churches, many homes and the deaths of 13 persons.

Catholic immigrants became more insular and turned to the urban parish churches for their physical and spiritual welfare. After the Irish, the second largest group of immigrants were Germans. Many of them settled in the Philadelphia area. They needed priests and nuns who understood their language and culture. They needed Catholic schools. In 1843, there were 50 German priests in the United States that served a German-American population of 300,000. By 1869, these priests increased to over a thousand who served a population of more than a million. One of these priests was Father John Neumann who would later become Bishop of Philadelphia and the founder of the American Catholic parochial school system.

16. Saint John Neumann and German Immigrants

Born	March 28, 1811 in Prachatitz, Czechoslovakia (Bohemia)
Died	January 5, 1860 in Philadelphia, Pennsylvania
Canonized	June 19, 1977
Feast Day	January 5

Founded the Third Order of St. Francis of Glen Riddle, a religious order for women.
Organized the first diocesan schedule of the Forty Hours' Devotion in the United States.
Established the first unified system of Catholic schools under a diocesan board.
First American Bishop to be canonized.

"Among the shepherds of the flock in Philadelphia, the figure of Venerable John Neumann is pre-eminent. It was mainly through his prodigious efforts that a Catholic school system came into being and that parochial schools began to rise across the land. His holy life, his childlike gentleness, his hard labor and his tremendous foresight is still fresh and green among you. The tree planted and watered by Bishop Neumann now gives you its fruit."
Pope Pius XII on the occasion of the 150th anniversary of the founding of the Diocese of Philadelphia.

Baltimore Archbishop Francis Patrick Kenrick walked down to St. Alphonsus' Rectory in Baltimore, Maryland. He entered the priest's residence to tell him the news that the priest had been appointed as Bishop of Philadelphia. But the priest wasn't home. So the Archbishop went into

147

his room and laid out on the table the Bishop's ring and pectoral cross that he himself had carried for 21 years as Bishop of Philadelphia. Then he went home without saying a word to anyone.

When the priest returned to his room and saw what Archbishop Kenrick had done, he understood that he was now to become the Bishop of Philadelphia himself. He was dumbstruck and fell to his knees in prayer. He was found the next morning still there and still praying. Father John Neumann was soon to be Bishop John Neumann.

"I would rather die tomorrow than be consecrated Bishop," said Father Neumann to a friend on the night before his consecration set for March 28, 1852 at St. Alphonsus' Church. Archbishop Kenrick had recommended Father Neumann to the Pope because he was a simple, humble, obedient and holy priest who spoke German in an area where there were thousands of German immigrants who did not speak English. Archbishop Kenrick had asked other bishops their opinion on appointing Father Neumann as its Bishop. When Father Neumann learned about this, he pleaded with him in tears to withdraw his name from consideration, but Archbishop Kenrick refused to do it. Father Neumann obeyed and became Bishop of Philadelphia. Two years later, Pope Pius IX received him in an audience and said, "Isn't obedience better than sacrifice?"

Formation

"If you believe yourself called by God, we shall put no obstacle in your way, but you must not take leave of us." This was the instruction that John Neumann's father gave him as he discerned his vocation to the priesthood as a young man.

John Nepomucene Neumann was born on March 28, 1811 in Prachatitz, Bohemia (now Czechoslovakia), in the Austro-Hungarian Empire. He was named after Bohemia's patron saint and martyr, Saint John Nepomucene. He was the third of six children of Philip and Agnes Neumann, both of whom were faithful Catholics. His father moderately provided for his family and ran a small stocking knitting business. The family spoke German and said daily morning and evening prayers together with the Rosary. His mother attended daily Mass and gave alms of food and clothing to her poorer neighbors. John later imitated her compassion when he saw a poor boy going from door to door with a bag on his back.

His heart was touched and he exclaimed, "Oh, if I only had a bag, I would go about begging with the poor boy, and then he would get more!"

When he was three years old, John fell through an open cellar door but landed unharmed 15 feet below. His mother said that his Guardian Angel protected him and taught him to pray to him for protection. In his childhood, John made a toy altar out of lead, decorated it with candles and flowers and said make-believe Masses for his small friends. He was a quiet and serious boy and enjoyed reading. "My mother," he said, "used to chide me, and call me book mad, a bibliomaniac." He was friendly with his parish priest who instructed him in the Catholic faith and introduced him to the natural sciences, particularly botany which remained a life-long hobby.

John served as an altar boy at daily Mass but, in his humility, he thought that the priesthood was beyond his reach. Later in his life he wrote, "I cannot say I felt a decided inclination to the priesthood in my childhood. It is true that I had an altar made of lead and that I served Mass almost every day, but the idea of being a priest was so exalted that it did not seem within my reach."

Vocation

When John was 12, he attended high school and college in the nearby town of Budwies and boarded with local families. God didn't call him to the priesthood with a very loud voice. This is how John described the strange and subtle process of how he discerned his vocation:

> When the time came, at the end of the philosophy course, for me to decide either for theology, or law or medicine, I felt more of an attraction for the last. This was all the more so because, out of eighty or ninety applicants for theology, only twenty were to be accepted. For this, along with the best scholastic transcript, recommendations were also required, and I wanted to have nothing to do with them.
>
> In this uncertainty about the choice of a profession, I came home in the autumn vacation of 1831 and found that my father was not against letting me study medicine in Prague, even though the expenses involved were great.

My mother was not too happy with this. Even though I pointed out to her that I did not know anyone who would back my request for admission into the institute for the study of theology, nevertheless she thought that I should give it a try. I then wrote a letter of application and sent it to Budweis by a special messenger. Shortly after that I received the letter of acceptance into the Budweis Theological Seminary.

From that moment on, I never gave another thought to medicine and I also gave up completely the study of physics and astronomy on which I preferred to spend time, and this without any great difficulty.

On All Saints Day in 1831, John enrolled at the Diocesan Seminary of Budweis when he was 20. His academic record was excellent. While he was there, his missionary zeal was inflamed by reports from the United States from another Austrian, Father Frederic Baraga, who served among the Ottawa and Chippewa Indians in Michigan and Wisconsin. John later wrote, "The letters of Father Baraga and other German missionaries charmed me. One day as [a friend] and I were walking the thought came to us to set out for America as soon after ordination as we should have obtained some practical knowledge of our priestly duties. From that day my resolution was so firm, my desire so lively, that I could think of nothing else."

Seminary Preparation

Thereafter, John changed his lifestyle to prepare himself for the hardships of the American missions. He increased his prayers and fasts, became less social and studied more, particularly languages including Italian, Czech, French and English. He even spent entire nights outside in the cold air. He decided to learn English and applied and was accepted for the Archepiscopal Seminary at Prague University where he thought that English was taught. However, when he arrived he was disappointed to learn that it was not taught there. So John learned it on his own.

Moreover, he was disappointed to learn that some of the professors were dissenters from the teachings of the Church and expressed anti-papal views. At that time, the teaching of Prague University was influenced by "Josephinism," named after Austrian Emperor Joseph II. Josephinism was a movement that was modernist, worldly and anti-papal. Soon John began keeping a spiritual journal that gives us a glimpse of his spiritual journey.

He wrote, "at [that] place I met a great disappointment. Nor was I satisfied with the professors of dogmatic, moral and pastoral theology. The first was more against the Pope than for him. The second was too philosophical to be understood by his hearers. The third was a thorough Josephinist. I had to do violence to myself even to listen to them, for the absurdity of their treatment of those subjects I fully understood; much less could I accept their opinions as heterodox. It is a matter of regret that in such institutions so much is done to maintain simply the appearance of learning, instead of diffusing good and useful Catholic knowledge."

It was difficult to be an orthodox Catholic among liberal professors but John taught himself and armed himself with 38 volumes of his own extracts from the writings of saints and doctors of the Church. He defended the true teachings of the Church and the dogma of papal infallibility, even before the dogma was proclaimed.

John's greatest disappointment was that he had no spiritual direction, something he expected to find at a supposedly Catholic seminary. In 1834, he began to write in his journal a daily outpouring of his soul to God. "The president's sermon," he wrote, "has wounded my heart. I like him now even less than ever. O Jesus, Thou knowest my sad condition. Here I am without a guide, without an advisor. Lord, teach me how to pray that I may obtain what is so necessary for me, a guide in the spiritual life. I have none to console me in my falls, to counsel me in my doubt as to whether I should enter an Order or Congregation where I might live in perfect obedience; none to direct me in my efforts to amend my life, none to point out how I may become more pleasing to Thee. O my Jesus, in my desolation I cry to Thee! Hear my prayer, send me a good confessor!"

Apparently no one was sent and John plodded on in spiritual darkness without a guide. However, he persevered in his vocation even when his teachers and fellow seminarians, affected by the prevalent modernist attitudes, belittled him.

He struggled against many temptations in his effort to be perfect as Jesus taught. He wrote, "Give me the graces which will aid me to obtain the perfection which You desire." His prayer was answered and Jesus granted him the grace to overcome his final temptation before coming to America. Just before his graduation from the seminary, John was urged by governmental and seminary officials to accept a prestigious position as secretary to a governmental agency because of his knowledge of languages. Much to their chagrin, he declined the offer with the explanation that he intended to devote his life as a missionary to America. If he had accepted the offer, America would have lost a saint.

After his graduation, John suffered from further disappointments. He learned that his closest friend suddenly changed his mind and decided not to accompany him to America. Then, through some confusion, he learned that the money that he expected to receive for his journey was not available. After that, he learned that the Bishop had postponed all ordinations in Budweis indefinitely because there was an over-abundance of priests in his diocese. Moreover, the Bishop would not release John to another diocese. Now John had to decide whether to go to America or not, in spite of his lack of ordination and release and, if so, should he tell his parents?

This was a very painful decision to make. He wrote, "While pondering last evening on my resolution, separation from home appeared to me so bitter that I burst into tears. My Jesus, if it be Thy will, increase my sufferings, but hear my prayers! Let my resolve be put into execution. With no other guide than Thyself, O Lord, I stand on the outskirts of an immense region full of dangers and difficulties. The final step once taken, there will be no looking back. No fond parents, no devoted brother and sisters, no kind of friends will greet my landing on those far-off shores. I shall meet none but strangers. There, indeed, I shall find unbelievers who scoff at Thee, my Jesus, but many souls also hunger to know Thy Word, O most merciful Savior!"

He decided to apply to become a priest of the Diocese of Philadelphia and that he would sacrifice the consolation of saying his first Mass with his parents and giving them his priestly blessing. When he finally told them of his plans, his parents and sisters were very sad and tried to dissuade him from leaving them. But since he hadn't received an answer from Philadelphia's Bishop Kenrick, and since his own Bishop would neither ordain him nor release him from his diocese, John could do nothing but wait.

Finally, a local priest who knew of the need of German-speaking priests in the United States advised him that he should go there in trust and hope to be ordained there. So, with great courage, but without ordination or release from his Bishop, John abandoned himself to Divine Providence and left for America on February 8, 1836.

John only told a sister that he was leaving and left a letter for his parents. He wrote, "By my sudden and unexpected departure, I have tried to lessen the mutual pain of separating from you as much on my own account as on yours. Convinced that your parental blessing will accompany me wherever I go, I did not ask it of you before leaving for the reason above stated."

His departure pained John and his family very much, even though John had literally followed his father's instructions. He had said, "If you believe yourself called by God, we shall put no obstacle in your way, but you must not take leave of us." So he didn't take their leave and he left for America with about $40 in his pockets. He did not know if or when he would become a priest or where he would undertake his missionary service. He never saw his mother again.

The Journey to America

For the next two months, John traveled west to France, hoping to receive a commitment from the United States. To save money, he often traveled by foot and at night to avoid coach and hotel bills. The trip across Europe brought more disappointments. He was misinformed and told that the Bishop of Philadelphia no longer needed German priests. But John courageously walked on asking himself, "Will I ever get to America? Will I ever be ordained? Who will ordain me? Where will I serve? Will my mother ever forgive me for not saying good-bye?"

Finally, with just enough money to buy his passage, John boarded the ship *Europa* at Le Havre, France. For 10 days he had to live uncomfortably on the ship in the harbor while the captain waited for passengers to fill it before he sailed.

On April 20, 1836, the ship set sail for New York. It had no comforts for its passengers. John had to supply his own food for the voyage and a pot to cook it in. He purchased a straw mattress on which to sleep on deck and suffered from seasickness for the first three days. The voyage struggled through a four-day storm, waited out a calm and evaded dangerous icebergs. One day, while John was standing alone on the deck during a storm, he heard an interior voice telling him to move. As he did so, part of a sailing yardarm crashed down onto the very spot where he had stood. His Guardian Angel had protected him once again.

The voyage lasted 40 days and when the ship arrived outside New York harbor, it had to wait out a storm. After three days, the Captain let John off in a rowboat on which he went to Staten Island. There he boarded a small steamboat and ferried to Lower Manhattan. He was alone in a new and strange world, unfamiliar with the language, in tattered clothes, with one dollar, unexpected and nervously apprehensive about his uncertain future.

He wrote in a letter, "It was the Feast of Corpus Christi, about 11:00 o'clock, when I landed in America. You can imagine how I felt. My first care was to find a Catholic church. But, not having brought along any address, I had no hope of finding a priest by asking in an entirely strange land. In spite of a constant downpour, I walked the mile-long streets of the city until evening. I found a number of churches, chapels, etc. but no Catholic church wanted to show itself. I had to put all my philological knowledge together to comprehend the inscriptions on these buildings, many decorated with ideal beauty. Often there was nothing on the church roof; often a weathercock; sometimes a Cross, indeed, but over the Cross a weathercock. The devil, I thought, may present himself ever so beautifully, but still he must let his cloven foot be seen a little!"

The next day, John found his way to the residence of Bishop John Dubois. He was now 72 years old. He was the same Bishop who helped Mother Seton and Mother Rose Duchesne establish their apostolates. He overlooked John's lack of a release from the Bishop of Budweis and said, "I can and must ordain you quickly, for I need you." Bishop Dubois' diocese covered the entire state of New York and part of New Jersey and he had only 36 priests to serve 200,000 Catholics. He had a great need for German priests because of the language barrier that faced the great influx of German immigrants who settled there. John was so thankful that he promised the Blessed Virgin Mary that he would say a daily Rosary in thanksgiving for the rest of his life.

Finally, John felt his years of spiritual darkness vanishing. He wrote, "Thanks, a thousand thanks to Thee, my Jesus, for having prepared a place for me in Thy sanctuary. Doubt and uncertainty have vanished like mist before the rays of the sun."

Ordination

Two weeks later on June 25, 1836, at the age of 25, Bishop Dubois ordained John to the priesthood. Father John wrote the following prayer in his diary the next day:

> O Jesus, You poured out the fullness of your grace over me yesterday. You made me a priest and gave the power to offer You up to God. Ah! God! This is too much for my soul! Angels of God, all you saints of Heaven, come down and adore my Jesus, because what my heart says is only the imperfect echo of what Holy Church tells me to say. I will pray to You (O Lord) that You may give to me holiness and to all the living and the dead, pardon, that some day we may all be together with You, our dearest God!

Father John celebrated his First Mass that day. He was unable to give his parents his priestly blessing, but he happily gave First Holy Communions to 30 German children whom he had been instructing during the previous two weeks.

Three days later, Father John traveled the reverse of the water route that Father Isaac Jogues had made from Auriesville to New York City during his escape from the Mohawk Indians almost 200 years before. Father John was on his way to Buffalo, New York, by way of the Hudson River north to Albany and from there west to Lake Erie and Buffalo on the Erie Canal, the longest man-made waterway in the world. He traveled by Hudson River steamer, railroad, stagecoach and canal boat and headed for the remote area of the state where an inrush of immigrants had followed the opening of the Erie Canal, the gateway to the West by the inland waterways.

The vast "parish" of Buffalo was spread over 900 square miles from Lake Ontario south to Pennsylvania. There was only one priest to serve all of the Catholics scattered throughout this broad frontier area. On the way to Buffalo, Father John stopped at Rochester where he began his priestly ministry. He wrote this prayer in his diary:

My Lord and my God! Have mercy on me and those
sheep who, for the time being, have been entrusted to
me. Give to my tongue words of life. Purify their hearts
and make them heed all sound advice and every
admonition. Your grace must do everything because I
can do nothing but sin – O Jesus, my Redeemer; I am
taking Your place. Let me be a redeemer for this parish!

After his first Baptism, Father John wrote, "If the child baptized today
dies in the grace of this sacrament, then my journey to America has been
repaid a million times, even though I do nothing for the rest of my life."

The Buffalo Frontier

Buffalo was a boom city in 1836 and its pastor, Father Pax, gave Father
John the choice of serving there or in the outlying settlements. Father
John chose to minister in the outlying settlements while his pastor, the
only other priest, ministered in the city. Much of the land was only recently
cleared of woodland and put into cultivation for the first time. Families
were poor and widely scattered and towns were no more than a handful
of houses.

Father John's territory of 900 square miles had only four small churches
where 400 families worshiped, of whom 300 were German. Father's
fluency in German and French were a great help to the people and he
even learned Gaelic. Some of his parishioners had not received the
sacraments for years. Many had lost their faith or joined Protestant
churches. Father John keenly desired their salvation. He wrote:

O my Jesus, I, a poor, ignorant young man, have
become a shepherd in Thy sheepfold. Grant that not one
of those confided to me is lost. Teach me to live, and, if
needs be, to die for my people that they all may be saved,
that they all may love Thy dear Mother! Mary, thou who
art ever victorious over heresies, pray for all who are
walking in the paths of accursed error! My Jesus, what
shall, I, a poor creature, do to lead many souls — yea, all
souls — to Thee?"

After living with families for two years, Father John moved into a log cabin built for him by the people of North Bush, a settlement near present-day Kenmore, New York. It was a simple structure with two rooms, four chairs and two trunks. He led a severely penitential life. He slept only a couple of hours a night in the cold without a fire. He ate simple meals and once went for four weeks on bread alone. He wrote, "Only a poor priest, one who can endure hardship, can labor here. His duties call him far and near. He leads a wandering life. There is no pleasure, except the care of souls. The Catholic population is continually increasing but many are in extreme poverty. They live in miserable shanties, some with not even a window."

The economic depression of 1837 left the Catholics in the area without work and with little food or money. Father's money support diminished and was replaced by gifts of vegetables. He wrote to a friend, "If you want to be a missionary, you have to love poverty and be entirely disinterested."

He taught the children the catechism, prayed the Divine Office, celebrated Mass, administered the sacraments, and mediated disputes among parishioners. His fervent prayers for conversions were productive of a rich harvest of souls. His journal tells of whole families under instruction, either for Baptism or reception into the Church. He said, "The recitation of the Rosary for my stray sheep is always productive of abundant fruit. I will redouble my zeal in this sweet and efficacious devotion." His fruits were noticed by Bishop Dubois who visited his parish and complemented him on his accomplishments after only one year in ministry.

His ministry faced anti-Catholic opposition from Protestant "heretics," as he termed them. They discriminated against Catholics and allured them with promises of financial security if they renounced their faith. Unfortunately, many left the Church. Father Neumann's heart was pierced with sorrow. He wrote, "Today has been a very painful one for me. I heard of the apostasy of one of my parishioners. My heart is pierced with sorrow. O my Jesus, [for his soul] I will pray, fast and with the help of Thy grace, sacrifice life itself."

Another problem in his ministry was scandal from bad priests. He wrote about them, "Much scandal has been given in these parts by the arrival of unworthy priests who come here merely to lead a reckless life amid the confusion of heresies. That the evils existing among our people are very great is, indeed, only too true. Still, we must allow that apostasy from the Faith, considering the evil influence exercised everywhere by heretics, is not so frequent as one might suppose; nay, the number of those who return to the bosom of the only saving Church balances the loss sustained by such defections. The gain would surely be greater if earnest priests were more numerous."

In 1839, Father John's brother, Wenzel, came to America to join him as a lay helper. His help was greatly appreciated, but it also allowed Father John to increase his labors. He tirelessly traveled his parish in his zeal for the salvation of the souls of his parishioners, walking and riding over muddy and rutty roads, through swamps and uncut forests, by day and by night, in the summer heat and winter cold. On he went from village to village, cabin to cabin, and church to church. On his back he carried an altar stone, vessels, vestments and books. The nearest of these outposts was two hours away, while the furthest was twelve hours. Since there were often no accommodations at the outposts, he frequently had to make a roundtrip and return home the same day.

One day, while he made his rounds through the forest, he collapsed in exhaustion at the foot of a tree. He was found by a band of Indians who carried him on a blanket to the nearest homestead. Eventually, his heavy labors exhausted him. He wrote, "I am a strong Bohemian mountain boy. It will not hurt me." But he was only five feet, three inches tall, he was not really very strong and his labors did hurt him. Even he finally realized this and said, "Father Pax, I must give up; my health is gone."

Father John had labored on the Buffalo frontier for four years, but in 1840 he suffered a complete breakdown in health. It took him three months to recover during which he agonized over his vocation. As in the seminary, he still yearned for spiritual advice and companionship. In spite of all his accomplishments, all his prayers and penances, he was convinced that he was but a wretched sinner, isolated and alone without any guidance. He even suffered from temptations of running away. He wrote, "To escape the terrible responsibility resting upon me, I sometimes thought of abandoning my flock, of fleeing to some distant solitude where I might lead a hidden, penitential life."

The Redemptorist Vocation

Father John was impressed by the missionary work among the German immigrants of several priests of the Congregation of the Most Holy Redeemer, popularly called the Redemptorists. He came to feel that he might be more effective in nourishing the spiritual life of the people if he were a member of a religious community rather than a lone missionary-pastor.

Providentially, Father Joseph Prost, the Redemptorist Superior, wrote Father John a letter confirming his thoughts. Father Prost closed his letter with the scriptural admonition, *"Vae soli!"* ("Woe to him who is alone!"). Father John thought that the only way that he could save his soul was to entrust it under perfect obedience to the guidance, care and protection of a religious order. So he decided to enter the Redemptorists. On October 13, 1840, he left Buffalo for Pittsburgh, Pennsylvania. His brother Wenzel followed him and became a lay brother in the Congregation.

Father John wrote to his parents and explained his reasons for joining the Redemptorists. "I think that this is the best thing I can do for the security of my salvation. The constant supervision of religious superiors and the good example of fellow religious spur one to lead a life more pleasing to God than one can lead in the world." This proved to be only wishful thinking.

On January 16, 1842, at the age of 31, Father John was professed as a member of the Redemptorists in Baltimore. He wrote his parents that the "mutual bodily and spiritual help, edification and good example, which one has around him, till his death in such a spiritual society, make my life and my office a great deal easier for me."

On November 30, Father John became the first novice of the newly established American branch of the Redemptorists. He had hoped for a novitiate of peace and quiet consisting of study, spiritual solitude, and spiritual direction. Once again, he was disappointed. The Redemptorists were needed for mission work. Father John's novice master was sent away to Baltimore and Father John was left alone once again to be his own spiritual director.

A Redemptorist chronicler reported, "The first novice of our American Province did not enjoy the advantages found in the regular instruction and careful discipline of a well-regulated novitiate. He was entrusted with duties which usually fell to the charge of a professed religious only;

nevertheless he distinguished himself by a faithful observance of rules, unaffected love for the Congregation, and the practice of eminent virtues."

Years later, Father Neumann commented on his so-called "novitiate" in a letter. "There was no novitiate in America at that time, and no novice master, but an overwhelming amount of work to be dispatched. I daily made two meditations and two examens of conscience with the community, spiritual reading in private, and a visit to the Blessed Sacrament. I also recited the Rosary, and that was all."

That was all of his interior life, but his active life consisted of the busyness that he had tried to avoid – preaching missions, assisting parish priests, settling disputes, changing residences frequently and traveling 3,000 miles on horseback, on bumpy stagecoaches, railroads, steamers and canal boats crowded with raucous immigrants heading West. When he complained about this to his busy, absent novice master, Father Tschenhens, he was firmly told, "You had better return to your former missions; you will never persevere with us."

Once again, Father John felt that he was a failure when all of his hopeful reasons for joining the Redemptorists were frustrated. But, God gave him a prophetic vision for his future. During his novitiate, Father John told Father Tschenhens about a strange dream that he had. He was in Baltimore and a Bishop was trying to force him to become a bishop against his will. As the Bishop dragged him to a church for his consecration, he awoke. Father Tschenchens rebuked Father John for entertaining such proud ambitions.

The Baltimore Mission

On January 16, 1842, after a long and arduous "novitiate", Father John became the first Redemptorist to make his vows in America. He was first assigned to St. James Parish in Baltimore. His parish work included administering the sacraments, hours in the confessional, visiting the sick, preaching simple, but solid sermons, instructing children in the catechism and baptizing converts. Sometimes there were as many as 30 non-Catholics taking instructions in the faith.

He also traveled to distant mission posts administering the sacraments to the vast numbers of immigrants, who long had been deprived of them in the New World. Most of them lived in isolation and poverty where they drifted into a state of religious indifferentism just trying to eke out an existence without benefit of sacraments or priests. Father John commented on the enormity of his task, "The few [priests] we have are sadly out of proportion to the ever-increasing wants of the faithful. There are Catholics who have not been to Confession for many years, and there are young people of nineteen or twenty who have nothing of Catholicity about them, saving their Baptism and all this from the want of priests. The longer this need continues, the more difficult it will be to reanimate faith and the fear of God."

Two other difficulties to reanimate the faith were the secret societies and the Protestant influence. Father John described the first difficulty: "Secret societies have been formed lately among infidels and non-Catholics; for instance, the Freemasons, the Odd fellows, and the Order of Red Men. All assert that the only object of their association is fraternal benevolence and mutual support. But this is merely a specious cloak. The very oath tendered by them, viz., secrecy as to what goes on in their meetings, is a sufficient reason to suspect their intention, and to warn Catholics against communication with them. Under pain of exclusion from the sacraments, the Provincial Council has forbidden Catholics to join such societies. Notwithstanding the prohibition, many have been enticed into them, and the sad consequences are that they have fallen away from the Faith." Father Neumann urged Catholics "from joining secret societies, from too intimate intercourse with heretics, from the reading of Protestant and immoral books, etc." He encouraged them to join new Catholic societies such as the Confraternity of the Rosary and the Confraternity of the Sacred Hearts of Jesus and Mary.

The other difficulty was the Protestant influence. A common practice of poor Catholic parents was to entrust their children to the homes of wealthy Protestants who could provide for their material welfare, since the Catholic parents could not. Father Neumann wrote, "This is a crying evil. American Protestants use every means to check the spread of Catholicism. They receive Catholic children into their homes with the secret intention of destroying their faith. And as they make fair promises, the foolish parents think themselves fortunate in having so well provided for their little ones. They will one day weep over their folly, but then it will be too late!" His proposed remedy was to entrust the care of these children to Catholic institutions and religious orders.

Father John spent about two years in Baltimore working in the main parish and riding the circuit throughout the countryside and ministering to the German families, organizing them if possible into parishes. Then, in March of 1844, he was assigned his first pastorship of St. Philomena's in Pittsburgh.

The Pittsburgh Mission

St. Philomena's was a nearly completed new church and Father John's first job was to finish the church and pay for it. It was a poor parish but his parishioner's contributed five cents a week towards the building fund to finish the construction of their church in 1846. Bishop O'Connor remarked years later that Father Neumann "built a church without any money." In order to bring a sense of community to his parish, Father John organized the new Catholic confraternities. These knitted the parish together weaving what was a disjointed group into a united parish.

Father John's work included the completion of the church and rectory, administering three schools and ministering to the outlying missions. In addition to his pastoral and missionary work, he stayed up late at night praying and writing catechisms and notes for a Bible history. Eventually, it was too much work and he got sick again. The doctor said that if he continued working in that way, he might face an early death.

His Superior ordered him to leave Pittsburgh for Baltimore to rest. The rest was a short one. At the end of two weeks, on February 9, 1847, Father John was named Superior of the American Redemptorists. He was only 35 years old, younger than many of the priests under him. He was responsible for the administration of 10 Redemptorist houses and over 70 missions.

Redemptorist Superior

This appointment stunned and terrified the humble Father John, who judged himself incompetent for it. The Congregation was heavily laden with debts when he assumed command. He lacked substantial sources of revenue, but somehow managed to ease the financial difficulties, erect additional Redemptorist foundations, new churches and new schools. His achievements as Superior justified his Provincial's description of him as "the wisest, the greatest, and the best among all the Redemptorists in America."

However, his authority as Superior was severely limited; his instructions were often disobeyed and his European superiors were disunited because of the European revolutions of 1848 that resulted in questionable orders issued from them. Father Neumann commented on his tenuous position, "Let it go. Do not be sorry for me. I have never done anything to become a Superior and I will not do anything to remain one. On the contrary, I will thank God if I am relieved of this responsibility."

In spite of all this, during his 23-month term, Father Neumann furthered the stability of the Congregation in the United States. He became a citizen of the United Sates and in 1847 he welcomed the School Sisters of Notre Dame to the United States and helped them to get established. He offered them the Redemptorist's property in Baltimore and they agreed to teach in St. Alphonsus' School. He also interceded for the Oblate Sisters of Providence, a congregation of African-American nuns, who were about to be dissolved by the Bishop for lack of numbers. He provided them with Redemptorist spiritual directors and confessors, the order revived and the Bishop changed his mind.

After his term as Redemptorist Superior, Father Neumann returned to his pastoral work from 1849 through 1851 in parish work, teaching the faith and as a confessor to nuns. One of them later said, "Father Neumann contributed much to the perfection of our Sisters. His instructions and exhortations were animated by his own enthusiasm for the honor of God, the sublime end of the religious state. They inflamed our hearts with an ardent desire for religious perfection, for a total oblation to God."

Father Neumann also became the confessor to Baltimore Archbishop Francis Patrick Kenrick, former Bishop of Philadelphia, which now had a vacancy. The Vatican asked Bishop Kenrick to recommend his successor. He recommended Father Neumann.

Bishop of Philadelphia

Father John was so alarmed over the prospect of being made a Bishop, that he wrote to the Procurator General of the Congregation in Rome, urging him to use all power within his means to prevent the appointment. He begged friends to pray against his consecration and asked religious houses to pray novenas to avert what he termed as "a great danger from one of the dioceses in America" and "a calamity for the Church."

However, the prayers were not heard and Pope Pius IX appointed Father Neumann as Bishop "under obedience and without appeal."

Father Neumann was asked to write under obedience a short autobiography for the Redemptorists. He ended it with these lines, "Tomorrow, March 28th, my birthday, which this year falls on Passion Sunday, I shall, if nothing prevents it, be consecrated Bishop in St. Alphonsus' Church, by Most. Rev. Archbishop Kenrick. But do Thou, O Lord, have mercy on us! Jesus and Mary, pity me! Passion of Christ, strengthen me!" With this last sentence as his Episcopal motto, Father John was consecrated as a Bishop of Philadelphia on Passion Sunday of 1852. It was his 41st birthday.

After his consecration, Bishop Neumann returned to his rectory clothed in his new robes of office. As his companions admired his clothing, Father Neumann said with a smile, "The Church treats her Bishops like a mother treats a child. When she wants to place a burden on him, she gives him new clothes."

Since the creation of the Diocese of Philadelphia in 1808, its Bishops had all been Irish. Many Catholics were upset over the appointment of Bishop Neumann because he was German, unsophisticated, diminutive in appearance (5'3"), spoke in an accent and was unimpressive in speech. In short, he was not a worldly man. Years later, his vicar-general, Father Edward J. Sourin, said, "He knew well when he came to this proud city there were many not only among those who differ from us in religion but hundreds of our own faith who wished as an occupant for the episcopate of this diocese a man more according to the judgment of the world."

The Diocese of Philadelphia was then one of the largest and most important in the United States. It included the eastern half of Pennsylvania, all of Delaware and the southern part of New Jersey for a total of over 35,000 square miles. It consisted of 113 parishes, with only 100 priests to serve a population of 170,000 Catholics. And it offered many a trying challenge to its new shepherd. The greatest need was for more churches and schools for the increasing numbers of Irish and German immigrants, but the diocese was burdened by debt.

Soon after his arrival in Philadelphia, Bishop Neumann got to work. He had taken a vow never deliberately to waste a moment of time. But his work was the fruit of an intense interior life of prayer and sacrifice. He rose before five a.m. and prayed until Mass at six which was immediately followed by another Mass. He then heard confessions and had a light breakfast before the work of the day.

His room was simple and he often slept on the bare floor. He had only one suit of clothes. He wore a cilicium (belt of iron wire) under his clothes as a mortification of his flesh. His residence was furnished very plainly. He maintained no secretarial staff. Instead, he personally answered all the voluminous correspondence that arrived on his desk. Visitors at all times of the day called and were graciously received by the Bishop himself.

Bishop Neumann was generous to the poor, personally giving them alms. He became one of them and went without clothes, linen and shoes. One Sunday a priest scolded him for his shabby appearance and pleaded that he change into a better coat. "What shall I do?" asked the Bishop, "I do not have another."

Once on a visit to a rural parish, the parish priest picked him up in a manure wagon. Seated on a plank stretched over the wagon's contents the Bishop joked, "Have you ever seen such an entourage for a Bishop!"

During a visit to Germany, he came back to the house he was staying in soaked by rain. When his host suggested that he change his shoes, the Bishop replied, "The only way I could change my shoes is by putting the left one on the right foot and the right one on the left foot. This is the only pair I own."

On another occasion, a priest found him in his room obviously very ill, but lying on a bare plank. He told him that he should be in bed. The Bishop replied, "Oh, I am very well here." "No," the priest responded, "You must go to bed. You are a Bishop and you belong to your diocese." Bishop Neumann obediently left his board and went to bed.

Soon after his arrival in Philadelphia, Bishop Neumann directed that all the religious communities, orphanages, hospitals and other Catholic institutions in the city evaluate their spiritual and temporal conditions. He began his pastoral visitation to every parish where he would remain for several days, examining the overall state of the parish and making a careful inspection of the church, altar and sacred vessels. While he was there he would conduct a mission, preaching to the parishioners, hearing confessions, visiting the sick and giving special instruction to the children. He personally examined candidates for Confirmation and would postpone it for those who were not prepared. He would prepare them himself.

Many immigrants had no priest who could hear their Confession in their native language. Bishop Neumann was a Godsend to them because he spoke so many languages. He had taught himself Gaelic, the language of many of the Irish immigrants. One of them made her Confession to him and later said, "It's an Irish Bishop we have at last!"

Bishop Neumann privately worshipped at St. Peter the Apostle, a German Catholic church that was staffed by the Redemptorists. His weekly custom was to walk about a mile and a half from his residence to make his Confession at St. Peter's. He spent his monthly and annual retreats, as prescribed by the Redemptorist Rule, at the nearby old rectory. When he came, he avoided all display of rank or special privilege and mingled with the people. No one would take him for a Bishop.

A memorial plaque in the church now reads: *St. Peter's is more than Bishop Neumann's resting place. He walked its aisles; he often knelt here, lost in prayer. His crozier rang on the sanctuary stones. His little feet moved up and down these aisles as he bore the Blessed Sacrament in Forty Hours Processions. The walls recall his voice; preaching at High Mass, catechizing little ones before Confirmation, complimenting the nuns who taught them – the School Sisters of Notre Dame. St. Peter's was very close to his heart.*

Next door to Bishop Neumann's official residence, construction was underway on Philadelphia's imposing new Cathedral. Work had been started six years before he came to the city. The brownstone building would later become the largest and most costly cathedral in the nation, but in 1852 construction was not one-third completed. They needed a lot of money to complete the project. Many people urged Bishop Neumann to hurry up and finish it. But he thought that parish churches and schools should be constructed first. So the Cathedral was never completed until four years after his death.

In 1852, Bishop Neumann attended the First Plenary Council of Bishops to be held in the United States. The Bishops approved the catechisms composed by him for distribution in the nation's dioceses. These became the standard catechisms in the United States for the next 35 years until the Baltimore Catechism replaced them. After the Council, one of the Bishops remarked about him, "I had an opportunity during the Council in Baltimore to admire Bishop Neumann's wonderful memory and extraordinary theological attainments. He had a solution for every question posed. What edified me most of all was his unruffled composure, which betokened deep humility and perfect self-control. I always regarded him as a saint."

The Catholic School System

Bishop Neumann believed that only Catholic schools could save the Catholic youth. He was critical of public education and wrote years earlier, "The public school system in the United States is very liberal in theory; but in reality it is most intolerant towards Catholics. It cannot be doubted that the young mind is influenced by the irreligious dispositions of the teacher. Even the textbooks selected for use are injurious to Catholic children. They are merely heretical extracts from a falsified Bible, and histories which contain the most malicious perversion of truth, the grossest lies against the doctrines and practices of the Catholic Church. These circumstances combine for the spiritual ruin of Catholic children."

Bishop Neumann's first project was the establishment of a Catholic school system in 1852. He set up a central diocesan board of education consisting of himself, the pastor and two laymen from each parish. The board recommended a general curriculum and raised funds to help the parishes build the schools. Then the pastors hired and paid the teachers. Bishop Neumann started building schools and churches as they were needed, in spite of the diocesan debt, trusting that God would provide for them. Within three years of his arrival, the number of children in Catholic schools increased from about 500 to 5000 and he completed construction of 42 churches. He was the Father of the Catholic Parochial School System.

Bishop Neumann's first love was for the poor, the simple and children. He always had something in his pockets to reward the students who gave correct answers to his catechism questions. He never lost his love for botany and he would often explain to the children the wonders of nature such as flowers and lead them up from there to appreciate the love of their Creator.

One day, two young girls came to deliver to the Bishop a message from their teacher. He found them waiting in an anteroom admiring a marble statue of a child lying in a cradle. He jokingly said that he'd give it to the one who could carry the heavy statue home. One of them took him seriously, left and returned a little while later with a wagon to haul it away. The Bishop was true to his word and let her keep it. The enterprising little girl later became the Mother General of the Holy Cross Sisters and the statue was venerated in their motherhouse in Notre Dame, Indiana.

The Forty Hours' Devotion

Bishop Neumann fostered devotion to the Blessed Sacrament by encouraging the Forty Hours' Devotion. This is a devotion of prayer before the exposed Blessed Sacrament over a period of 40 hours that represents the traditional time that Jesus was in the tomb from His death on the Cross until His Resurrection. He was the first Bishop to set up this devotion on an organized diocesan schedule so that Jesus was never left alone and someone was always there to adore Him.

However, several priests advised Bishop Neumann against instituting the devotion on the grounds that the Blessed Sacrament might be profaned. They thought that the anti-Catholic Nativists might burn down the churches as they did in the riots of 1844 when two churches were burned down. This troubled him, but his scruples were relieved by a revelation that he received from Jesus.

One night Bishop Neumann fell asleep at his desk while meditating on this issue of profanation. When he woke up, he saw that his still-burning candle had burnt down and charred some of his papers but that he could still read the words. He knelt in prayer to give thanks that a serious fire was averted and he received a locution from Jesus. "As the flames are burning here without consuming or injuring the writing, so shall I pour out my graces in the Blessed Sacrament without prejudice to my honor. Fear no profanation, therefore, and hesitate no longer to carry out your design for my glory." So Bishop Neumann established the devotion and it soon spread throughout the United States.

The Lay Trustee System

A recurring problem in early American Catholic churches was the issue of who should run the churches – lay trustees, as in the Protestant churches, or the pastors and Bishops. Under the Lay Trustee System, many Catholic churches were administered somewhat like Protestant churches. Title to the church property was vested in a board of lay trustees and not in the diocese as it is today. This system fostered tension in the church administration between the board and the pastor.

Bishop Neumann faced this tension head on. Holy Trinity church in South Philadelphia was under an interdict ordered by former Archbishop Kenrick that forbade the administration of the sacraments there because some rebellious trustees claimed title to the property and wouldn't convey it to him. In 1852, Bishop Neumann informed the trustees that he would lift the interdict if they would convey title to him as Bishop. Instead, they sued him and won title in a lower court. Thousands of Germans were now without church, priest or sacraments. Bishop Neumann appealed the case to the Supreme Court of Pennsylvania on the grounds that the rebellious trustees were not Catholics in a true sense and that therefore they could not be trustees of a Catholic church. The appeal was finally heard two years later.

The judge told the trustees, "You had an Irishman for Bishop, an American and now you have a German. You are satisfied with none, obedient to none. If you want to be Catholics you must obey the Pope and the Bishops in all ecclesiastical affairs. You cannot expect that the court will protect your disobedience." Bishop Neumann won the case and regained title to the church. This was an important decision for the Catholic Church in America and helped to end the system of church administration by lay trustees.

The Immaculate Conception

Bishop Neumann was devoted to the Immaculate Conception, the Patroness of the United States. He went to Rome to witness the proclamation of the dogma in 1854. Before he left, he wrote a Pastoral Letter in which he announced the proclamation and urged devotion to Our Lady under the title of the Immaculate Conception. He wrote, "Henceforth and forever, all generations of true believers shall invoke Mary, Mother of God, as the ever immaculate virgin, conceived without stain of original sin."

After the proclamation of the dogma on December 8, Bishop Neumann wrote, "I thank the Lord God, that among the many graces He has bestowed upon me, He allowed me to see this day in Rome."

The Sisters of the Third Order of St. Francis

While Bishop Neumann was in Rome in 1854, Pope Pius IX suggested training a new group of religious to work with the poor. He suggested that it be placed under the patronage of St. Francis. Providentially, at that very time, Bishop Neumann learned that three Philadelphia women had established a hospice for working girls and were seeking permission to form a Franciscan community. Before leaving Rome, Bishop Neumann obtained the authority to found the Sisters of the Third Order of St. Francis of Glen Riddle and to receive the Philadelphia women as its first members. After he returned home from Rome, he invested them with the habit of novices and later heard their final vows on May 26, 1856.

The Sisters began devoting much of their time and energy to the care of the sick. After their numbers increased, they established St. Mary Hospital and, at the request of Bishop Neumann, they became teachers as well.

Bishop Neumann also helped to establish the Sisters of the Immaculate Heart of Mary and encouraged the School Sisters of Notre Dame to come from Germany to the United States. Many of these pioneer religious women staffed the new Catholic schools of his diocese.

Business Administration

Bishop Neumann was well aware of the deficiencies of his administration of the Diocese of Philadelphia. His gifts did not include financial wisdom, business administration, social affability and cultured manners. These were the qualities that would have been appreciated by the wealthy Philadelphia socialites and their sophisticated clerical friends.

Bishop Neumann's gift was simplicity. His nature was shy and retiring rather than outgoing and social. The poor masses of his diocese appreciated this. But, they had no voice and everyone listened to the loud complaints of the rich.

A symbol of the conflict between his nature and the expectations of the rich was the Cathedral project. This project was a visible symbol to the whole city of what the rich said were the Bishop's faults. He was criticized for being often outside the city visiting his flock in the outlying missions, while the uncompleted Cathedral project languished for lack of leadership and funds and became an eyesore to the city. Bishop Neumann didn't defend himself against their criticism. Instead, he seemed to humbly agree with them. He sent a letter to Cardinal Franzoni in Rome and suggested that he transfer him to a smaller diocese. He wrote:

> Day and night I am filled with uneasiness and perpetual fear. The debts left me by my venerable predecessor

cause me much anxiety. Because of circumstances here, a man of sharp insight, brave and accustomed to direct temporal affairs is required. I, however, am timid, always hesitant, and possess a horror of business and pecuniary transactions. The City of Philadelphia, which has more than five hundred thousand inhabitants and (if you will pardon the statement) a very worldly character, needs someone else instead of myself who am too plain and not sufficiently talented; besides I love solitude. Since there is a proposal to erect many new dioceses, I thought it my duty to inform Your Eminence that I am most willing to be transferred to another See where a less gifted man would be required. For more than fifteen years I was occupied on the North American missions; I have loved corporal labors and journey in the mountains and through the forests. Visiting Catholic families separated from one another by long distances and preaching to them, etc. has been my greatest pleasure.

Bishop Neumann's offer of transfer was not accepted. Pope Benedict XV later declared his letter as an example of heroic virtue. He said, "This offer of Bishop Neumann to leave Philadelphia was positive proof of his magnanimity of soul."

The Coadjutor

Archbishop Kenrick also wrote to Rome and made a more prudent suggestion in order to satisfy Bishop Neumann's critics. He wrote:

It seems to me that he should by all means be retained in the See of Philadelphia since he is a shining light because of his piety and his labors. I, indeed, confess that he is wanting a little in managing affairs, but I believe that he can appoint a vicar general, consultors and helpers, whose assistance will enable him to clear the debts and to smooth out matters. He is beloved by the clergy and people, although certain ones would like to see more urbane and polished manners.

On December 9, 1856, Rome adopted Archbishop Kenrick's suggestion and decided that Bishop Neumann would remain as Bishop of Philadelphia with another Bishop as coadjutor, an assistant who would help him in diocesan administration. Bishop Neumann wrote, "We give all thanks to God for the provision He has made for the welfare of this diocese."

Coadjutor Bishop James Wood was an answer to Bishop Neumann's critics. He was tall and distinguished in appearance, educated in Rome, sophisticated, a good public speaker and experienced in financial matters. His business administration of the diocese freed Bishop Neumann for his pastoral work of visitations to religious houses and the remote areas of his diocese, administering the sacrament of Confirmation and establishing new parishes and schools. One day he spent the entire day riding 25 miles through mountainous terrain to confirm a single child.

The Chalice

Bishop Neumann said in a speech at Illinois Bishop Juncker's consecration reception on April 26, 1857:

> You have scarcely any idea how difficult and painful the office of Bishop is, especially here in America. Catholics come from all parts of the world, all nationalities mingle with one another and the Bishop is supposed to please all – an impossible task. Where are we to gain strength: Where will Bishop Juncker receive the strength he needs: From the Blood of Christ, from the Chalice.

This strength soon ran out for Bishop Neumann and he drank from the Chalice in full. On January 5, 1860, he remarked to a visiting priest, "I have a strange feeling today. I feel as I never felt before. I have to go out on a little business and the fresh air will do me good." Then he added strangely, "A man must always be ready, for death comes when and where God wills it."

He went out on foot to visit a lawyer about property deeds. Then he went on a mission of mercy to the express office to inquire about a lost chalice that one of his rural pastors had sent to Bishop Wood to consecrate. On his way there, Bishop Neumann suddenly collapsed on the sidewalk. Two men carried him into a nearby house where he died. Bystanders notified Bishop Wood. A priest hurried to administer the sacrament of Extreme Unction (Anointing of the Sick) but it was too late. In a stranger's house, without benefit of the sacraments of the Church, the Bishop of Philadelphia died, three months short of his 49th birthday.

Deep shock and disbelief swept the entire community when the news spread, followed by an unprecedented display of the peoples' respect and affection for their Bishop. Thousands came to bid him farewell at the Cathedral chapel where his body first was placed. Two days later, the streets were thronged as the funeral procession moved through the city. Four black horses decked with sable plumes pulled the glass-sided hearse past weeping mourners. That night St. John's was filled with men and women of many faiths and from all walks of life coming to see the Bishop for the last time.

Another solemn funeral cortege moved through packed streets from St. John's to St. Peter's. Far into another night, German parishioners filed by the casket of the little Bishop whom they had known so well and loved so deeply. On the next morning, there was a second funeral Mass and a sermon preached in German by a Redemptorist. Then his body was carried to a vault beneath the floor of the sanctuary of the lower church.

Father Edward Sourin preached at the funeral, "He has labored through every part of the diocese, and has, undoubtedly, done more for its better organization and for the spread of piety throughout the various congregations than might have been otherwise done in even ten or twenty years by another individual. He spared himself in nothing."

Archbishop Kenrick gave permission for the Bishop's body to be buried at the Redemptorists' St. Peter's Church instead of the graveyard of St. John's Pro-Cathedral. He said, "Gladly I'll consent to Bishop Neumann's finding a resting place in death where he could not find one in life."

In November 1962, Bishop Neumann's body was exhumed and found to be very much intact and flexible. A wax mask was made and his body remains today under the Mass Altar in the Lower Church of St. Peter the Apostle in Philadelphia.

Virtues

Over the corpse of Bishop Neumann, Archbishop Kenrick declared, "His people appreciated his zeal and his learning, yet he possessed accomplishments of which the world knew not and virtues of which Heaven alone took comprehensive cognizance." He never worked miracles during his lifetime. His works were ordinary and simple. On December 11, 1921, Pope Benedict XV declared Bishop Neumann Venerable. He said, "Works, even the most simple, performed with constant perfection in the midst of inevitable difficulties, spell heroism in any servant of God. Just because of the simplicity of his works we find in them a strong argument for saying to the faithful of whatever age, sex or condition: You are bound to imitate the Venerable Neumann."

St. John Neumann is often called "the common man's saint" not so much for his extraordinary accomplishments, but for his extraordinary simple faith. Through all of the discouragements and disappointments of his weary career, through the long spiritual droughts that parched his soul, through his never-ending uncertainty of whether he was giving his best to God's work, his remarkable faith never wavered. His simple faith alone inspired his ordinary works to be done in an extraordinary way.

Faith, humility and obedience were Bishop Neumann's greatest virtues. His faith carried him through the darkness of discerning his vocation, being subjected to heretical teachings in the seminary and traveling to the United States as a hopeful missionary priest without benefit of ordination. His humility helped him to be silent about his many gifts such as his ability to speak several languages and his knowledge of the natural sciences. His humility also helped him to abhor his appointment as Redemptorist Superior and his ordination as Bishop. He agreed with his many detractors that he was incompetent. His obedience led him to accept his consecration as Bishop as Pope Pius IX ordered, "under obedience and without appeal."

Fruits

Bishop Neumann founded one religious order and welcomed seven others in his eight years as Bishop – one for each year. He built churches and schools, established the Catholic Parochial School System, provided for the spiritual welfare of immigrants and published a catechism. He built 40 new schools and 80 new churches in 8 years – almost one church for every month of his service. He encouraged popular piety through the Forty Hours' Devotion, confraternities and societies in honor of Our Lady and the saints and parish missions.

When Father Neumann was the Redemptorist Superior and pastor of St. Philomena in Pittsburgh, Pennsylvania, his assistant pastor was Blessed Father Francis Xavier Seelos, a fellow Redemptorist. Father Seelos worked for nine years at St. Philomena's, first as assistant pastor with Father Neumann, the Superior of the Religious Community, and later as Superior himself and for the last three years as pastor. During this time, he was also the Redemptorist Novice Master. Father Seelos also preached missions.

From 1863 until 1866, Father Seelos dedicated himself to the life of an itinerant missionary who preached in English and German in the states of Connecticut, Illinois, Michigan, Missouri, New Jersey, New York, Ohio, Pennsylvania, Rhode Island and Wisconsin.

In 1866, he was assigned to the Redemptorist community in New Orleans, Louisiana. He was known as a pastor who was always available to his faithful and concerned for the poorest and the most abandoned. He contracted yellow fever while visiting and caring for its victims. After several weeks of patiently enduring his illness, he died on October 4, 1867, at the age of 48.

Regarding his relationship with Bishop Neumann, Father Seelos said, "He has introduced me to the active life" and "he has guided me as a spiritual director and confessor." Pope John Paul II beatified Father Seelos on April 9, 2000. His Feast Day is October 5.

Saint

Soon after Bishop Neumann's burial at St. Peter's, people who visited his tomb were cured of diseases, the lame walked, the deaf heard and the blind saw. The first miracle that was proved was a healing from acute peritonitis. Eleven-year-old Eva Benassi lived in Sassuolo, Italy. In May of 1923, while she was at boarding school, she became ill with acute diffused peritonitis and death was imminent. One of the school's nuns had a devotion to Bishop Neumann. While Eva was on her deathbed, she placed a picture of him on Eva's stomach and prayed with her community and Eva for a healing. During the night, Eva awoke and said that her pain was gone. By morning she was entirely cured.

In July of 1949, 19-year old James Kent Lenahan was severely injured in an automobile accident near Philadelphia. He was admitted to the hospital with a crushed skull, an eye torn from its socket, three broken ribs and a broken collarbone. He was near death when his parents brought a piece of Bishop Neumann's cassock and placed it upon him. He immediately improved and was fully healed within a month.

The Holy See approved both of these cures as miracles and Pope Paul VI beatified Bishop Neumann on October 13, 1963.

In October of 1962, young Michael Flanigan of Philadelphia was diagnosed with cancer and given six months to live. His parents began taking him to Bishop Neumann's Shrine at St. Peter's Church. He showed immediate improvement and was totally healed within five months. Pope Paul VI canonized Bishop Neumann on June 19, 1977. His Feast Day is January 5, the date of his death.

Intercessor for United States' Bishops

Bishop Neumann's intercession is appropriate for the Bishops of the United States because he was a witness to hope through his pastoral ministry centered on the three basics of a Bishop's role in sanctifying, teaching and governing the Church. Pope John Paul II emphasized this in an address to the United States Bishops on April 2, 2004. He said:

> The exercise of this prophetic witness in contemporary American society has, as many of you have pointed out, been made increasingly difficult by the aftermath of the recent scandal and the outspoken hostility to the Gospel in certain sectors of public opinion, yet it cannot be evaded or delegated to others. Precisely because American society is confronted by a disturbing loss of the sense of the transcendent and the affirmation of a culture of the material and the ephemeral, it desperately needs such a witness of hope. It is in hope that we have been saved (cf. Romans 8:24); the Gospel of hope enables us to discern the consoling presence of God's Kingdom in the midst of this world and offers confidence, serenity and direction in place of that hopelessness which inevitably spawns fear, hostility and violence in the hearts of individuals and in society as a whole.

Opening Prayer for the Mass in Commemoration of Saint John Neumann

Almighty God,
you called St. John Neumann
to a life of service, zeal and compassion
for the guidance of your people in the new world.
By his prayers
help us to build up the community of the Church
through our dedication to the Christian education of youth
and through the witness of our brotherly love.
Grant this through our Lord Jesus Christ, your Son,
who lives and reigns with you and the Holy Spirit,
one God, for ever and ever.

Shrine:

The National Shrine of Saint John Neumann
Saint Peter the Apostle Church
1019 North Fifth Street
Philadelphia, PA, 19123
Telephone: 215-627-3080
Website: www.stjohnneumann.org
The shrine of St. John Neumann houses his body exposed on the altar.

17. New Union

Bishop Neumann's death was soon followed by the Civil War. It was an atrocious and brutal conflict that ended in 1865 with the assassination of President Abraham Lincoln, over a half million deaths and hundreds of millions of dollars in property destruction. It also ended with the emancipation of the slaves, a re-united nation and a land of new inventions.

In 1869, the Union Pacific Railroad, built from the West, and the Central Pacific, built from the East, met at Promontory, Utah. Now it was possible to travel by rail from coast to coast. In 1875, Andrew Carnegie perfected the conversion of iron ore into steel which was used in the expanding railroad lines and in farm machinery. In the 1830s Cyrus McCormick had invented a mechanical farm reaper that replaced the scythe for harvesting grains. It became more effective with steel.

In 1859, the first successful oil well was drilled and in 1870 John D. Rockefeller formed the Standard Oil Company. In 1876 Alexander Graham Bell invented the telephone and in 1879 Thomas Alva Edison invented the electric light bulb. All of these inventions and developments led to increased manufacturing, more factories and more industrial workers in the cities. These workers worked long hours for low pay in miserable, filthy and dangerous conditions. Many children had to work and were not educated. Workers were laid off or got hurt and received no unemployment or worker's compensation benefits. Many got evicted and became homeless. Some got killed and left destitute widows and orphans. Living accommodations were often in crowded, dark and dirty buildings that caused diseases and epidemics that killed many. Because of the large number of foreign immigrants, the workers outnumbered the jobs because of which they could not make demands for better wages, hours and working conditions. They were simply fired and replaced by someone else.

In 1887, Cardinal James Gibbons, Archbishop of Baltimore, reported all of these abuses to the Pope. This led to Pope Leo XIII's Encyclical

Letter *Rerum Novarum* (*The Condition of the Working Classes*) which set forth Catholic principles of justice and fair treatment of workers. It also pointed out the evils of both Communism and unrestrained capitalism.

Like the Irish before them, Italian immigrants were poor and settled in the cities where they hoped to find work. However, unlike the Irish, they could not speak English, they seemed culturally strange and more foreign than the Irish and they faced all of the abuses pointed out by Pope Leo XIII.

On October 28, 1886, President Grover Cleveland dedicated the Statue of Liberty in New York Harbor. It was a gift from France and symbolized the liberty for which the United States was famous. It was one of the first sights that many Italian immigrants saw as they sailed into the United States. Emma Lazarus wrote a sonnet, "The New Colossus," celebrating the statue as "a mighty woman with a torch" who is named "Mother of Exiles" and cries with silent lips to the Old World:

> Give me your tired, your poor,
> your huddled masses yearning to breathe free,
> The wretched refuse of your teeming shore.
> Send these, the homeless, the tempest-toss'd to me.
> I lift my lamp beside the golden door.

About 200,000 tired, poor, huddled masses of Italians arrived each year in the United States "yearning to breathe free" only to face the abuses that Pope Leo XIII wrote about. They needed a saint to help them.

18. Saint Frances Xavier Cabrini and Italian Immigrants

Born	July 15, 1850 in St. Angelo, Italy
Died	December 22, 1917 in Chicago, Illinois
Canonized	July 7, 1946
Feast Day	November 13

Patroness of Immigrants
Missionary of the New
Evangelization
Foundress of the Missionary
Sisters of the Sacred Heart of Jesus.
First United States citizen to be canonized.

"She was not a humanitarian; she was a heroic lover of God. In her missions of charity, in her achievement of the impossible, it was not genius; her secret was Divine Love. This is the wonderful story – a romance that is gripping and striking. It is the story of a woman who lived among us, who saw the things which we see, a woman in whose soul Divine Love had consumed the last remnant of self, who came to love only God, and who saw God in every poor man, woman and child. She loved us. She was our benefactor. She went begging in our streets. She rode our street cars. Through alleys she went in search of little hungry children who were homeless and friendless. "

"Our Saint issues a challenge to each of us, no matter how gloomy the world about us may be; we can smile the serene smile of our Saint."

Samuel Cardinal Stritch of Chicago, *Radio Address*, July 7, 1946, the day of the canonization of Mother Cabrini.

The small young nun with beautiful large blue eyes entered the presence of the elderly Pope Leo XIII. She knelt before him and told him of her ambition to go to China. He shook his head and said, "No, not to the East, my daughter, but to the West." He decided that Mother Francis Cabrini should go to the United States and not to China. This began a missionary service that resulted in the largest number of missionary foundations in the United States.

Formation

A prophetic, swiftly moving cloud of white appeared above the Lombard plains in Sant'Angelo di Lodi in northern Italy, as Agostino Cabrini waited for his 52-year old wife, Stella, to deliver their last child. The white cloud turned out to be a flock of white doves that circled their home. The flock of doves landed on Agostino's courtyard to pick at the grain that he had threshed there. He caught one, carried it into the house to show his wife and set it free. It seemed that the dove was a symbol of his new daughter who was born prematurely shortly afterwards. She was baptized on the day of her birth, July 15, 1850, and named Maria Francesca. Francesca was the last of the 13 Cabrini children. Only she and three others survived.

Agostino and his sons worked hard on his land plowing, sowing and reaping. The women weeded, fed the animals and carried the noonday meal to the men in the fields. It was a typical life on a family farm in 19th century Italy. Francesca's stern sister, Rosa, who was 15 years older, helped her mother to form and discipline Francesca. They called her "Cecchina", an abbreviation of the diminutive Franceschina.

Francesca was confirmed at the age of seven. She later described it as a mystical experience in which she felt wrapped by a mantle of heavenly light. "The moment I was being anointed with the sacred chrism," she said, "I felt what I shall never be able to express. I seemed no longer on earth. My heart was replete with a pure joy. I cannot say what I felt, but I know it was the Holy Ghost."

Her parents were devout Catholics whose piety influenced Francesca's future vocation. Her father read aloud to his children various Catholic works including the *Annals of the Propagation of the Faith.* This particular magazine inspired young Francesca with a desire to go to the missions in China. Because of her frailty and frequent illnesses, she developed a contemplative spirituality that fostered her desire to go to China.

One day while picnicking, Francesca took the waxed paper in which her lunch was packed, divided it and folded it into the shape of little boats that she filled with violets and sailed in a local canal. She told Rosa that they represented missionaries on their way to China. She hoped to sail to China herself when she grew up. One day she fell into the canal and nearly drowned. An unknown force pulled her safely to the bank. Her uncle attributed this to her Guardian Angel.

When she was 13, a visiting missionary related his experiences in the missions of China. She later mentioned her missionary desire to Rosa who replied scornfully, "*You*, a missionary? One so small and ignorant as you a missionary!" This helped Francesca to develop the virtue of humility. She continued to secretly cherish her missionary dream and geography became her favorite study. She spent hours looking over maps of the Far East.

Francesca had piercing blue eyes, a ready smile and a soft voice. She was short and slim, and her skin was fair and delicate. She was so attractive that Rosa used to plaster and comb her hair down to prevent any youthful vanity. She attended public school until she was 13. Then she attended a private Catholic school until she was 18. From the age of 13, she took an annual vow of virginity and made it permanent when she reached 18. She said that she made this vow, "Because God wants it."

Teacher

Francesca finished school and, like Rosa, obtained a teaching certificate when she was 18 in 1868. She applied for admission to a religious order but she was refused. The order believed that Francesca's constitution was too weak to stand up to religious life. She then lived at home and helped Rosa with the household chores. Together the sisters cared for their elderly parents until their deaths in 1870 when Francesca was 20 years old. Two years later, while nursing the victims of a smallpox epidemic, she contracted the disease herself. Rosa delicately and patiently nursed her back to health with a face free of any marring pox marks.

For the next two years, Francesca taught, practiced works of mercy as a Third Order Secular of St. Francis and lived at home. In spite of the government's anticlericalism, she was able to obtain permission from the mayor of Vidardo to reinstate religious instruction in the public school there. After her parents' death, she was free to follow her vocation but her dream of being a missionary to China was not to be realized.

Novitiate

Francesca applied for admission to religious orders two more times. Each time she thought that she was refused because of her health. But in fact, Father Antonio Serrati of Codogno suggested to the orders that she be rejected because he had his own need of her services. Soon he became Bishop of Codogno. There was an orphanage for girls there named the House of Providence. It was in desperate need of reform. Madame Antonia Tondini, the eccentric woman who founded and administered the orphanage, squandered its revenues and proved an unfit caretaker for the orphans. Bishop Serrati persuaded her and her staff to form a religious community in hope that the situation would improve. He took the profession of their vows but Sister Tondini said with a smile that she kept her vows in her pocket. The Sisters dressed like nuns, but they didn't act like them.

Bishop Serrati then asked Francesca to bring order into the chaos. At first she refused, citing her desire to be a missionary, and her lack of authority over the older Sister Tondini. Eventually, however, she took the opportunity at hand and agreed to go with the understanding that it was only for two weeks. She was 24 years old.

Three bleak years passed. Francesca brought cleanliness, kindness and a semblance of order to the orphanage. She gathered around her a small group of seven young women whom she trained as religious sisters. It became an anomalous, non-canonical novitiate within a novitiate. For her efforts, she was insulted and abused by Sister Tondini. On September 13, 1877, Bishop Serrati finally told Francesca that he wanted her to take vows. She did so and then he received the professions of seven of the orphans who became her novices. She became the Mother Superior of the House of Providence.

Sister Tondini then saw Francesca as a usurper. Three more terrible years passed. Sister Tondini terrorized the orphans who often fled to Francesca's room for protection as Sister Tondini shouted and banged on the door. Eventually, she even sued the Bishop in civil court for the return of the money that she had donated to found the orphanage. He finally excommunicated her and dissolved the House of Providence in 1880.

Francesca was 30 years old and had just completed her novitiate as a six-year trial by fire. She had begun her adult life teaching in the public school while living in the orderly, peaceful, quiet home of her parents. Then she went for six years to a place of noise and chaos. She had proved to be one courageous, tenacious and patient woman. She never learned how to run an orphanage, but she learned how not to run one.

Francesca wrote in her notebook, "Thy mercy, O Lord, urges me to desire to suffer something for love of Thee, and to imitate Thy life, O my Jesus, which was one continuous martyrdom of pure suffering. Thou dost also make me feel the longing to humble myself for love of Thee. Enlighten me regarding the manner of accomplishing it in so many circumstances when I scarcely have the courage to put into effect Thy holy inspirations."

The Foundress

After she left the dissolved House of Providence, her Bishop, Dominic Gelmini, urged Francesca to found her own community. He said, "I know that you want to become a missionary. I know of no such missionary order for women. Why not found one yourself?" This was a very unusual request for the Bishop to make at a time in Italy of severe anticlericalism. The Italian government was suppressing religious orders and it had appropriated most of the Vatican territory. Francesca simply answered the Bishop, "I will look for a house."

Bishop Serrati helped her to obtain an abandoned Franciscan monastery. Joined by seven of the former orphans, Francesca began her new congregation as a diocesan Institute with their first Mass on November 14, 1880. Bishop Serrati celebrated the first Mass in the chapel and placed an image of the Sacred Heart above the altar. This became a custom that would be kept in all of Mother's future houses. Mother's habit was a simple peasant dress. Her principal work was to be the Christian education of girls. The Institute was eventually called The Missionary Sisters of the Sacred Heart. Francesca also added the name "Xavier" to her own, in honor of St. Francis Xavier, the Jesuit apostle to the Far East where her heart had longed to go. She was now Mother Frances Xavier Cabrini.

Mother's first convent was poor and humble. The community started with no lights or beds. They prayed in the dark and slept on hay brought in from the fields. Young peasant girls from the neighboring towns soon joined them and they expanded their house, doing the bricklaying themselves. Mother accepted new candidates before she had any actual means of supporting them. She simply abandoned herself to Divine Providence and trusted in God. God in turn honored her trust.

One day, a Sister reported to Mother that a wine merchant refused to sell them any more wine until their past due account was paid in full. Mother asked the Sister to look in her pockets for some money. She did but they were empty. Mother said, "Look again." So, in obedience the Sister did so and amazingly she found the exact amount that the merchant demanded. On another occasion, a Sister reported that there was no milk. Mother said, "Take another look." She did so and found a full can of milk. However, these miracles were rare and most often the community suffered, sacrificed and relied on God's providence through natural means.

Mother credited these miracles to obedience. She said, "To become perfect all you have to do is to obey perfectly. When you renounce your personal inclinations you accept a mortification countersigned with the Cross of Christ." She assured her nuns that the acceptance of sufferings was the secret of interior joy. She wrote in the rules, "When they are not able, on account of illness, to attend to all the common practices, the religious should frequently raise their hearts to God, keeping united with Him and offering Him their sufferings without complaint."

Mother built on the nature of her young postulants who wanted to serve Christ. They were simple country girls, not educated intellectuals or mystical contemplatives. She prepared them for the hard work that she had already experienced in caring for and teaching young girls and orphans. Their rule was to say the Little Office, meditate, be humble and obedient and trust in Divine Providence. Mother took as her motto the words of St. Paul, "I can do all things through Him who strengthens me." She taught them that they should carry out their duties "serenely, in holy indifference since that is real love, practical love, stripped of all self-interest; the strong love you ought all to have. You are immolated to the Sacred Heart of Jesus; in this complete self-abnegation lies the very essence of sanctity."

The young postulants recognized in Mother a spiritual leader who could lead them to perfection as religious missionaries. She was a loving mother in forming them and they did not fail her expectations that they would love and serve God as she did. The miracles that God brought through Mother strengthened her postulant's faith in her leadership. Often they saw her face glow in a heavenly radiance when she was in prayer. One night, the Sister who shared her bedroom awoke to see it flooded with light. She called out, "Mother, Mother, did you see that?" "Yes," she calmly replied, "I saw it. It's nothing. Go to sleep."

Another time, a Sister was advised by a doctor to wear elastic stockings to relieve the suffering from her varicose veins. Instead, she obtained a pair of Mother's cotton stockings, put them on and was instantly cured. She told this to Mother who said, "I hope that you are not so foolish to say that my stockings cured you. I wear them all the time and they do me no good. It was your faith that did it. Say nothing about it."

Mother branched out in Lombardy and opened two more houses for young girl students and orphans. In 1884, she opened a home for prospective women teachers in Milan. In view of secularism, Mother saw that teachers needed to be grounded in Catholic values in order to pass them on to their students. Vocations came and within the first seven years, Mother opened seven houses in the diocese for schools, social-services, women students and orphans.

Mother had visions of a worldwide ministry, so she wanted to establish a house in Rome as its center and she wanted papal approval of her diocesan Institute. Bishop Serrati's response was, "Those things should be left to the saints to do!" He thought that she wouldn't succeed and that she'd make a laughingstock of herself and her Institute. Then the Infant Jesus appeared to her in a dream and said, "Go to Rome." Mother left Milan and wrote, "F. Cabrini, always burning with the desire to go on foreign mission, but on the other hand not wishing to go or send Sisters without the approval or blessing of the Sovereign Pontiff, the representative of Christ on earth, came to Rome in September, 1887."

The Great Commission

Mother traveled to Rome in 1887 at the age of 37, seven years after the founding of her community. She had an audience with Rome Vicar General Cardinal Parocchi and explained her plans. He said that it would take more time to approve the rule of her Institute and there was no need of another convent in Rome. He urged her to return to Codogno. His advice was prudent since Mother had only a short history of her Institute and no financial means to start a new house in Rome. Mother boldly asked the Cardinal to consult the Holy Father himself about her plans.

That surprised him so much that he later did it. Two weeks later, the Cardinal summoned her to another interview. Surprisingly, he asked her, "Now, Francesca Cabrini, will you be obedient?"

She replied simply and directly, "Obedient I am. Obedient I shall always be. Obedient unto my death."

The Cardinal smiled and continued, "Good. In that case, I shall not allow you to establish a house in Rome." He paused for effect and continued with a smile, "Instead, I order you to found *two* houses."

The Cardinal asked for a free school for the poor at Porta Pia and a kindergarten for the poor at Aspra. Mother agreed to establish the schools and to be responsible for most of the costs. Mother wrote to her Sister, "Pick out five Sisters, fill valises with linen and kitchen utensils, raise money for their train fare and send them to me. In the meantime, I will have managed (with His help) to rent a few rooms. Courage and forward in His love!"

The two schools quickly opened. Mother rented an unfurnished apartment and bought bargain used furniture. The Sisters slept on straw on the floor with hood and habit as sheet and blanket. For a table they used a plank stretched between two boxes. This became the Rome motherhouse of the Institute.

Then, on March 12, 1888, her diocesan Institute was approved by the Vatican. Pope Leo XIII dispensed with the usual formalities and approved her rule without many changes. While Mother was in Rome, she also learned from Bishop Scalabrini of Piacenza, about the plight of the Italian immigrants in the United States.

Bishop Scalabrini was the Founder of the Scalabrini Fathers who ministered to the Italian immigrants. He asked Mother if her community would go to New York to help his priests work with them. Italy suffered from an economic crisis in 1887 and the government encouraged poor people to leave the country. There was insufficient work for the men in Italy and many of them immigrated to the States where there was plenty of work for laborers. There were over a million immigrants who lived in ghettos, worked at low-paying menial jobs and had no priests, teachers or doctors to care for them or the orphans. The preceding Irish and German immigrants had assimilated into American society but the Italians had not.

When the immigrants arrived in the States, they faced minority discrimination, a language barrier in communicating for their daily needs and, more importantly, for their spiritual needs. Some came only for money. Mother said, "They had to come to the United States to earn a living. But what breaks my heart is to see how often they think of nothing else." Immigration endangered the immigrants' faith since there were hardly any Italian-speaking priests or nuns in the States to help them to practice it.

The Italian workers had no medical insurance, unemployment insurance, worker's compensation, welfare benefits or life insurance. Their crowded tenement homes helped to spread contagious diseases and there was no one to nurse them. Their children often got hurt at play and their fathers often got hurt working. There was no medical attention for them. Some died and left widows and orphans with nothing. Children had few Italian teachers. There was a great need to educate the children, to take care of the orphans and to conduct hospitals that would care for the sick and injured. Many immigrants lived and died without a priest, without teachers and without doctors. Bishop Scalabrini wrote in a pamphlet, *Italian Emigration to America*:

> I see those poor Italian immigrants in a foreign land, among people who do not speak their language, easily falling prey to cruel exploitation, fatigued, sick, sighing in vain for their quaint and humble little towns in Italy, and finally dying without the consolation of their dearest ones, without the enlivening words of faith which hold out to them the reward the Lord has promised to the good and the unfortunate. Yet those who do succeed in making a decent living – they are the very ones who, feeling aloof from their native country, forget every idea of the supernatural, every precept of Christian teaching, and each day they lose more of their former religious feelings, since those sentiments are not nourished with a good Christian life, and thus evil inclinations overcome the loftiest ideals.

In December 1888, Bishop Scalabrini asked Mother about going to New York. "But New York is too small a place for me", she answered.

"Well, what about the United States, Mother? You ought to find that large enough."

"No, Bishop," she replied. "For me the whole world is too small."

Pope Leo XIII summoned Mother to an audience. She had felt as if she could go anywhere in the world but, now that there was an actual prospect of going to United States, she felt timid. The night before her audience she had a dream-vision. She was on the bank of the Verna River placing flowers symbolic of her Sisters in a large paper boat to sail across the ocean, but she herself feared to get in the boat. Her mother appeared and said, "Francesca mine, and what is it? Afraid? Daughter, courage is wanting! Why did you say, 'I am going to be a missionary?' Did you mean it, or were you pretending? And now why are you reluctant to leave the Christian soil of your people?"

Then in silent procession came various saints and the Blessed Virgin Mary followed by the Sacred Heart of Jesus. He said, "My child and bride, what are you afraid of? Don't you know that your prayer brings passion and my love in return brings strength? I send you to bear my name in a distant land. Then, be courageous and fear not, for I am ever with you, and with me you can do all things."

Early in 1889, Mother knelt before Pope Leo XIII and told him of her ambition to go to China. But he decided that she should go to the United States and not to China because he foresaw that the United Sates would have great influence in the world. He wanted that to be a good influence through her missionary work

Mother's doctor had given her only two years to live but the Holy Father personally gave her his great commission, "No, not to the East, my daughter, but to the West." He entrusted to Mother the great need of the Italian immigrants – a superhuman task to a little, frail nun with no experience of working outside of the convent in large cities. Mother obediently received her commission from the Holy Father and got ready to leave for New York with six of her Sisters. She felt that obedience would take care of her health problems and everything else. "With the Pope's blessing," she said, "I would go with a feeling of security to the end of the world." Bishop Scalabrini promised to make the arrangements for the Sisters with New York's Archbishop Michael Corrigan.

The Mission Is Established

Mother arrived in New York on March 31, 1889, with six Sisters and 1,500 Italian immigrants on the ship *Bourgogne*. It was the end of an eight-day stormy voyage over the Atlantic from Le Havre, France on an old and slow ship. New York Archbishop Michael Corrigan had written Mother not to come, as he didn't approve of the site of her proposed orphanage. But Mother never received the letter and thought that they were expected. Since he did not expect them, the Archbishop had prepared no housing for them. So a priest led the Sisters to a shabby rooming house in Chinatown and they spent the night there. It was the closest that Mother would ever get to China. Weak and exhausted from the crossing, the Sisters spent the night on chairs in order to avoid the vermin-infested beds. This was a frightening change of pace for the Sisters. New York was a busy metropolitan city unlike rural Italy. They were strangers in a strange land.

The next morning they went to see the Archbishop to receive his welcome and their work assignment for the Italian immigrants and orphans in New York. He received them but appeared bewildered and embarrassed since he thought that Mother had received his letter. He advised her to return to Italy. Mother was stunned but calmly and firmly told the Archbishop that she had a commission from the Pope himself. She said, "No, your Excellency. No. We cannot do that. I came to New York under obedience to the Holy Father. And here I shall remain."

The Archbishop was impressed by her boldness and let them remain. He then personally led the nuns to a convent of the Sisters of Charity who provided them with food and shelter. They looked forward to opening their first orphanage.

The proposed orphanage was offered by a wealthy benefactress. However, she had acted without the Archbishop's authority. She had rented a building and had arranged for the Sisters to move to its location in mid-town Manhattan. The Archbishop didn't think that it was a suitable location since it was in the wealthy section and might stir up antagonism from the prejudiced wealthy against the poor Italians.

During the next three weeks, Mother prayed, begged and taught the children at St. Joachim's Church which was administered by the Scalabrini Fathers. Her humility, obedience and perseverance earned the Archbishop's admiration and he soon approved Mother's request to open the orphanage.

In a great sign of reconciliation and peace, the Archbishop personally went to the nun's convent on Palm Sunday carrying the palm branch that he had received at Mass in the Cathedral. He presented it to Mother as a blessed scepter for her mission. Mother's first orphanage began on May 3 with a Mass celebrated by the Archbishop.

A newspaper article told the story:

> This week young ladies with radiant faces dressed in plain black religious hoods and robes were seen coursing the overcrowded streets of Little Italy between the Ghetto and Chinatown, befriending and soliciting the Italians. They left no stones unturned, climbing the dark narrow-hallways of poverty to the top floors, descending murky cellar-ways into filthy basement flats, boldly entering questionable alleys, backyards and obscure areas into which not even the police would venture. They are the pioneers of a congregation called the Missionary Sisters of the Sacred Heart, and in the short period of a month have already founded a school and orphanage. It is not unlikely that after their devoted rounds these young religious ladies are rewarded with scant alms and the care of more of our vaunted city's shamefully neglected orphans.
>
> These young nuns hardly speak English. The Directoress of their congregation is "Madre Francesca Cabrini," a diminutive, youthful lady with great eyes and an attractive smiling face. She does not know the English language, but she knows the universal language of the human spirit.

Within four months, 400 orphans were sheltered at the Asylum of the Holy Angels supported by Mother's begging expeditions to the merchants and workers in "Little Italy." Mother and her Sisters visited the immigrants in their crowded tenement homes, their hospitals, workplaces and prisons. They taught religion to their children and prepared them for the sacraments. They taught evening classes in English for the adults and found food, clothing, shelter and jobs for them. They tended the sick, consoled the dying and buried the dead. The immigrants were happy to receive these works of mercy from nuns from their own country who spoke their own language.

In July, Mother returned to Italy for more Sisters to expand the American mission. While she was in Codogno a demented man set fire to the convent's woodshed. The wind was blowing towards the convent and the fire threatened to destroy it. Mother went up to the fire, prayed and made the Sign of the Cross. Then the wind changed direction and a heavy rain fell to smother the fire.

Mother also visited her houses in Lombardy and Rome. Once again, she received the Pope's blessing and sailed back to New York with seven Sisters.

The Archbishop's prudential judgment that the Manhattan orphanage location was unsuitable proved to be correct. Mother wanted to move and soon had a prophetic dream of a suitable site which she described to the Archbishop. He recognized the description as a site owned by the Jesuits near Peekskill on the Hudson River. They drove up there by carriage and she looked west across the River and recognized the place of her dream.

New York's West Park

The Jesuits ran a novitiate there named "Manressa" with 450 acres, country houses, barns and stables. The Jesuits agreed to sell it because it had a poor water supply. Mother raised the money to purchase it, renamed it "West Park" and moved hundreds of orphans into it from the slums of the city in the carriages of the rich. These children had never before seen country land and were filled with joy. The nuns taught them how to saddle horses, milk cows and goats and feed the chickens and pigs.

Mother prayed to Our Lady of Grace to help her locate water. Then Our Lady appeared to her in a dream and showed her where a well should be dug. Mother obeyed the dream, showed the well driller where to drill and he uncovered a mountain spring that assured the orphanage a limitless supply of clear water. Mother left a statue of Our Lady at the well site in thanksgiving.

In the meantime, her Sisters were working in Manhattan's "Little Italy" teaching in St. Joachim's church building since there was no school building. They taught amongst the interruptions and distractions of the use of the church for prayer and liturgies. Mother taught over 200 children there as well as catechism to the public school children there on Sundays.

Mother never waited until everything was perfectly in place before she started working. She started and worked with whatever was available. Soon, benefactors came to her aid and praised her for her works. She simply replied, "I am merely watching God perform wonders through us."

She wrote to her Sisters:

> Let us not be deterred by blind men's laws. Let us not shirk and dream and wait to help His children who are this moment in pain, in want, crushed and abandoned by the society of men who are mortal microscopic things compared to Christ! Let our bride's small hands do the work of a hundred hands and bring His love and aid to the lost souls, to the poor in prisons, tenements, streets, mines, hospitals, fields, and wherever is suffering! Missionary Daughters! If, then, we do not burn with intoxicating love, we do not deserve the beautiful title, "Bride of Heaven" which ennobles us, elevates us, makes us great and even a spectacle to the angels!

There were more than 200,000 Italians living in New York and each boat brought hundreds more. Mother wrote, "We are a small group that is swallowed up in such an infinite sea." Mother sailed the sea of the Atlantic Ocean on 25 occasions. Some of these crossings were dangerous.

One night her ship had to stop for repairs in the middle of the ocean. In the morning light they saw that the ship was surrounded by icebergs. Had the ship not needed to stop in the night, it probably would have collided with some of them.

On another voyage, her ship encountered a hurricane. Mother prayed. Other ships were wrecked but her ship was saved. Mother's faith in God's providence and the confidence with which she confronted her voyages earned her the name of "The Good Sailor."

Nicaragua

Mother returned to New York in September of 1891 with 29 Sisters. They brought the total of Mother's nuns in the United States to 50. She then sailed for Nicaragua with 14 Sisters on October 10 to open a school in Granada that a wealthy woman had requested. This was the beginning of her expanded mission to teach wealthy girls in Central and South America. Her only concern was to save souls, and she knew that the wealthy needed spiritual help just as much or more than the poor. Mother explained, "The world is only a small ball for the Missionary Sisters. See how the Infant Savior holds it in His hands!"

In Nicaragua, the Sisters endured stifling heat, insects, reptiles, earthquakes and typhoid fever. Three Sisters fell ill with this dreaded disease and Mother nursed them for days and nights during their delirium. She also noticed the results of social sexual promiscuity in the many illegitimate children. Mother refused to admit these children as students until their fathers had made them legitimate by law. This was to protect them so that they would be equal in the eyes of both God and society.

Mother then traveled through Nicaragua south towards Costa Rica with another nun by 12 steamers and some canoes and continued to suffer the same tropical miseries. She wrote, "We had as fellow passengers rats and all sorts of cheeky rodents. As Sister Cepeda and I had not much confidence in the designs of these small adventurers, we passed the nights dodging them, standing on boxes, and cheerfully finding motives in our fright to laugh at their antics."

She visited the Indians of the Mosquitia Riviera and wrote about them. "Overcoming their shyness and yielding to their respect for the 'Black Gowns,' as they called the Sisters and the priests, they begged us to send them Sisters and priests to instruct them and save them. The poor things! How I felt for them! I would have opened a house at once had I the means to do so." But she wasn't able to do so and two years later the nuns of the Nicaragua mission were expelled by a new anti-clerical government on two hours notice. As they walked away from the mission carrying their crucifixes one of the children said to the Superior, "Mother you are not crying! You are leaving us so calmly." The Mother gestured towards her crucifix and said, "We arrived with Him, and we are leaving with Him."

New Orleans

Mother Cabrini then went to New Orleans to help the Italians there. Many Italians had moved to New Orleans to work on the cotton plantations. However, they were subject to much discrimination. A raging mob of thousands battered down a local jail, shot nine Italian immigrants and publicly hanged two more. Two months later, Mother sent three nuns who begged their way there. When they reached New Orleans, they begged $17 and wired to Mother, "Success, please come!"

Mother came and joined them and they took up residence in a multifamily tenement. Mother bought it a week later. The tenement overlooked a courtyard which at night was a center of debauchery for the locals who drank, gambled, screamed, cursed and fought while the nuns tried to pray and rest. Soon the courtyard was turned into a center for Mass and religious instruction. Their house served as convent, church, day school and orphanage. It was also a center from which they visited, nursed and prayed for mothers in labor, the distraught, the prisoners, the sick and the dying. They also visited the plantation fields to bring mercy to the workers there.

New York's Columbus Hospital

In the spring of 1892, Mother returned to New York to check on the management of a small hospital. In 1891, the Scalabrini Fathers had asked her to take charge of this hospital for them to help bring mercy to the poor sick and injured Italians. Mother was reluctant to do so but she had a dream that convinced her otherwise. She saw the Blessed Virgin Mary with her sleeves rolled up and her skirt pinned back, going from one bed to another in a hospital ward as a nurse changing repulsive bed sheets and cleansing patients' ghastly wounds. As soon as Mother recognized her, she sprang forward offering her help. Mary said, "I am doing what you refuse to do." So Mother agreed to help the hospital.

However, the Scalabrini Fathers had mismanaged it and incurred debts that they wanted Mother to assume while they remained in control. Rather than to continue to take on the burden of the hospital, Mother prudently and charitably took on the burden of the patients. She removed 10 of them from the Scalabrinis' hospital and took them to a new one of her own. She begged and received $250 and used it to rent two adjoining houses. The Sisters bought old beds, made mattresses and cut out the sheets themselves. They bought food at a restaurant, warmed it on the stove and slept on the floor. A doctor donated some medical equipment and his services and Columbus Hospital was founded. It was named in honor of the Italian hero, Christopher Columbus, because the Italians were celebrating the fourth centenary of his discovery of the New World in 1892 and he was the first Italian immigrant.

Soon other doctors came and the public rallied to support the hospital. It was more than just an institution, it was more like a home where the patients were loved and refreshed both physically and morally. The nuns read them letters from their families in Italy and encouraged the patients to help each other and to develop friendships among themselves.

Italy

In late 1892, Mother was back in Italy where she remained for nearly two years visiting her houses, begging, opening a house and founding a college in Genoa. She visited Pope Leo XIII several times in private audience. On one occasion, he placed his hand on her head, drew her to himself and blessed her. Mother said, "It is like the Church opening its arms to the Missionary Sisters in an embrace."

On another occasion, she asked Cardinal Rampolla, the Secretary of State, to ask the Holy Father for a personal gift from his private funds for her work. The next time that she saw the Pope he said, "I hear that you want some of my own money. Here is a trifle I have for you," as he handed her a thousand dollars.

In the summer of 1894, she went to say good-bye to the Pope before returning to the United States. He blessed her and the Sisters with her and urged Mother to keep on working towards Heaven.

Mother smiled, "But I like work so much, Your Holiness, that I sometimes wonder whether it gives me any merit. Will work get me to Heaven?"

"Certainly it will," the Pope responded. "Heaven was made for all those who work like you! Courage, Cabrini, forward! Work onward until death! Let us work, and God bless you Cabrini. Let us work!"

New York

Mother sailed for New York in September. On the way home she wrote some exhortations for her Sisters:

> The Kingdom of God has no limits; its limits are those
> of the globe itself. Come, and let your glory be the glory
> of your celestial spouse, the working out of that celestial

talent – the sublime vocation of cooperating with Christ for the salvation of souls. Come, for in the Vineyard of the great Father of the Family we are to gather rich and copious sheaves. There are some who think they are too poor, ignorant and weak to undertake such work. Do not fear; mistrust yourselves and confide in God.

Mother returned to New York and opened a new and expanded Columbus Hospital in March of 1895. The nuns moved into it before its renovations were completed, worked manually with the construction men by day and slept in the unheated rooms at night when rain and snow blew through the broken windows. The new hospital was a vast improvement over its smaller predecessor. It had more than 100 beds, modern equipment and an excellent staff.

South America

Next Mother sailed for South America. She wrote, "I travel, work, suffer my weak health, meet with a thousand difficulties, but all these are nothing, for this world is so small. To me, space is an imperceptible object, as I am accustomed to dwell in eternity." On her way, she visited the nuns of the Nicaragua mission who had re-settled in Panama. From there she planned to travel to Buenos Aires, Argentina, where she had been invited to open a school by its Archbishop. She planned to sail down the coast of South America with Sister Chiara to Chile and from there cross the Andes Mountains to Argentina.

After four and a half months at Panama, she left for Argentina on October 11, 1895. During a frightening storm at sea she wrote, "The winds roar, heavens darken, the waves arise and threaten to turn the steamer topsy-turvy. All this matters nothing. I have given my trust, I must keep my word of honor, and with faith and confidence."

When they reached the end of the railroad line near the Andes, they were transferred to mule-drawn coaches and later to the backs of mules for the ascent. In her modesty, Mother would not let the mule leader hoist her into the saddle. She insisted that he get a stool for her and Sister Chiara to mount the mules. They climbed the cold, snowy, winding path on the edge of a precipice. She wrote, "Sister Chiara lost her speech. Her appearance of the most ultimate dejection, a picture of the world's end, made me laugh. No matter how often I told her to bravely sit up straight, she lay like a wet sack of flour on the mule's back, her head plunged down in refuge on the little animal's neck."

When they reached a deep crevice, the mules jumped across alone followed by the jumping nuns. Mother's jump was short but she was saved by the hand of the mule leader who pulled her to safety while Mother dropped exhausted and fainted onto the snow. She wrote, "I was very pleased to have ascended such high mountains, which gave me an inducement to incite myself to ascend the heights of spiritual perfection, a peak much higher than any in the Andes." Then they rode and slipped with their mules down the perilous mountain passes and took the train to Buenos Aires.

After Mother arrived in Buenos Aires, she trudged the city streets until she found a suitable school building. She bought it and then cabled to New York and Italy ordering Sisters to come immediately. This astounded the local priest who thought that she should wait to see if the school enrollment would justify their presence. Mother smiled and said, "Don't worry, Father, if I were to think too much about procuring the means, the Lord would withhold His graces. Just send the cables for me." Fifty students came and the Academy of St. Rose opened on March 1, 1896.

Mother was satisfied that its foundation was successful and sailed for Italy on August 8. Once again, she visited Pope Leo XIII. He had told a couple of her Sisters, "Mother Cabrini is truly a saint!" He inquired about all of her missions, confirmed her commission to go all over the world as a missionary and blessed her. After her audience she said, "The Pope has spoken! God has spoken through him. I shall go everywhere without fear. Oh, how powerful is the blessing of the Pope!" Three weeks later she was in Paris where she opened a ladies' boarding house on September 29.

United States

In 1898, Mother was back in the United States and established Catholic schools in the cities of New York, Newark, Scranton, Chicago and Denver. She opened an orphanage in Arlington, New Jersey and established Mother Cabrini High School in New York City. Mother Cabrini High School began as a boarding school for wealthy Italian girls called Sacred Heart Villa. Mother emphasized that the young girls of today were the wives and mothers of tomorrow and should be trained in sports, music, drama, domestic skills, good manners and good morals as well as scholastic subjects. Regarding the difference between educational quantity and quality, she said, "It is better to teach a few rightly than many wrongly, for the properly educated girl is the first link in a chain of interminable good." She wrote, "My Daughters, in your hands are the new generations. As educators you are obliged to form not only Christians for the glory of Christ and perpetuation of Holy Church, but also solid, patriotic citizens for the prosperity of the Nation and the felicity of the family. Thus it is yours to mold the decorum of spirit, State, family, and society."

The Newark school consisted of two empty adjoining stores divided by glass partitions into rooms that were very hot in summer and without heat in winter. The Sisters started out with 60 cents as their capital and gathered 400 students there who had no prior schooling.

Europe

In 1900, Mother established her mission in Spain. It consisted of a school and college in Madrid and two orphanages at Bilbao. She even had an audience with the Queen of Spain who provided her a good house and furnishings and asked her to be the personal governess of her children. Mother declined the offer but she opened a house for the daughters of the upper classes. This would serve as a reservoir for Spanish speaking Sisters to serve in South and Central America.

Mother went on to Italy and opened a boarding school and rest home for her nuns in Turin, two other convents and an orphanage elsewhere and a school and a chapel in Rome. She visited ninety-year-old Pope Leo XIII again and told him that she wanted the whole world for the Heart of Jesus.

"The Heart of Jesus!" cried the Pope. "Deepest in my heart is this devotion. The Heart of Jesus is the hope of the world! Cabrini, I say to you, you are the instrument of God. He has elected you to propagate this devotion!"

Next, Mother sailed for Genoa, Italy, while some of her Argentinean Sisters opened a house in Sao Paulo in Brazil. Then in November she sailed for Buenos Aires, Argentina, where she stayed for seven months. The nuns who had suffered from expulsion from Nicaragua and Panama joined her there in three new houses. Then she sailed back to Rome sick and exhausted.

Finally, she began to relieve herself of the administrative burdens that she had carried alone. She appointed delegates to represent her in each of the countries where her order served and gave instructions for the administration of the Institute. She was an invalid in Rome for weeks until one day Pope Leo XIII sent her a basket of oranges picked from his private grove. Soon after she had eaten some of them, she got out of bed and went to visit him for the last time. The oranges renewed her energy and she visited all of her houses in Italy and Paris, established her first house in England and set sail for the United States.

United States

In July 1902, Mother went to Denver, Colorado. The Bishop invited her to minister to the Italian mining colony there. His diocese consisted of the whole state and it exceeded the size of Italy. Mother opened a school for wayward children and a mission for the Italian miners. She went down into the mineshafts with them in cage hoists hundreds of feet into the dark bowels of the earth. She walked by candlelight through miles of low shafted tunnels to reach the miners. The Sisters also ate and talked with them in their camp shacks and built them a chapel for their Masses. The forgotten miners were thankful to hear in their own language that God loved them and that the nuns would teach their children.

Mother returned East where she opened an orphanage in Arlington, New Jersey, and added an annex to the overcrowded Columbus Hospital in New York. Then she left for Chicago in 1903 to found another Columbus Hospital. Chicago was the main city of the Midwest with stockyards filled with cattle shipped from the West and meat packing houses where the Italian laborers toiled and got injured. They and their families needed medical services. Mother begged for funds and purchased a former hotel for her hospital. Before the closing, she prudently inspected the boundaries. She had two of her Sisters measure the lot with a clothesline with knots a foot apart. They discovered that the sellers tried to keep for themselves a 25-foot wide strip of land on one end. Mother got title to the full plot.

Then she took a train for Seattle in the Wild West. She wrote, "What a place! Here, tempestuous men, wearing pistols like soldiers shoot each other without ceremony. In these wild and virgin territories there is no dearth of troublemakers, cheats, and violence." She built a house for a small church, a school and an orphanage. There was no bell to summon the people to Mass so the nuns climbed the hills calling the residents to come to Mass. Soon whole families happily followed the nuns to the church. Mother wrote, "Deprived of parish, priest and Altar, our Italians here have been many years away from God. Still, I found the Faith deeply rooted in them. Therefore, by means of kindness and courtesy it is not difficult to bring them back to God."

While in Seattle, Mother also became a United States citizen. She had a deep love for the United States. She wrote, "America? The Vicar of the Lord sent me here. Codogno is my heart and Rome is my intellect, but my wish is to die in this vast field of Christian hope."

From Seattle, she traveled on to New Orleans where she opened a new orphanage and then returned to Chicago. She learned that she had been cheated by the contractors who did the construction renovations for the hospital during her absence. She was overcharged for poor workmanship. She fired the contractors and became her own contractor, hired her own workers, supervised their work and completed the project four months earlier than the estimate of the original contractors. Chicago's Columbus Hospital opened on February 26, 1905.

Mother then received news from Italy that a small group of headstrong young nuns protested her manner of managing the Institute. They wanted to change the rules, modernize and liberalize it by rejecting total obedience to Mother who was an elderly Foundress. They presented their case to the Vatican. The Secretary of the Congregation answered them, "By the fruit is known the tree. Mother Cabrini's works blossom from the hand of God. She is a woman who by herself bears the weight of many houses. Your Mother Cabrini, dear Daughters, is a superior woman. I not only revere her, but humble myself at her feet."

Mother calmly wrote to her Daughters:

> Do not waste further time, Daughters always so dear to me, in vain fantasy. Keep your feet on earth, for fairy castles in the air you can never adorn. There is no easy way, no substitute for goodness and the imitation of your Spouse. I pardon you with my entire love no matter what you have said or done, but I do wish that your contrition and sacrifices come gladly from your willing hearts. In penitence make a Holy Communion after my intention,

and then let us think no more of the incident as though it had never occurred. The good Jesus blesses you and encloses you very well in His Sacred Heart.

This message of love and forgiveness converted the rebels back to loyalty to Mother.

By 1905, Mother's main centers of operations in the United States were in New York, New Orleans, Chicago, Denver, Seattle and Los Angeles. There she opened a school and an orphanage. In nearby Burbank, she opened the first tuberculosis sanitarium for girls in California.

In 1907, Mother celebrated the 25th anniversary of the Institute and Pope Pius X granted its final approval. At that time it had more than 1000 Sisters who cared for 5000 children in schools and 100,000 patients in hospitals. The Italian Ambassador to the United States said, "As Ambassador, I consider the illustrious Mother General of the Missionary Sisters a priceless collaborator; for while I work for the interest of Italy among the powerful, she succeeds in making it loved and esteemed by the humble, the infirm, and children."

Mother's Houses

Upon her arrival in Italy, Mother was received in audience by Queen Margherita with the *Grand Prix* in recognition of her work for the Italian immigrants. She decided to make a personal visit to each of the houses that she had founded so as to promulgate the Constitutions in person. So, at the end of 1907 she sailed to Buenos Aires which she had first visited 12 years before on the back of a mule. This time she went more comfortably by boat from Barcelona, Spain, after founding an orphanage at Canillas. In Argentina she also visited Sao Paulo, where the Italian immigrants formed one-third of the entire population.

Cardinal Arcoverde of Rio de Janeiro also called her. He said, "Mother, I have a million souls to save; come and help me." She arrived sick from malaria from which she suffered for the rest of her life. But this didn't slow her down. She said, "The doctor tells me I must have absolute rest, but the only absolute rest I hope for will come with my death. See, that is how it goes. When I had a great deal to do I had no time for the luxury of sickness, but as soon as I slacken my pace, I fall. The best medicine for me is to tackle a lot more work and to move faster – for when I move at high speed sicknesses can not catch up."

So she opened a school there on June 25, 1908 on the Feast of the Sacred Heart. Soon an epidemic of smallpox broke out there which brought down two of the Sisters. Mother nursed them herself as her sister Rosa had once nursed her for the same disease. She bathed them and applied cream with a feather to the pustules on their skin. One of the Sisters testified to her delicate care. She also testified that when she was sick at a later date Mother suddenly appeared to her, although she was then in Chicago. Mother bi-located to her, removed the wet bandages from her forehead and said, "Why are you lying here, my daughter? Get up and go about your duties!" Upon this the nun awoke, found her bandages gone and was perfectly healed.

Mother continued to establish houses seemingly out of thin air. Somehow, a hospital, an orphanage or a school sprung up from nothing. In the mystery of God's providence, He allowed Mother Cabrini's successes just as He had allowed Mother Duchesne's pioneering failures. She returned to the United States from Argentina and spent the next two years visiting all of her American houses.

In 1910, Mother was back in Chicago to establish another hospital. The Chicago Columbus Hospital was so successful that patients came to it from all over the United Sates. The Archbishop requested that she open another hospital strictly for charity patients. Mother picked out a large suitable property in a wealthy residential area. On impulse, she rang the bell and asked if the property could be sold. The wealthy owner sold it to her but the wealthy neighbors did not want a charity hospital in their neighborhood. They tried to scare her away because they thought that their property values would decline. They put political pressure on Mother to no avail.

Then some people tried to sabotage the project. They cut the water pipes in mid-winter and caused a flood of water that turned to ice. Mother and the Sisters broke up the ice with picks and axes. A few days later, her enemies started a fire in the basement. Mother and the Sisters fought the flames until the firemen arrived. Mother defended her property by moving 16 patients in before the completion of the project. "Our enemies," she said, "are not going to carry the fight to such lengths as to roast the sick poor to death in their beds." The hospital was then completed without further incident.

Mother for Life

In March of 1910, when Mother was 60 years old, sick and tired, after 30 years of arduous work, she sailed to Rome and requested permission to retire. She intended to return to the Mother House in Codogno, Italy, and spend her time in prayer and writing meditations for her Sisters. Unknown to her, the Sisters had collected ballots from the Sisters in all of the houses throughout the world and unanimously voted her as Mother for Life. They told this to Cardinal Tuto, the Prefect of the Sacred Congregation of Religious. So he prepared a decree for her lifetime appointment, dated it July 15, 1910, her 60th birthday, and summoned her for an audience.

As Mother stood and expected his acceptance of her resignation, he solemnly said, "Mother Francesca Xavier Cabrini, you petition to retire?"

"Yes, Your Eminence," she replied.

"Will you obey me Mother?"

"Of course, I have always been obedient."

"Very well," he said with a smile, "Since you have run your Institute so badly up to now, I have decided to give you another chance, in the hope that you will do better in the future. You are to remain the Superior General for the rest of your life as voted unanimously by your Sisters, this Congregation and Pope Pius X!"

She was now Mother for Life. Her Sisters presented their Mother with an album containing the signed names of everyone in the Institute and a long letter that expressed their love of her. But she had the last laugh. She asked, "But what about all of those who wanted to become Mother General? Now they have lost all hope!"

Mother sailed on to England where she transferred her Sisters to a large residence in a suburb of London. Then she returned to Codogno for a retreat after which she organized the archival documents of the history of the Institute. She was putting her houses in order. Then she called for her old nemesis Madame Antonia Tondini to be brought to the convent. She was the eccentric former Superior of the House of Providence where Mother began her novitiate. In a beautiful scene of reconciliation, Mother knelt before her.

"But why do you kneel?" Madame Tondini asked in astonishment.

Mother replied, "I want you to forgive me for anything that I did that grieved you."

Madame Tondini put her arms around Mother and drew her to her feet. "No. Francesca, I should kneel to you. I always knew you were a saint."

"Reverend Mother," Francesca said, "you must not say that. Just tell me that you have forgiven me."

"Child, child!" Madame cried as the tears flowed.

"*Child!*" said Francesca, "Call me that again! It's so long since anybody called me anything but *Mother*. And that's what I am, though I don't want to be. I was a bad child to you, Antonia."

They laughed and embraced as Antonia said, "Just you and I are left now, Francesca. They are all dead and I am over 80. But you did me good, my little daughter. You saw where the embittered woman was going. You prayed for me?"

"Every day I have prayed for you, Antonia. And now you make me so happy."

"I'm happy too," replied Antonia, "hearing of all the wonderful things you do in America and all over the world. You always wanted to be a missionary. But if I had been a good nun, you would still be stuck in the House of Providence. You see how God works, Francesca!"

Later, a Sister who had witnessed the moving scene asked Mother, "Didn't she cause you much harm Mother?"

Mother replied, "Madame Tondini was a gift to me from God. He allowed her not to know any better and she thought that her treatment of me was for my own good and, in fact, God allowed that it was."

Mother then returned to Rome where she convalesced for months from chronic anemia and a severe malarial attack. One day she decided that work would be her medicine so she got out of bed and packed for New York. She decided that it needed a new Columbus Hospital to replace the overcrowded original. She left Italy on March 22, 1911 for the last time.

Mother spent months in New York trying to raise $200,000 to get the Columbus Hospital project started. She was not successful and exhausted herself. She collapsed in her room nearly dead. Her Sisters decided to move her to Colorado to convalesce where she settled in a log cabin on a mountain. After weeks of rest and prayers, she decided that the children of Los Angeles needed another school. When she got there, she learned that an amusement park was scheduled for demolition. She gathered her Sisters and an army of workers to salvage the buildings. For 31 days they salvaged and moved all of the building materials to her school site.

In 1904, Mother had established the Queen of Heaven Orphanage in Denver, Colorado. It was located in a residential neighborhood. Mother desired a rural property to give her orphans recreation in a natural outdoor environment. So in 1910, she purchased some rural land on the east slope of Lookout Mountain in Golden, Colorado. A farming operation with poultry, dairy cows and other livestock was established and maintained by three of the Sisters. During the summer months, girls from the inner-city orphanage came to enjoy several weeks of freedom at the farm. On her last visit there in 1912, Mother Cabrini gathered some white stones and formed an outline of the Sacred Heart on the highest point on Lookout Mountain, overlooking the city of Denver. Later, a 22-foot statue of the Sacred Heart was constructed there.

Early in 1913, she went to Seattle to establish another orphanage. She had a dream of a house for her orphanage. She saw a beautiful house on a hilltop. The next day, she placed a map of Seattle in front of her Sisters, pointed out a location and asked them to go there to see what they'd find. They came back and reported that they had found a beautiful hilltop villa.

The next day, Mother went with some Sisters and saw for herself that it was the property that she had seen in her dream. The owner said that it belonged to his wife and that she was very attached to it. The nuns left for their convent and while walking back, Mother waved down a chauffeur-driven limousine and asked for a ride. The woman in the limousine was happy to help the Sisters and gave them a ride. As they drove, Mother told her about the house of her dream for her orphans. When they later arrived at the convent and were saying good-bye, the woman told Mother, "Mother Cabrini, that house you dreamed of is mine, I own it. I never thought of parting with it, but if I may be allowed to enter your Holy House for a moment and receive from your hands a glass of water in the name of Our Lord, your little orphans shall have their home with my blessing."

When asked later by the Archbishop how she had obtained such a beautiful property, Mother said, "I paid for it with three treasures: my love, a dream, and a glass of water in His Name."

As World War I broke out in Europe on June 28, 1914, Mother's heart was with her suffering Sisters in France and England. She wrote to them:

> Dearest Daughters, let the mantle of your charity cover
> all without question. Gather all the dependents of the

dead and wounded and homeless. Now is the hour to stretch out your hands to all victims of disaster, the poor, the rich, the believing, and the unbelieving. From your bastion of Christ's love Providence will not be lacking, but will abide with you in abundance. Take to yourself the abandoned babies, for they are His emissaries of the future on earth, the Christian fathers and mothers of a better tomorrow.

Mother's last major acquisition was of the Perry Hotel in Seattle in the summer of 1915. She was ill when she set out from New York and she remained ill throughout the hot, fatiguing five-day trip. She understood that God wanted her to begin a new orphanage and said, "If God wants this mission accomplished, He will return to me the strength that I have lost. He will give me the strength for it."

She decided to buy the Perry Hotel in the center of the city. She learned that the major stockholder was a certain Mr. Clarke in New York. She made no further inquiries since she didn't want to alarm the other stockholders who would probably prevent the acquisition. She telegrammed the Sisters in New York to locate him and ask for the hotel as a gift. The Sisters telephoned every Mr. Clarke in New York until they found the owner of the Perry Hotel. Then they went to him and asked him to give the hotel to their Institute. He understandably declined. Then they negotiated a bargain price of $150,000 that he accepted, to the dismay of the other stockholders.

Mother then begged and applied for loans but she only received $30,000 and no loans. She still needed another $120,000. The other stockholders, who were influential Seattle businessmen, frustrated all of her attempts to get a loan from a local bank. Mother struggled on for five months and still couldn't raise the money. So she turned to the Blessed Virgin Mary.

In her other house in Seattle, there was a statue of the child Mary standing and reading a book that was held in one hand of her standing mother, St. Anne, who pointed to the book with her other hand. Mother wrote on the book, "A hundred and twenty thousand dollars" and said, "There! Now she can't help seeing it." Soon after, on the eve of her deadline to fulfill her sales contract, the president of the Scandinavian Bank appeared at her convent door. Mother received him and told him of her need for a loan of $120,000. He agreed to loan her the money and she finally bought the Perry Hotel the next day on April 21, 1916.

Rest

In her lifetime, Mother established 67 elementary schools, high schools, hospitals, orphanages and other missions. She established one institution for every year of her life. "Rest?" she would exclaim, "We will have all eternity in which to rest. Now let us work." But all of her work was the fruit of her prayer. She once wrote, "I would become weak and languid and risk losing myself if I were to occupy myself only with exterior things or if I were to be without the sleep of prayer in the heart of my beloved Jesus."

Her only rest was on her long sea cruises where she also had the time to write letters to her Sisters. They would read these at recreation time for their education, inspiration and entertainment. Mother wrote, "How sweet and good it is to go to sea, tired and drained from the work of the missions!"

In 1917, Mother was still "tired and drained from the work of the missions" and her health deteriorated. She had contracted malaria when she was in South America in 1908 and its effects were still debilitating her. She rested in the warm climate of Los Angeles until spring when she returned to Chicago. She staggered off the train nearly dead from exhaustion and malaria. The Sisters hoped that a stay at the Columbus Hospital would cure her. They took her for automobile rides in the country every morning. She was reminded of her early farm life and the beauty of God's creation. So she bought a farm for the Institute to help to supply the hospital with farm products.

As Christmas neared, Mother learned that the local priest was unable to distribute the usual Christmas candy to the children because of the sugar shortage during the war. Mother said, "What! No candy for the little ones? Christmas would not be Christmas! We'll provide the candy as usual, war or no war."

So she spent the day of December 21 with her Sisters, wrapping Christmas presents and filling bags of candy for the children. She wrapped a special gift of a desk set for a long time friend, Cardinal Mundelein of Chicago. Shortly before noon on the next day, December 22nd, she was found collapsed in a chair in her room, her clothes stained with blood.

There was just enough time for a priest to come and administer the sacrament of Extreme Unction. Then Mother turned a last look on to her Sisters and died at age 67. Fourteen years after her death, two Sisters went to China and began to work in the country that had originally held Mother's heart as a child.

Interior Life

All of Mother's missionary activity was carried on in an un-hurried manner. In the midst of her whirlwind activities she maintained her recollection in the presence of God. She was never in a hurry and always in a spirit of detached peace. Her prayer life nourished her active life and provided the wisdom and prudence to make her decisions in conformity and obedience to the will of God.

Mother continually practiced prayer in the midst of all of her activities. She wrote, "Pray, pray always, and ask unceasingly for the spirit of prayer. What is the spirit of prayer? It means praying according to the Spirit of Jesus, in Jesus and with Jesus. The spirit of prayer means praying in accordance with the divine good pleasure, willing only what God wills. It means that we have our minds fixed on prayer at all times, in all places, working, walking, eating, speaking, suffering; habitually and always."

We should pray habitually and always, she wrote, because:

> The salvation of mankind does not depend on material success, nor on sciences that cloud the intellect. Neither does it depend on arms and human industries, nor on sterile and diplomatic congresses, nor worldly means. Pray much, for the conversion of sinners and the sanctification of souls does not depend on human eloquence, or the grace of style and rhetoric, but upon our Spouse Jesus alone, who enlightens the mind, moves the will, sows virtue, and animates us to undertake perfect works.

One day she confided to one of her Sisters, "If I followed my secret desires I would go to West Park and there, far from all distractions, do many beautiful things for the Institute. But because I see that the Lord does not wish this of me for the time being, I forget solitude and attend to the affairs of the Order. In this way I carry out God's will, even on the street, on the train, aboard ship – everywhere I feel as though I were meditating in my cell."

One of the Sisters once asked Mother what to do when her prayers were not answered. "Do?" Mother replied, "Thank God all the more!" At such times she herself would say, "I thank Thee, dear Jesus, that Thy will and not mine has been done."

Mother's interior life was the life of a crucified victim soul who practiced the presence of God in a state of constant interior recollection while focused on the present moment, abandoned in confidence to God's providence. She practiced and recommended the "crucifixion of the spirit" against self-will and self-love. Her life was one continuous mortification and self-discipline. She cheerfully endured chronic ill health and said that we should "walk on thorns and let it not be seen, to love humiliation, to love the Cross." However, an even quicker way was to fly. She said, "Free yourselves; put on wings and fly. The road to Heaven is so narrow, steep and thorny that only by flying can one travel over it."

She did not practice nor recommend austere penitential methods, such as the wearing of a hair shirt. She said, "Contradictions, there is the real, sharp hair shirt! If you love penance, there is a penance that has made saints and which all can practice, even with the weakest health. It is a hair shirt that you can wear not for an hour but all day long."

Mother was also docile to the voice of Jesus and promptly obeyed. She said, "Jesus speaks and passes by. The Sacred Heart of Jesus acts so quickly that I can hardly follow Him." Her confidence in Jesus was increased by her humility. She said, "I am imperfect and full of failings, what shall I do? Discouragement, anxiety and worry keep us away from our merciful Jesus. It is an offense to the Sacred Heart, this lack of confidence in His love and gracious bounty."

All who met Mother received the impression that they were the most important person in the world, and for the moment nothing else mattered to Mother but them. While she talked to them she seemed focused only on them, but she was continually in intimate communion with Jesus. She kept an interior cloistered heart in the midst of a bodily whirl of exterior activities. She wrote, "The soul learns that there is no necessity to look for her Beloved outside her own being, and that she can find Him within herself, as in His own throne and in His tabernacle."

She wrote, "The science of suffering is the science of the saints. My book will be the crucifix, and I will always keep it before my eyes to learn how to love and to suffer. I wish to die of love after a life of total surrender to God. Oh Jesus, I love You so much, so much! I am being consumed by Your love; for You I languish and die; but in spite of such intense ardor, I see – I feel – that it is only a pale shadow compared to the fire of love with which You surround me. Give me a heart as large as the universe, so that I may love You, if not as much as You deserve, at least as much as I am capable of. I am Your victim, ready to be sacrificed; do with me as You will."

Virtues

Mother Cabrini was very patient in following her vocation. She completed her unorthodox "novitiate" after six years with the eccentric Madame Tondini. Then she had the faith to found a new order of missionary nuns when there was no precedent for them. She accepted new candidates before she had any way to support them. She simply abandoned herself to Divine Providence and trusted in God. In the same way, she founded all of her institutions. She was faithful to God's inspiration and went forward without the means trusting that He would provide. God in turn honored her trust.

Her deep love of God was shown in her love of neighbor by her heroic practice of the works of mercy in teaching, caring for orphans, feeding the hungry, nursing the sick and visiting prisoners.

In her humility, she forgave her rebellious Sisters who tried to usurp her as Superior. She also forgave Mother Tondini for her ill-treatment at the House of Providence and even went so far as to beg her forgiveness for any wrongs that she had done to her.

She was always obedient to those in authority over her, even to the extent of accepting her appointment as Mother for Life when she had hoped to retire and rest from her exhausting labors. Mother was ever docile to the voice of Jesus and promptly obeyed Him. Her confidence in Him increased her humility. She could see all of her failings and all of His successes.

Fruits

Mother was as pragmatic as a stereotypical American. She got things done in an efficient, quick, economical and productive manner. Her journeys and accomplishments, in spite of great difficulties and obstacles, are almost unbelievable and seem humanly impossible considering her limited education, lack of business training and experience and her frail health. Although she lacked all of these, she was still a shrewd, iron-willed businesswoman when she needed to be. She listened, studied, inspected and contemplated, so that she could find the best location for a new school, hospital or orphanage. But these works were mainly the fruits of her prayer. Her prayer was, "Convert me, Jesus, convert me completely to yourself, for if you do not make me a saint, I will not know how to work in your vineyard and will end by betraying your interests, instead of rendering them successful."

Her lack of learning and experience did not intimidate her. "Neither science nor speculation has ever made, or ever will make, a saint," she claimed. "Better to be an idiot capable of love, because in love he will sanctify himself."

Mother's Institute expanded to over 1000 Sisters who served in 67 institutions in eight countries on three continents. Her charitable institutions seemed to sprout from nothing in a whirlwind of activity. It was an extraordinary demonstration of her faith and her works of mercy in cooperation with the mighty power and works of God. With no money or means and little help from others, she bought, furnished, staffed and administered her institutions.

Mother simply went forward with the means at hand confident that God would supply what was lacking. "Don't worry," she would say with a smile, "if I were to think too much about procuring the means, the Lord would withhold his graces. We have nothing, yet we spend millions." No obstacle could stop her. She wrote, "Difficulties! What are they, Daughters? They are the mere playthings of children enlarged by our imagination, not yet accustomed to focus itself on the Omnipotent. Who is not weak? But with God's help you can do everything. He never fails the humble and faithful." This little frail woman demonstrated the truth of her motto, the words of St. Paul, "I can do all things through Him who strengthens me."

At the time of her death, Cardinal Mundelein recalled the paradox of her dynamic power in so frail a body. He said, "When we contemplate this frail little woman, in the short space of two-score years, recruiting an army of 1,000 women under the banner of the Sacred Heart of Jesus, dedicated to a life of poverty and self-sacrifice, fired by the enthusiasm of the Crusaders of old, burning with love of their fellowmen, crossing the seas, penetrating into unknown lands, teaching them and their children by word and example to become good Christians and law-abiding citizens, befriending the poor, teaching the ignorant, washing the sick, all without hope of reward or recompense here below – tell me, does not all this fulfill the concept of a noble woman?"

Saint

Mother was beatified in 1938 after Pope Pius XI waived the rule requiring a lapse of 50 years after death. She was canonized in 1946 and was the first United States citizen to be canonized. Her Feast Day is celebrated on November 13, which is the day before the anniversary of the foundation of the Missionary Sisters of the Sacred Heart.

When Pope Pius XII canonized her, he said, "May the nations learn from her, who loved her homeland with an ardent love and who spread to other countries the treasures of her charity and her works, that they are called to form one family. This family must never spread unrest and rivalries, nor the enmities eternally engaged in seeking revenge for old insults. This family must be united in the fraternal love whose source is found in Christ's commandment and His divine example."

One of the miracles brought through Mother's intercession was the complete cure of a baby boy at Columbus Hospital. He was blinded by an overdose of silver nitrite solution poured into his eyes by a careless nurse. His eyes burned out, but his eyesight was restored after prayers for Mother's help.

A second miracle was the cure of a Sister who was given only days to live. However, after prayers for Mother's help, she too was cured and continued to live for another 20 years.

After her canonization, the Holy Father spoke to some American pilgrims and described Mother Cabrini's life as "a vast, marvelous epic of struggles and victories." "Crossing oceans and continents," he said, "conquering the world for Christ, she could say, 'The world is too small to satisfy my desires.' "

Before he became Pope Pius XI and beatified Mother in 1938, Achille Ratti once remarked to his housekeeper and asked her a question that applies to everyone. "Did you see that little nun who came for advice here? She has crossed the Atlantic Ocean more than twenty times; she has also founded many institutions of charity in Europe and the United States of America. A great missionary, yes, and a saint! And what have *we* done, for the glory of God during our whole lifetime?"

In 1996, on the 50th anniversary of her canonization, Pope John Paul II called Mother Cabrini "Missionary of the New Evangelization." Mother's intercession is necessary in the New Evangelization particularly for the many immigrants still coming to the United States from foreign lands. They come as refugees from persecution, war and famine as well as the immigrants who come illegally from Latin America and the Caribbean as refugees from poverty. Mother wrote in one of her letters a prophecy of her intercession for them and for us, "In the adorable Heart of Jesus, I can always find you. He is our comfort, our way, our life. To Him I shall confide all your needs. I will speak to Him of each one of you in particular. I know the wants of every one of you. I will take a great interest in you and keep you close to my heart – you may be sure of this."

Opening Prayer for the Mass in Commemoration of Frances Xavier Cabrini

God our Father,
you called Frances Xavier Cabrini from Italy
to serve the immigrants of America.
By her example teach us concern for the stranger,
the sick and the frustrated.
By her prayers help us to see Christ
in all the men and women we meet.
Grant this through our Lord Jesus Christ, your Son,
who lives and reigns with you and the Holy Spirit,
one God, for ever and ever.

Shrines:

Mother Cabrini Shrine
20189 Cabrini Boulevard
Golden, Colorado 80401
Telephone: 303-526-0758
Website: www.den-cabrini-shrine.org/index.htm

Mother Cabrini High School
701 Fort Washington Avenue
New York, NY 10040
Telephone: 212-923-3540
Website: www.cabrinihs.com
The chapel of Mother Cabrini High School houses the body of Mother Cabrini. It is exposed at the foot of the altar enclosed in glass.

19. New Needs – Those Left Behind

The American Dream of success and fortune through education, equal rights and opportunity was realized by many but also left many behind, notably the Western Native Americans and the African-Americans.

Western Native Americans

The peoples of the United States became an amalgamation of Native Americans, African-Americans and Europeans. The first Americans arrived in a series of migrations from the Asian continent across the Bering Strait thousands of years ago. They divided into different tribes and populated all of America. When Christopher Columbus discovered America, he mistakenly called them Indians because he thought that he had discovered the Indies. Now they are also called Native Americans.

By the 20th century, the collision, diseases and conquests of the Europeans and their descendants decimated all of the Indian tribes in the United States. The Eastern woodland Indians whom the Europeans first encountered, were virtually extinguished. The great tribes of the Algonquin, the Iroquois and the Huron nations no longer hunted and fished in the eastern woodlands.

The Cherokees in the South, who lived like American settlers with houses, farms, roads and churches, written language and an organized tribal government, were forcibly removed to a so-called "reservation" in Oklahoma because whites discovered gold on their land in 1828. Three thousand whites settled onto their land and mistreated the Cherokees. In 1838, the United States Army forced the tribe to march at gunpoint to Oklahoma. The Cherokees joined the Choctaws, the Creeks and the Chickasaws who had already been forced to leave their lands to settle in the so-called "Indian Territory." On the long arduous journey, thousands of Cherokees died. It is called the Trail of Tears.

In 1860, the American West comprised about half the total area of the United States. It was mostly unsettled wilderness and the territory of Indian tribes – the Sioux, Blackfoot, Nez Perce and Crow of the northern plains; the Ute, Cheyenne and Kiowa of the middle region; the Comanche and Apache of the south and the Pueblo, Hopi and Navajo of the southwest.

Mother Duchesne's friend, Father De Smet, was a missionary to the Western Indians in Montana, Idaho, Oregon and the Great Plains. He traveled 250,000 miles on foot, horseback and boat, promoting peace and establishing missions. From 1851 to 1868, he mediated peace treaties between the various Indian tribes and the United States. However, the Indians soon went on the warpath because the government broke many of these treaties and the railroads crossed Indian lands with "sport" hunters who annihilated the buffalo which was the Indians' food, clothing, shelter and tool supplier. Then gold was discovered and prospectors invaded the Indians' territory and cattlemen and sheep men claimed vast grasslands to feed their livestock. The United States Army was sent to forcibly remove these Indians to reservations. Many Indians were killed including men, women and children. They grew tired of fighting, starving and freezing. They were sick at heart.

Nez Perce Chief Joseph best expressed this in his surrender message to General Oliver Howard in 1876. "I am tired of fighting. Our chiefs are killed. The old men are all dead. He who led the young men is dead. It is cold and we have no blankets. The little children are freezing to death. Hear me, my chiefs, I am tired. My heart is sad and sick. From where the sun now stands, I will fight no more forever."

The Western Indian wars continued until the late 1880s. The United States Army defeated the Indians everywhere and placed them on reservations. They were utterly defeated.

On December 15, 1890, Chief Sitting Bull was murdered by federal Indian police when they attempted to arrest him at his home on the Standing Rock Reservation. His followers fled with his half-brother, Chief Big Foot, to seek refuge at the Pine Ridge Reservation in South Dakota. Chief Red Cloud had invited him to come there to help make peace. The Seventh Cavalry intercepted Chief Big Foot and about 356 of his followers and escorted them to a campsite at Wounded Knee Creek. The Indians were surrounded and harassed all night. A trader from Pine Ridge brought a barrel of whiskey and the officers and troopers got drunk celebrating Big Foot's capture.

On December 29, they attempted to disarm Chief Big Foot's band. The women and children were separated from the men. The soldiers were very abusive. Chief Big Foot was sick with pneumonia and flying a white flag of truce next to his tent. The Indians were almost completely disarmed and completely surrounded by the soldiers. When the soldiers attempted to take the rifle of a deaf mute, it discharged and the soldiers opened fire on the Indians. About 300 Indians, men, women and children were killed along with 30 soldiers, many of them shot in their own crossfire. Some women and children were later found as far as two miles away, gunned down by soldiers.

On January 3, a burial party finally picked up the bodies of the dead Indians after a raging blizzard swept through the massacre site. They dug a mass grave and buried the dead, stomping on the bodies to fit them into the mass grave. This was the United States' last battle against the Indians. The Indian wars were over and so was the Indian way of life.

By 1891, most Indians lived on reservations and most of these were west of the Mississippi River. Reservation life was supposed to civilize and educate the Indians to become useful citizens. However, the reservation policy of the United States is a history of good intentions and a legacy of failure.

African-Americans

The European Atlantic slave trade was the largest forced migration in world history. Millions of Africans were forcibly removed from their homeland into slavery. From the mid-15th century to the mid-19th century, about 15 million Africans were captured and brought across the Atlantic Ocean in chains on ships in coffin-like quarters for forced labor throughout America. The United States imported about 750,000 of these from 1619 to 1808.

Europeans captured Africans and marched them to the African coast. There they were placed into pens like animals, branded and later placed aboard a ship. The average ship held about 400 slaves, chained in groups and stacked below decks like cadavers in a mortuary. About 15% of them died on the way because they had below decks temperatures of over 100 degrees, little food or water, and many diseases and punishments. When they arrived in the United States, they were again placed in pens, freshened up and put on the auction block for sale to labor in the fields and homes of Americans.

The auctioneers broke up families and many slave owners encouraged promiscuous relations among their slaves so that the children born of such relations could replace older or weaker slaves. Many slaves died from exhaustion, disease and poor diet. It was cheaper for the slave owners to buy or breed new slaves to replace them than to provide adequate food, clothing, shelter and care for the slaves that they owned.

Venerable Pierre Toussaint was an African-American Catholic slave born in Haiti in 1766. His parents raised him as a Catholic and his master, Jean Berard, taught him to read and write. In 1787 his master moved to New York City to escape the social unrest among the Haitian slaves after the French Revolution. He thought that Pierre should have a profession in New York, so he apprenticed him to a hairdresser. Pierre was a contemporary of Mother Seton in the early 19th century and a very successful hairdresser for New York socialites.

At that time, wealthy women had their hair decorated in elaborate fashions and a good hairdresser like Pierre made a decent living. Moreover, he had a quiet wit and was discreet. These qualities led his clients, who included Mrs. Alexander Hamilton, to confide in him and seek his advice. Pierre heard about these women's problems such as sickness and errant husbands and children.

When people tried to pry some gossip from him, he said, "Toussaint dresses hair; he is no news journal." He frequently quoted the Beatitudes and *The Imitation of Christ* in the spiritual guidance that he gave to his clients and he encouraged them to pray and patiently trust in God. They also supported Pierre in his charitable works. For 60 years, he attended daily Mass at six in the morning at the same church where Mother Seton later worshipped. Later, he cooperated with her new order and established one of the first orphanages in New York.

Pierre's master died and a slave rebellion on Haiti destroyed his widow's support and left her in a deep depression. Pierre then supported the Berard household while still their slave. He refused to let the widow Berard lose her dignity or be burdened with the concerns of running a household, so he personally took over all the household expenses. He bought his sister's freedom, but decided to remain a slave himself so that he could care for Madame Berard. Often he put on great parties for Madame, paid for everything, yet dressed as a butler and served the guests. He even postponed his own wedding to care for Madame.

When his sister criticized him for supporting Madame while still her slave, Pierre answered, "I never felt enslaved but felt compassion for a lonely woman who was considered my owner." Madame Berard finally gave Pierre his freedom on her deathbed. Pierre "thanked God he was able to keep this woman from knowing want and thanked God for giving her the courage to set him free."

At last, at the age of 41, Pierre was free. He bought the freedom of his sister's best friend, Juliette, whom he married. Together, they continued the charitable works that Pierre had begun. They helped refugees find jobs, cared for orphans and opened a school to teach black children a trade. They also provided financial help to the Oblate Sisters of Providence.

When New York was hit with a plague, Pierre risked his life and nursed the sick and dying without regard to his own safety. His sister Rosalie said, "You think of everyone but yourself. Now that you are free, you are still acting like a white man's slave."

Pierre answered, "I have never felt I am a slave to any man or woman but I am a servant of the Almighty God who made us all. When one of His children is in need, I am glad to be His slave."

When Rosalie died leaving a young daughter, Pierre and Juliette welcomed her into their home. They had no children of their own and took abandoned boys into their home, educated them and found them employment.

Pierre walked to his hair appointments with his rheumatic knee rather than subject himself to the discrimination of public transportation. He kept on working and gave a substantial part of his considerable income to the poor, telling a friend who urged him to retire, "I have enough for myself, but if I stop working I have not enough for others."

Pierre's wife died in 1851 and two years later he died on June 30, 1853 at age 87. His last words were, "God is with me," and then, when asked if he wanted anything, "Nothing on earth." General Schuyler said, "I have known Christians who were not gentlemen or gentlemen who were not Christians – but one man I know who is both – and that man is black."

At Pierre's funeral Mass, attended by an overflowing crowd, he was eulogized from the pulpit by the pastor, Father William Quinn. "A stranger would not have suspected that a black man of his humble calling lay in the midst of us. Though no relative was left to mourn him, yet many present would feel they had lost one who always had wise counsel for the rich, words of encouragement for the poor, and all would be grateful for having known him. There are few left among the clergy superior in devotion and zeal for the Church and the glory of God, among laymen, none."

Pope John Paul II visited St. Patrick's Cathedral where Pierre is buried in October 1995, and said, "Beneath the high altar of this Cathedral, together with the former Cardinals and archbishops of New York there is buried the Servant of God, Pierre Toussaint, a married man, a one-time slave from Haiti. What is so extraordinary about this man? He radiated a most serene and joyful faith, nourished daily by the Eucharist and visits to the Blessed Sacrament. In the face of constant, painful discrimination he understood, as few have understood, the meaning of the words, 'Father, forgive them; they do not know what they are doing.' " Pope John Paul II declared Pierre Venerable in 1996.

In 1839, Pope Gregory XVI condemned the slave trade, but on March 6, 1857, in the Dredd Scott decision, the United States Supreme Court ruled that a Negro is not a citizen of the United States under the United States Constitution. President Lincoln soon answered, "We think the Dredd Scott decision is erroneous."

Slavery finally ended after the terrible suffering of the Civil War. God said, "For your own life-blood, too, I will demand an accounting . . . and from man in regard to his fellow man I will demand an accounting for human life." (Gen. 9:5). Echoing this, President Abraham Lincoln referred to the Civil War and to slavery in his Second Inaugural Speech on March 4, 1865:

> Woe unto the world because of offences! . . . this terrible war [is] the woe due . . . . Yet, if God wills that it continue, until all the wealth piled by the bond-man's two hundred and fifty years of unrequited toil shall be sunk, and until every drop of blood drawn with the lash, shall be paid by another drawn with the sword, as was said three thousand years ago, so still it must be said, "the judgments of the Lord, are true and righteous altogether."

Although slavery finally ended after the Civil War, discrimination against African-Americans continued and was even legalized by the same United States Supreme Court that had previously legalized slavery. In the 1896 case of *Plessy v. Ferguson*, the Supreme Court ruled that there could be "separate but equal" public facilities and accommodations for whites and African-Americans. These facilities and accommodations included public schools, restaurants, hotels and transportation. They were certainly separate but never equal.

20. Saint Damien de Veuster and Lepers

Born   January 3, 1840
Died   April 15, 1889
Canonized   October 11, 2009
Feast Day   May 10
              "Servant of Humanity"

"The sacrifice is great indeed for one who tenderly loves his parents, his family, his brother and the land of his birth. But the voice that has called upon us to make a generous sacrifice of all is the voice of God Himself." October 30, 1863 letter from St. Damien to his parents before his departure for Hawaii.

Leprosy

The first Europeans to reach the Hawaiian Islands arrived in 1778 with English Captain James Cook. There were then about 250,000 inhabitants but this number was reduced to 60,000 within 100 years because of the diseases that the Europeans brought with them such as smallpox, syphilis, tuberculosis and leprosy.

Leprosy, now known as Hansen's disease, was the most terrifying of the diseases encountered by the Hawaiians. The biblical solution was segregation. When a leprosy epidemic broke out in Hawaii in the 1860's, they employed the same solution. The government ordered that anyone with leprosy, regardless of age or gender, be exiled to a narrow peninsula on the island of Molokai. This peninsula was a natural prison since it was surrounded by the sea and high cliffs. No one could swim or climb away.

The lepers had poor food and shelter and there was no law and order. It was survival of the fittest with thefts, fights, rapes, drunkenness, sexual immorality and orgies. The weak, especially women and children, were easily abused and exploited. The dead were thrown into shallow graves that pigs and dogs dug up to eat the corpses.

Into this living graveyard came Father Damien De Veuster, a former Belgian farm boy, who became a priest in the Congregation of the Sacred Hearts of Jesus and Mary. He came to serve a life sentence, since living with other islanders was forbidden once he went to live with the lepers.

Father wrote, "I am bent on devoting my life to the lepers. It is absolutely necessary for a priest to live here. The afflicted are coming here by the boatloads." For the next 16 years, Father Damien taught the lepers to farm, to raise animals, to play musical instruments and to sing. He organized a band and a choir. He restored their sense of human dignity. He was a skilled carpenter and he taught the lepers to build everything from cottages to coffins. He organized the lepers into the Christian Burial Association to provide funerals and decent burials for the dead. He reverenced the dead and fenced the cemetery to protect their graves from the animals. He ministered to the sick bodies and administered the sacraments for their souls. He was not afraid to touch them, heedless of the danger to himself. He finally caught the disease and died from it by doing so.

Formation and Vocation

Father Damien was born and baptized with the name Joseph in Tremolo, Belgium, on January 3, 1840. His parents nicknamed him Jef. He was the seventh of eight children. His father pulled him out of school at age 13 to work on the family farm, but five years later he sent him off for more education to prepare for a future in grain dealing. His father was a grain farmer and he and his wife raised Jef and his siblings in the Catholic faith. Joseph's mother edified her children and read them *The Lives of the Saints*. Two sisters became nuns and one brother a priest.

Jef enjoyed tending the family's small flock of sheep and contemplated the beauties of nature as they grazed in the meadows by the banks of the river. This was the beginning of his reticence which led his friends to nickname him "Silent Joseph".

When Jef was 18, he attended a mission preached by Redemptorist priests and heard the voice of God calling him. He decided to become a priest. His father asked him to wait. He waited about six months until Christmas day, 1858, when he announced to his father, "Don't think this idea of entering the religious life is my idea! It's Providence, I tell you, that is inspiring me. Don't put any obstacles in my way. God is calling me. I must obey. If I refuse I run the risk of going to hell. As for you, God will punish you terribly for standing in the way of His will."

His father yielded and, one month later, Jef asked to be admitted as a lay brother with the Congregation of the Sacred Hearts of Jesus and Mary and of the Perpetual Adoration of the Blessed Sacrament of the Altar. His brother Pamphile had already entered before him. He began his novitiate at the age of 19 with the new name of Brother Damien.

Unlike Pamphile, Brother Damien was no scholar, but he compensated with sheer hard work. As a result of Pamphile's help in learning Latin, Brother Damien convinced his superiors to allow him to study for the priesthood. He was modest, amiable, brash and impulsive, yet quick to apologize. He was stocky, of medium height, with curly black hair and dark eyes. He was near-sighted and wore glasses, but he impressed everyone with his physical strength. During his novitiate he acquired a number of social skills and was transformed from his rough and brash manners. He carved the words "silence, recollection and prayer" into his desk.

In 1863, he received minor orders and learned that his brother Pamphile was ill and could not join the other missionaries going to Hawaii. Brother Damien's sister, Eugenie, was a nun who had died in her convent. Her sister, Pauline, volunteered to take her place as a nun. Now Brother Damien discerned that God was asking him to make a similar sacrifice and replace his brother Pamphile as a missionary to Hawaii.

So, Brother Damien volunteered to take Pamphile's place, even though he was not yet ordained. His request was granted and he left for Hawaii on October 29, 1863.

He later wrote his parents from the ship:

> Do not trouble yourselves in the least about us. We are in the hands of God, of an all-powerful God, who is taking us under His protection. All I ask you to do is to pray that we may have a good voyage, and that we may have courage to fulfill our tasks everywhere and at all times. That is our life! Good-bye, dearest parents.

Henceforward we shall not have the happiness of seeing one another, but we shall always be united by that tender love which we bear to one another. In our prayers especially let us often remember one another, and unite ourselves to the Sacred Hearts of Jesus and Mary, in which I remain ever your affectionate son.

Cape Horn is located at the southern tip of South America and often presents a treacherous rounding passage for ships with violent winds and mountainous waves. As they approached the Cape, a violent gale began and Brother Damien and the missionaries onboard began a novena (nine days of prayer) to end the gale. It ended exactly on the ninth day.

Brother Damien arrived in Honolulu on the island of Oahu after a journey of almost five months on March 19, the feast of St. Joseph, his namesake. He was 23 years old. He wrote his parents, "It would be impossible for me to tell you of the immense joy a missionary has when he comes to see his new country that he must water with his sweat to gain poor souls for God." He was finally ordained as a priest there by Bishop Maigret on May 21, 1864.

Hawaii Island Ministry

Bishop Maigret assigned Father Damien to the Big Island of Hawaii. It was 4000 square miles of a tropical paradise of beautiful beaches, plains and gardens mixed with mountainous terrain and active volcanoes. He ministered in the districts of Puna, Kohala and Kamakua. He made his pastoral rounds by walking and by riding horses and donkeys over the streams, rocks, lava fields and mountains. His food and shelter were the same as the native Hawaiians. He lived in thatched huts and ate the native fish, fruits and vegetables, especially *poi.* This is a paste made from the taro plant which looks and tastes like wallpaper paste. Father Damien described his diet when he wrote, "The calabash of *poi* is always full; there is also meat; water in quantity, coffee and bread sometimes, wine or beer never."

Father Damien described his ministry on the Big Island in a letter, "From one end of my district to another you have to walk on lava. I think I shall require fully three days to get from one end to the other. In every direction there are little villages scattered about, and for seven or eight years there has been no resident priest. Before leaving, the Bishop told me that I must remember the mission was quite in its infancy. Indeed, I found no church in which to say Mass, but two are now in course of construction."

Father Damien admired the simple kindness and hospitality of the natives but lamented their sexual promiscuity. Moreover, some sorcerers still led occult rites on the island.

One night, a native woman warned Father Damien that a sorcerer was at that moment in a burial cave practicing these rites against his life. Father went to see for himself. As he approached the cave, he heard the beat of drums and a wailing scream. He entered the cave and saw by its flaming torch light a half circle of 30 men crouched shoulder to shoulder with their eyes fixed on an old, toothless, evil looking man. He cut the neck of a dog and held its head while its blood spouted into a large open gourd. He stared into the gourd and screamed incantations as he swayed back and forth.

Then he held up an effigy of Father Damien himself. It was a wooden doll with a cassock-like gown, a wooden cross around its neck and Father's own rosary beads, stolen from him, fashioned around its waist. At that moment, fearless Father Damien seized the doll and tore it to pieces before the astonished group. He demonstrated to them that their evil rites could have no effect on him who was under God's protection. He admonished the participants to go home to their families as he safely left the cave.

Father Damien built several chapels on the island with his own hands. The natives admired his strength as they watched him climb mountains, cut down trees and haul them to the construction site. They marveled at his good example and came to help.

Father became a good farmer, architect, engineer and carpenter. The construction of each chapel concluded with a celebration that Father Damien described in a letter:

> As it is the custom of the country to give a big feast after bringing an important work to conclusion, my neophytes wanted to give one for their friends from the other districts, to match the hard work we did in building and finishing the church so well. Everyone was invited for the eve of the Epiphany. A good number of fat animals

had been killed and cooked in the kanaka oven, that is to say, in red-hot stones. At a signal the crowd goes to the church, which unhappily is too small to fit everyone in. After a short prayer, I give a sermon adapted to the occasion. Sermon and prayers over, everyone goes to the place prepared for the feast, all around the church, on the grass.

Something like a thousand people are there to celebrate. At our kanaka, even the most civilized always eat with their fingers, no trouble about knives and forks and the rest of the table setting. Everyone brings his own with him. Just like the ancient Romans, they eat on the ground, legs crossed like tailors, a very economical way. No use for tables, chairs, seats.

However, Father Damien's life was not all celebration on the Big Island. It was a lonely life with only a few visits from other priests and Bishop Maigret. He also had to contend with the forces of nature. Hurricanes, earthquakes, tsunamis and volcanic eruptions destroyed houses and chapels. Father Damien helped to rebuild them, to rescue and feed the survivors and to bury the dead.

Leprosy Panic

A leprosy plague struck Hawaii without notice in 1862. Leprosy is now known as Hansen's disease, after Norwegian doctor G. H. A. Hansen, the discoverer of its cause. Throughout the centuries, people feared and shunned the ravaged bodies of lepers as "unclean". They were doomed to live lives of segregation and isolation without care or pity. In scientific ignorance, its cause was often attributed to sexual immorality. Its actual cause was an infectious microorganism which spread through respiratory droplets or skin contact only among the genetically predisposed, such as the native Hawaiian people.

Leprosy slowly attacks the skin and mucous tissue. It kills nerves, disables muscles, decalcifies bones and disfigures faces. The body becomes deformed, crippled, ulcerated, blinded and eventually unable to breathe. It destroys the body inside and out. Its Hawaiian victims had open sores and rotting flesh often infested with maggots. They exuded a terribly foul odor. There was no cure. After the first cases were diagnosed, panic ensued in the white community. They remembered the remedy of segregation against the contagion of leprosy from the Bible and applied the same remedy in Hawaii.

The government was heavily influenced by American businessmen and puritanical Protestants who attributed the cause of the Hawaiians' leprosy to their own sexual immorality. They persuaded King Kamehameha V to promulgate a decree on January 3, 1865, that made segregation the policy for Hawaiian lepers with the removal of the infected and their separation from their families.

Six months later, the government chose the island of Molokai as the site to which they would remove and segregate the lepers. Most families disregarded the decree and hid their sick from the government to care for them themselves. As a result of this, the government hunted the sick down like animals to forcibly remove them. The people physically resisted and several battles broke out with the police. By the end of 1866, approximately 150 men and women were finally apprehended and shipped out to Molokai.

Sheer volcanic cliffs rose up 3000 feet high from the bottom of a peninsula that jutted out to the crashing seas below. These cliffs and the sea barricaded ten square miles of land that would become the lepers' home. This was the Kalaupapa promontory on the north coast of the island of Molokai. It served as a natural prison for the banished, segregated and confined lepers.

The government idealistically believed that the lepers would become self-sufficient, building their own homes and producing their own food. However, the necessary supplies were not provided for them and this planned paradise never came to be. Lepers were initially settled at Kalawao, on the east side of the peninsula. But ships could not land on its stony beach, and it was necessary to bring the poor lepers and their even poorer supplies to shore by way of small boats in the big seas. Soon the windblown, scrubland became a place of horror where the strong ruled the weak, where only the fittest survived and where the lepers danced their nights away into alcoholic and sexually promiscuous oblivion. Lepers fought over scanty allotments of food and clothing. The weak lay untended in their huts until they died, often without any burial. Molokai was a land without law or order. Hawaiians called it "the Given Grave". Between 1866 and 1873, when Father Damien arrived, approximately 40% of the lepers on Molokai died without proper food, shelter, medical care or any hope of improvement.

During this time, Father Damien was still ministering on the Big Island of Hawaii. There he witnessed the spread of the leprosy, the great sufferings of the lepers, the separations of their families and the exile of the lepers to an unknown land. In April 1873, he wrote a letter to his Father General and said that he could "only attribute to Almighty God the undeniable feeling that soon I shall join them."

The lepers on Molokai complained to Bishop Maigret that they only saw a priest once a year which left "so much time to die in between visits." So, after nine years in the Hawaiian missions, Father Damien volunteered to become a full-time resident priest on Molokai and the Bishop accepted his proposal.

Molokai Island Ministry

Father Damien arrived on Molokai with Bishop Maigret on May 10, 1873. He was 33 years old and carried only a cross and his Breviary. Bishop Maigret told the lepers, "I have brought one who will be a father to you. One who loves you so much that he is willing to become one with you, to live and die with you." In the words of author Robert Louis Stevenson, "He shut to, with his own hands, the doors of his own sepulcher."

Father started life on Molokai with 600 lepers at the Kalawao leper settlement under the shelter of a pandanus tree. He had a big rock on its side for his dinner table. He wrote, "No house to shelter me. I lived a long time under the shelter of a tree." Later he commented on the poor housing and shelter in general, "A heavy windstorm blew down most of the rotten abodes, and many a weakened leper lay in the wind and rain with his blanket and wet clothing."

Six months after his arrival on Molokai, Father Damien described his situation in a letter to his brother:

> I found on my arrival a little chapel dedicated to St. Philomena, but that was all. No house to shelter me. I lived a long time under the shelter of a tree, not wishing to sleep under the same roof as the lepers. Later on, the whites of Honolulu having assisted me with their

subscriptions, I was able to build myself a hut, sixteen feet long and ten feet wide, where I am now writing these lines. Well, I have been here six months, surrounded by lepers, I have not caught the infection: I consider this shows the special protection of our Good God and the Blessed Virgin Mary.

Every morning, then, after Mass, which is followed by an instruction, I go to visit the sick, half of whom are Catholics. On entering each hut, I begin by offering to hear their confession. Those who refuse this spiritual help, are not, therefore, refused temporal assistance, which is given to all without distinction. Consequently, every one, with the exception of a very few bigoted heretics, look on me as a father.

The lepers boasted, "Here there is no law!" Indeed it was a lawless place where the conditions reduced the value of life and the dignity of human beings to brute survival and the pleasures of the flesh to dull the awareness of their misery, which finally ended when they died and were thrown in their rags into ravines or shallow graves where the animals ate what was left of their flesh.

This is how Father Damien described the lawlessness on Molokai:

Vice reigned instead of virtue. When new lepers came, the old ones were eager to impress them with the principle: 'in this place is no law.' I was obliged to fight against such defiance of Divine as well as human laws. Under primitive roofs they lived in the most revolting promiscuity, without distinction of age or sex, old or new cases, all more or less strangers to one another, these unfortunate outcasts of society. Many an unfortunate woman had had to become a prostitute in order to win care for her children. When she was attacked by the disease, she and her children were cast out and had to find another shelter; sometimes they were thrust behind a stone wall and left there to die, or they were carried to the hospital and deserted.

Father visited the bedridden cases. He changed their bandages and washed their sores. He described their appearance, "Nearly all were prostrated on the beds, in damp grass huts, their constitutions badly broken down. The smell of their filth, mixed with the exhalation of their sores, was simply disgusting, unbearable for a newcomer. Many times at their domiciles I have been compelled to run outside to breathe fresh air."

Father explained the great difficulty in getting accustomed to the atmosphere of leprosy. "One day, at Sunday Mass, I found myself so stifled that I thought I must leave the altar to breathe a little of the outer air, but I restrained myself, thinking of Our Lord when He commanded them to open the grave of Lazarus, notwithstanding Mary's words, 'There will be an odor.' Now my sense of smell does not cause me so much inconvenience. I enter the huts of the lepers without difficulty. Sometimes, indeed, I feel no repugnance when I hear the confessions of those near their end, whose wounds are full of maggots. Often, also, I scarce know how to administer Extreme Unction, when both hands and feet are nothing but raw wounds. As for me, I make myself a leper, to gain all to Jesus Christ." These proved to be prophetic words.

The infrastructure to care for patients at the new leprosy settlement was virtually nonexistent. There were no homes to live in and no doctors to treat the sick. There was no dock, so ships delivering new groups of people for quarantine would dump patients in the water and force them to swim ashore. The patients, many profoundly ill, had to forage for meals and sleep out in the open. Doctors, when they did come, would refuse to touch the patients.

In contrast, Father Damien aggressively lobbied the Hawaiian government and the Catholic Church for more help, raising public awareness about their plight. Over the years, he ceaselessly and incessantly appealed to the governmental authorities in Honolulu to help the lepers.

He needed to constantly implore them for basic necessities such as food, clothing, bandages and medicines. When a hurricane destroyed his people's flimsy huts, Father petitioned for lumber, built 300 houses for them and laid a pipeline to a distant spring to supply them water. Many lepers died not from their disease but from insufficient basic necessities. Even after 15 years, Father Damien was still begging for the "luxury" of milk.

Unlike Jesus, Father Damien did not miraculously heal any of the lepers. He simply practiced the corporal and spiritual works of mercy to a heroic degree.

He practiced the corporal works of mercy and helped them to build housing, to clothe themselves and to raise crops. He cleaned and bandaged their sores, bathed them, amputated their gangrenous limbs, and washed their clothes. He restrained the strong from brutalizing the weak. He put an end to the debauchery. He built orphanages and schools.

A longtime inmate of Kalawao summed up Father Damien in his rural grammar as "a vigorous, forceful, impellent man with a generous heart in the prime of life and a jack of all trades, carpenter, mason, baker, farmer, Medico and nurse, no lazy bone in the makeup of his manhood, busy from morning to nightfall."

Father also practiced the spiritual works of mercy and built a chapel to celebrate the Eucharist and the funerals of the lepers. He founded pious associations for men, women, and children and instituted perpetual Eucharistic adoration. He built approximately 1000 coffins and buried the dead. Father Damien brought hope where there was despair. He became a source of consolation and encouragement for his people as the doctor of their bodies and souls. He gave a voice to the voiceless and built a community where a once lawless place became a place where the law of love prevailed and he was the witness of that law. His Father General later wrote, "It is impossible to list here all that his charity inspired him to do, under the kindly gaze of God, who has written all in the Book of Life."

An Englishman named Edward Clifford visited Molokai in 1888. He noted that, unlike other leper colonies that exhibited filth and hopelessness, the settlement at Molokai was neat and tidy with small white houses, gardens, livestock and a cemetery. He wrote that he was told by the patients, "We are well off here . . . . And we like our pastor. He builds our houses himself; he gives us tea, biscuits, sugar and clothes. He takes good care of us and doesn't let us need for anything."

The "Decree Concerning the Process of the Beatification and Canonization of the Servant of God Damien de Veuster" stated:

> Damien always showed himself to be a man of God. Forgetting himself, he was always full of happiness and understanding. His pure life, extreme poverty, kindness and firm character expressed in his life what he proclaimed in his preaching. In order to make the others feel, in a

certain way, the presence of God, a God who is love (1
Jn. 4:16), he tried to make them see the generous and
omnipresent kindness of God: he was doctor and nurse,
carpenter and bricklayer, tailor and farmer. He comforted
and served his lepers, seeing and revering Christ in them.
In order to make their living conditions more human, he
did not blush in asking for money and he was very happy
when he could improve their situation. Very often he was
the only priest and religious on the island of sorrow. He
was ready to risk even his health for the sake of his
apostolate. In this way, he attracted to religion those
suffering brothers, and fortified their faith; he tried to
make those precious children of Christ understand that
their sorrows were a participation in the mystery of Jesus'
passion.

However, Father Damien also understood that his own sorrows were a
participation in the mystery of Christ's passion, particularly by bearing
wrongs patiently. Since leprosy was often judged by the morally righteous
as a punishment from God for licentious behavior, and his detractors could
not believe that anyone could be as selfless as Father Damien, they
slandered him and claimed that he was immoral and willing to endure his
segregation with the lepers in order to enjoy sexual pleasure with them.

Father had his critics even among his brother priests who found his zeal
indiscreet and his publicity an embarrassment. One wrote that he has "no
common sense and is ill-bred." Even his Bishop called him "over-animated
and tempestuous."

Another of Father's great sufferings was his loneliness and the lack of
a priest companion to whom he could confess. One day a priest came by
ship to hear his Confession but the captain refused to allow Father Damien
to board. Father had to humiliate himself and publicly confess from a
small skiff and yell up his sins to the priest on the ship.

In 1886, Father Damien reported to the government:

As there were so many dying people, my priestly duty
toward them often gave me the opportunity to visit them
at their domiciles, and although my exhortations were
especially addressed to the prostrated, often they would

fall on the ears of the public sinners, who, little by little, became conscious of the consequences of their wicked lives, and began to reform, and at last, thus with the hope of a merciful Savior, gave up their bad habits. Kindness to all, charity to the needy, a sympathizing hand to the sufferers and the dying, in conjunction with a solid religious instruction to my listeners, have been my constant means to introduce moral habits among the lepers. . . . I am happy to say, that, assisted by the local administration, my labors here, which seemed to be almost in vain at the beginning, have, thanks to a kind Providence, been greatly crowned with success.

Dr. G. W. Woods spent a week on Molokai in 1876 to make a special study of leprosy. In 1887 he wrote to Father Damien that he had visited all parts of the world where leprosy could be found, but he had never found a place where the lepers were so happy and where they were so well cared for than at the leper settlement of Molokai.

Becoming a Leper

In 1881, Queen Liliuokaline recognized Father Damien's sacrificial works of mercy and decorated him with the Cross of the Royal Order of Kalakaua. She wrote a personal letter to Father in which she said that she knew that he sought his reward only from God, but that she wanted to show her own appreciation. Father accepted her award and later wrote to his Father General in Rome, "I have been decorated by the royal Cross of Kalakaua and now the heavier and less honorable cross of leprosy. Our Lord has willed that I be stigmatized with it. I am still up and taking care of myself a little. I will keep on working."

In a letter to his Bishop he wrote, "It is the memory of having lain under the funeral pall twenty-five years ago – the day of my vows – that led me to brave the danger contracting this terrible disease in doing my duty here and trying to die more and more to myself. The more the disease advances, I find myself content and happy at Kalawao."

In 1884, Father Damien visited Honolulu. While he was at a Mission center with another priest, Father Fouesnel, he spilled a bowl of boiling water on his foot. Father Fouesnel was surprised that Father Damien did not yell out in pain or do anything about the severe burn that was readily apparent to Father Fouesnel but not to Father Damien.

He felt nothing because of his nerve damage caused by leprosy. Father's leprosy was soon officially diagnosed by a doctor. The diagnosis excluded the disease of syphilis which quieted the wagging slanderous tongues of his detractors who accused him of licentious behavior. Since there was no treatment for him, Father returned to Molokai.

As his disease progressed, he wrote that he drew his strength from the Eucharist which he needed to live his life of charity with great courage until the end and to bear his terrible disease as Christ bore His Cross. He wrote, "It is at the foot of the altar that we find the strength we need in our isolation . . . I am always happy and content. Even if I am ill, I have no other desire than to accomplish God's will." He wrote his brother Pamphile, "I myself have been chosen by Divine Providence as a victim to this loathsome disease. I hope to be eternally thankful to God for this favor."

Over the years, Father Damien's loneliness, lack of help and frustrations with the governmental authorities caused a harder edge to his personality. He could be hardheaded, quarrelsome, and impatient. Even priests who were sent to help him left after short periods of time. His Bishop wrote, "Father Albert would still be with him if he (Damien) were a little more accommodating with his fellow-priests, and less of an autocrat."

However, after he contracted leprosy, Father's personality softened. He wrote, "There are signs of it on my left cheek and ear, and my eyebrows are beginning to fall. I shall soon be quite disfigured. I have no doubt whatever about the nature of my illness, but I am calm and reason I'm very happy in the midst of my people. I daily repeat from my heart, 'Thy Will be done.' ". He became more cheerful, smiled more often and was less bitter and hostile.

The news of Father Damien's leprosy was kept from his 83-year old mother by her family. However, she soon found out from news stories that sensationalized his symptoms, particularly the flesh falling from his body. She withdrew into a state of grief and eventually died of a broken heart on April 6, 1886.

Brother Joseph Dutton

Three months after the death of Father's mother, "Brother" Joseph Dutton arrived on Molokai as a volunteer to help Father Damien. He was a Civil War veteran who divorced his unfaithful wife and lived several years as an alcoholic. In 1883, he turned to sobriety and he converted to Catholicism. Then he read a news article about Father Damien's work and was inspired to go to help him. He never took religious vows but Father Damien fondly called him "Brother".

Brother Joseph was a great help to the leprous Father Damien. His calm temperament softened Father Damien's impulsiveness. They worked together from early morning until late at night nursing the sick and building homes, furniture and chapels. Eventually, Brother Joseph became the administrator of the colony. Since he was so close to Father Damien on a daily basis for almost three years, Brother Joseph is the most important and reliable witness of his virtues and faults. After Father Damien's death, Brother Joseph wrote about him:

> He had a great natural strength and vitality. These powers, coupled with his zeal, seemed to enable him to be ever ready to pursue with vigor whatever seemed to him ought to be done. . . . Father Damien had in his heart, when tranquil . . . a most tender feeling, as I often have been made to know. You will bear me out in stating the fact that no one found it pleasant at all times to be with him for a very long period. If my intimate association with him was longer continued than that of others, it was partly because I admitted my own faults in that regard, and partly because I ever saw him place in me the most entire confidence, and had in his heart a deep love, no matter what his exterior might be. And also, I used to be quite open with him in speaking of all these things; he likewise to me, and this seemed to give confidence in each other. . . .
>
> Father Damien was very devout, and in his tranquil moments he seemed to take a supernatural view of things, I may say of almost everything. His meditation in the morning was generally of about an hour's duration, and

he had a regular practice of making a visit to the Blessed Sacrament, at night before going to bed. He offered the Holy Sacrifice long after he seemed to be unable to do so, and recited his office nearly to the last, for some time after being dispensed, and while his one eye was hardly able to see. . . . It seems to me that the recitation of his office under the circumstances showed marked heroism. His devotion had many ways of showing itself in his last days; reciting the rosary, every evening asking for spiritual reading, etc.

His love for these people of the leper settlement – for all of them – was great. He gave himself freely for them. A sudden call of charity – one in distress – would cause him to drop at once what he might be engaged upon (except when at the altar) and quickly to give his aid.

In his ministrations with the natives he was untiring. Especially in attendance upon the dying was he earnest and helpful. So frequently being with him in this office, I was particularly impressed with it, and often thought that he must have been a great comfort to many souls in these moments.

When he felt that his end was approaching, and having quite a number of pieces of unfinished work about the new church, etc., he strained every nerve and muscle to get them completed. I'm sure that those engaged upon the work, all who noted his efforts in those last weeks, will join me in asserting the belief, that by these extra exertions he considerably hastened his end. . . .

Brother Joseph stayed at Molokai for more than 40 years as "brother to everybody" and director of the orphanage for leper boys. Near the end of his life he wrote, "I am an old, old relic, still on duty and happy. Almost ashamed to say how jolly I am." He died on March 26, 1931 in Honolulu, but his body was returned and buried on Molokai.

In 1886, Father Damien returned to Honolulu where he met a charitable nun, Mother Marianne Cope. Two years after that, she was on her way to Molokai to help him.

Blessed Marianne Cope

In 1883, Mother Marianne Cope arrived in Honolulu with six of her Sisters. They expected to travel on to Molokai to help Father Damien.

They were members of the Sisters of the Third Franciscan Order at Syracuse, New York, an independent branch of the larger foundation that Bishop John Neumann established in 1855. Mother Cope was born Barbara Koob in Germany in 1838. She immigrated to Utica, New York as a child and worked in a woolen factory for nine years before joining the Franciscans in 1862.

Her first service was as a schoolteacher but she soon became nurse-administrator of the Franciscans' hospital in Syracuse, which introduced new standards of cleanliness. Seven years later she was elected Provincial Superior of her Order.

After Mother Marianne and her Sisters settled in Honolulu, the Board of Health decided that they should not serve the lepers on Molokai, but should begin their work with those lepers who were at the Branch Hospital in Honolulu.

This "hospital" was actually a collection of poorly built wooden buildings located on a salt marsh which often flooded. The few attendants treated the lepers as prisoners There were no sanitary facilities and the stench was vile. The nuns brought order and cleanliness and three years later welcomed Father Damien as a patient and provided him with the luxury of sheets for the first time in years.

The nuns wept at the pitiable state of Father's disfigurement and treated him with the utmost care helping him with newly invented baths. Unfortunately, Father had little patience with their constant care or with spending time bathing. He worried about the lepers on Molokai and returned there within two weeks.

On November 14, 1888, Mother Marianne and two other nuns finally landed at Molokai to care for the female lepers. As Father Damien had done before them, they washed and bandaged the lepers' wounds.

One day one of her Sisters asked her, "Mother, what will you do with me if I become a leper?" Mother calmly answered, "You will never become a leper. I know we are all exposed, and I know, too, that God has called us for this work. If we are present, and do our duty, He will protect us. Do not allow it to trouble you, and when the thought comes to you, drive it from your mind. Child, remember, you will never be a leper, nor will any

Sister of our Order." This proved to be a prophecy that time has fulfilled. No Franciscan Sister at Molokai ever contracted leprosy.

Mother Marianne came to the Hawaiian Islands for an expected short period, but she stayed there until her death at age 80, on August 9, 1918, after 35 years of service. In 1889 she wrote to her Superior in Syracuse, "Will I ever see those I love again? God's will be done."

Soon after Mother Marianne died, a woman wrote in the *Honolulu Advertiser*, "Seldom has the opportunity come to a woman to devote every hour of 30 years to the mothering of people isolated by law from the rest of the world. She risked her own life in all that time, faced everything with unflinching courage and smiled sweetly through it all."

Mother Marianne was the first person beatified by Pope Benedict XVI on May 14, 2005. She was a woman who spoke "the language of truth and love" to the world, said Cardinal José Saraiva Martins, prefect of the Congregation for Saints' Causes. Cardinal Martins, who presided at the beatification Mass, called her life "a wonderful work of Divine grace." Speaking of her special love for persons suffering from leprosy, he said, "She saw in them the suffering face of Jesus. Like the Good Samaritan, she became their mother." Her Feast Day is August 9.

Last Days

Father continued to follow his own personal spiritual counsels: "Be severe toward yourself, indulgent toward others. Have scrupulous exactitude for everything regarding God: prayer, meditation, Mass, administration of the Sacraments. Unite your heart with God. . . . Remember always your three vows, by which you are dead to the things of the world. Remember always that God is eternal and work courageously in order one day to be united with him forever."

As his leprosy progressed, sores developed on Father's face and body and his eyebrows fell out. He kept working but fatigued easily. He suffered from acute diarrhea. He became partially blind because of the infection of his eyes. The bridge of his nose collapsed and his eyeglasses looked askew as they rested on his rotted ears.

In the silence of the night, when loneliness, discouragement and depression set in, he made rosary walks through the cemetery known as the "Garden of the Dead" where many bodies of those who died of leprosy were buried. He had difficulty sleeping because of the damage to his larynx which affected his ability to breathe so that he only got two hours of sleep a night. Gradually his senses left him until he was only able to hear.

As the end approached, he prepared for death by prayer, and the sacraments of Penance and Extreme Unction. He said, "Do you see my hands? All of my wounds are closing, and the crust is turning black. It's a sign of death, as you well know. Look at my eyes too; I have seen so many dying lepers that I cannot be mistaken. Death is not far off. I would very much have liked to see the Bishop once again, for the Good God is calling me to celebrate Easter with Him. May God be blessed."

He told Father Moellers, an eyewitness, "Work for the lepers is assured; I am no longer needed, so very soon I will go up there. . . . If I have any influence with God, I will intercede for all who are in the leprosarium."

Father Moellers then asked Father Damien to leave him his mantle, as Elijah did to Elisha, so that he would have his big heart. Father Damien responded, "Eh! What would you do with it, it is full of leprosy!"

Father Moellers admired Father Damien's admirable patience. He wrote, "He who was so ardent, so alive, so strong . . . to be nailed in this way to his poor sickbed . . . but, however, without suffering very much. Like the simplest and poorest of lepers, he was lying on the ground on a poor straw mattress, and we had a lot of trouble getting him to accept a bed. And what poverty! He who had spent so much money to care for the lepers had been self-forgetting to the point of not having sheets or a change of underclothing."

Father Damien died on April 15, 1889 at the age of 49. He died peacefully without any effort, as if he had fallen asleep. Father Moellers observed that all signs of leprosy had disappeared from his face and that the wounds in his hands were dried. The next day, he celebrated the funeral Mass and led the funeral procession to the cemetery. Father Damien's coffin was carried by eight white lepers. He was buried, according to his wishes, under the same pandanus tree beneath which he slept on his first nights at Molokai.

English author Robert Louis Stevenson wrote regarding Father Damien's ministry, "It was his part, by one striking act of martyrdom, to direct all men's eyes on that distressful country. At a blow, and with the price of his life, he made the place illustrious and public. And that, if you will consider largely, was the one reform needful; pregnant of all that should succeed. It brought money; it brought (best individual addition of them all) the Sisters; it brought supervision, for public opinion and public interest landed with the man at Kalawao. If ever any man brought reforms, and died to bring them, it was he."

Legacy

Finally, in 1969, 80 years after the death of Father Damien, the mandatory segregation and isolation policy decreed for the lepers by King Kamehameha V was officially ended. The site of the former leper settlement is now a part of the United States National Historical Park system. Some lepers, now more charitably known as victims of Hansen's disease, still live there because they freely chose this familiar ground as their home.

In 1893, the American power elite overthrew the Hawaiian monarchy in favor of an American-dominated republic. Five years later, the United States annexed Hawaii as a territory. Statehood was granted in 1959.

In 2005, the Belgian public broadcasting service, VRT, polled Belgians as to who was the Greatest Belgian of all time. The list was topped by Father Damien.

A statue of Father Damien, bearing the scars of leprosy, is displayed in the Rotunda of the Capitol in Washington, DC in Statuary Hall in honor of his virtues and service to the state of Hawaii. It was unveiled on April 15, 1969. Honolulu's Bishop John Scanlon addressed the assembly:

> His statue will stand here among the statues of the great men who each in his own way contributed to the building of America. This humble but sturdy farmer's son from the plains of Flanders takes his place here because his contribution to Hawaii, America, and to all mankind was the greatest. . . .
>
> Damien's greatness is in the heroic example of Christian living which he gave to all. Life, liberty and the pursuit of happiness are human rights. For Damien, life meant losing it for the sake of Him who said "he who loses his life for my sake shall find it." Liberty meant shutting himself up in his prison at the foot of the cliffs of Molokai for sixteen years, that he and his charges might possess the liberty of the sons of God.

His pursuit of happiness was paced for eternity, for his faith told him the age-old experience of mankind that the human spirit is not satisfied with even the best that this life can offer. Accordingly, he witnessed to his Divine Master in an extraordinary degree. . . .

Our country today is blessed beyond measure with the material things made possible by the intelligence, energy and industry of our people, but we need greater values for the human spirit. We need the understanding of and the dedication to the values to which the life of Damien gives witness. We need the recognition of the value of human life itself from its very beginnings. We need the recognition of the dignity of the human person, even the poorest and most wretched. We need a humanity possessed of a pity which is not condescending and of a humility which thinks of duties before rights.

Damien, human in his short temper and impatience, human in his stubbornness, but with the mark of divinity in his love and concern for the most wretched of men and women, speaks now from this seat of civil government of the Nation, and the word that he utters is the Hawaiian word which expresses what is noblest and greatest in us all-it is Aloha (Love).

Father Damien's remains were moved from Molokai to Belgium in 1936 and interred in a marble tomb in the crypt of the church of the Congregation of the Sacred Hearts at Louvain. A relic of his right hand was later returned to his original grave on Molokai after he was beatified by Pope John Paul II in 1995. Church leaders picked Damien's righthand to bring back because it's the one he used to bless, care for, and bandage the sick.

After his canonization, a heel bone relic of the new saint was presented to the Bishop of Hawaii. Encased in a closed metal container, it was enshrined at Our Lady of Peace Cathedral in Honolulu where Damien was ordained in 1864.

St. Damien is the only healthcare worker in Hawaii who ever contracted leprosy. It finally became fully curable with antibiotics in 1981. However, two to three million people worldwide have been disabled by the disease, which remains endemic in East Africa, Brazil, India, and Southeast Asia. The emergence of HIV as a global threat has expanded Damien's relevance. AIDS sufferers have adopted St. Damien as their patron.

Saint

On July 7, 1977, Pope Paul VI declared Father Damien was of "heroic virtue," and gave him the title of Venerable. He said, "In the endless variety of the manifestations, those who have emerged as saintly figures have but one characteristic in common: love in its purest essence. Love expresses itself in giving. Saints have not only given of themselves, but they have given of themselves in the service of God and their brethren. Father Damien is certainly in that category of an extraordinary man. He lived his life of love and dedication in the most heroic yet unassuming and self-effacing way. He lived for others: those whose needs were greatest."

A nun in France was totally healed in 1895 from a slow and agonizing terminal intestinal illness after she prayed a novena to Father Damien. This led to his beatification on June 4, 1995 by Pope John Paul II. He gave him the title of Blessed Father Damien—Servant of Humanity.

Recognizing Blessed Damien's imperfections, the Pope said during his beatification homily, "Holiness is not perfection according to human criteria; it is not reserved for a small number of exceptional persons. It is for everyone; it is the Lord who brings us to holiness, when we are willing to collaborate in the salvation of the world for the glory of God, despite our sin and our sometimes rebellious temperament."

Later, a second miracle was approved that led to Father Damien's canonization. Audrey Toguchi, an 80-year-old Hawaiian, was diagnosed with incurable cancer but was miraculously cured after she prayed for Father Damien's intercession.

Audrey Toguchi's devotion to Father Damien started when she was a Catholic schoolgirl and continued throughout her life. In 1998 she was diagnosed with pleomorphic liposarcoma, an aggressive form of fat tissue cancer that spread to her lungs. The doctors told her that she had only six months to live, at best, and suggested chemotherapy as the only option.

"I'm going to Molokai to pray to Father Damien," Mrs. Toguchi calmly told Dr. Walter Y.M. Chang after hearing her death sentence. "Mrs. Toguchi," he replied, "prayers are nice and it's probably very helpful, but you still need chemotherapy."

Defying Chang and the pleas of her husband and two sons, Mrs. Toguchi caught a flight from Honolulu and made a pilgrimage to Blessed Damien's grave in Kalawao, on the island of Molokai. "Dear Lord," she prayed, "you're the one who created my body, so I know you can fix it. I put my whole faith in you. . . . Father Damien, please pray for me, too, because I need your help."

On a later doctor's visit on Oct. 2, 1998, a month after cancer was first detected in her lungs, doctors expected that the tumors would have grown. Instead, they had shrunk, and by May 1999 tests confirmed that they had disappeared without treatment. In 2004, Mrs. Toguchi made a pilgrimage of thanksgiving back to Blessed Damien's grave to thank him and God for her healing. The Vatican conducted an extensive review and concluded that her recovery defied medical explanation. On July 3, Pope Benedict XVI agreed and approved her miracle for Blessed Damien's canonization.

Mrs. Toguchi said, "I talk to him (Blessed Father Damien) constantly and I ask him for help for other people. There are people from all over asking for help and so I ask for help for them." She added, "It's the good Lord that helps us, but Father Damien puts the good word in."

On October 11, at St. Peter's Basilica in Rome, Pope Benedict XVI canonized Blessed Damien and declared him a saint. During the papal homily at the Canonization Mass, he preached, "His missionary activity, which gave so much joy, reaches its summit in charity. Not without fear and repugnance, he chose to go to the Island of Molokai to serve the lepers who were there, abandoned by all; thus he exposed himself to the disease they suffered from. He felt at home with them. The Servant of the Word thus became a suffering servant, a leper with lepers, during the last four years of his life."

Now the Church knows, as Robert Louis Stevenson said more than a century before, that Father Damien shared "all the grime and paltriness of mankind" yet was "a saint and a hero all the more for that."

Opening Prayer for the Mass in Commemoration of
Saint Damien de Veuster

Father of mercy, in Blessed Damien
you have given a shining witness of love for the poorest and most
abandoned. Grant that, by his intercession, as faithful witness of the
heart of your Son Jesus, we too may be servants of the most needy
and rejected. We ask this through our Lord Jesus Christ, your Son, who
lives and reigns with you and the Holy Spirit, One God,
forever and ever. Amen.

Shrine:

Cathedral of Our Lady of Peace
1184 Bishop Street
Honolulu, HI 96813
Website: http://www.fatherdamien.com

20. Saint Katharine Drexel and Western Native Americans and African-Americans

Born	November 26, 1858, in Philadelphia, Pennsylvania
Died	March 3, 1955 in Cornwells Heights, Pennsylvania
Canonized	October 1, 2000
Feast Day	March 3

Foundress of the Sisters of the Blessed Sacrament. Second native-born United States citizen to be declared a saint.

"When nobody else did, she loved us."
A Navajo Indian man after the funeral Mass for Mother Drexel.

The young Philadelphia socialite knelt at the feet of Pope Leo XIII, just as Mother Frances Cabrini would do three years later. In her girlish fancy, Katharine Drexel thought, *surely God's Vicar will not refuse me.* So, she pleaded with the Pope for missionary priests for the Indians of the United States. To her astonishment His Holiness responded, "Why not, my child, yourself become a missionary?"

Discrimination Continues

Discrimination against Western Native Americans and African-Americans continued as millions of immigrants poured into the United States. The mass migration of peoples who immigrated to the United States in the 19th and early 20th centuries dramatically changed American life and the Catholic Church in the United States. These peoples, principally from Ireland, Germany, Italy and Poland, flocked to urban parishes where they preserved their native languages and cultures as they began the process of entering into the American melting pot and fulfilling the America Dream of a better life. Many priests, sisters and brothers ministered to them, notably saints John Neumann and Mother Cabrini.

These immigrants started at the bottom of the economic work ladder, worked hard and left greater opportunities for their children. Eventually, they were amalgamated into American society. While all of this was happening to them, many other United States citizens were left behind. Among them were the most neglected, the Indians and the People of Color, those later called Native Americans and African-Americans. God responded to their needs by calling to their aid a wealthy, young woman with no formal education or training in business administration. He called Katharine Drexel of Philadelphia, Pennsylvania.

The first African-American priest in the United States, Father John A. Tolton, diocesan priest of the Archdiocese of Chicago wrote her:

> It took the Catholic Church 100 years here in America to show forth such a person as yourself . . . . In the whole history of the Church in America we cannot find one person that has sworn to give her treasury for the sole benefit of the Colored and Indians. As I stand alone as the first Negro priest of America, so you, Mother Katharine, stand alone as the first one to make such a sacrifice for the cause of a downtrodden race.

Formation

"There is no hope for her recovery," said the doctor to Francis Drexel about his wife, Hannah Jane, as he kept vigil at her bedside. She died of complications from the birth of her second daughter, Katharine, on December 30, 1858. It was the day after Katharine was baptized and a month after her birth on November 26. Katharine was forever grateful to her mother who lay down her life for the life of her daughter. Later, Katharine would give up her own life for the sake of the neglected Native

Americans and African-Americans.

Francis Drexel was a self-made millionaire. His father emigrated from Austria to Philadelphia in 1817 and opened a currency brokerage business in Philadelphia after the financial panic of 1837 resulted in various currencies in circulation. Francis frequently acted as a night watchman and slept under the counter. He supplemented his income by playing the organ in church on Sundays. He has to walk six miles each way. Later he became a wealthy banker in the prominent family that established Drexel Institute, a vocational school, and supported charities such as schools, hospitals, orphanages and homes for the elderly. He expressed his grief over the loss of his wife in these words:

> I am again alone in the world with two children, the youngest five weeks old [Katharine] - my bereavement, though very afflicting, lately had not been unexpected. After three weeks of intense suffering, although she may have been unconscious of it, having lost her reason, my beloved one was taken from me. If I know myself I am resigned to this dispensation of the Almighty. His will in all things be done, for He ordereth all things wisely and well. . . . I have every assurance that my beloved one has gone to her heavenly Father.

For the next 14 months, Katie and her sister Elizabeth (Lizzie) lived with her aunt and uncle. When their father remarried Emma Bouvier, they returned to live with him and their stepmother in their luxurious home on Walnut Street in Philadelphia. Both Francis and his new wife were devoted Catholics. They built a special oratory in their city home where the family gathered for daily prayer. In the summers, they rented a country estate in Nicetown, Pennsylvania, that they called "the nest." Here the family enjoyed the wonders of nature and the children learned the faith at their stepmother's knee.

In later life, Mother Katharine remembered her family's prayer life:

> Prayer was like breathing, there was no compulsion, no obligation, it was natural to pray. Night prayers were always said together. We were usually in bed by eight o'clock when we were children. Then in our little night

dresses we would go to the top of the stairs and call down, "Mama! Papa!"

Then Papa (we did not call him "Dad") would leave his organ or is paper and Mama her writing and both at the call of the children would come up and kneel for night prayers in the little oratory. Sometimes, Mama would be sleepy, she would be worn out from her work with the poor and would doze off and say, "Hail Mary, Mother of God." No matter how often this would happen she would begin all over again when Pap would gently say, "Dear, it is Holy Mary, now, Holy Mary, Mother of God." Yes, he knew she was tired after her day.

Archbishop Wood and the local pastor, Father James O'Connor, blessed the family oratory. Afterwards, they discussed President Grant's plan to provide a Christian education for the Indians. This planted a seed for Kate's vocation at the age of 13. Father O'Connor became Kate's lifelong spiritual director and the Bishop of Omaha, Nebraska, where he served the Indians. Father O'Connor told Kate that her predominant passion was scrupulosity and that she was always to pray fervently to God each day that He might aid her to know her vocation in life.

When she was 15, Kate began to express her resolutions and, later, her disappointment at not keeping them. She was somewhat scrupulous, always tried to do better, often failed, but never gave up. She wrote in her diary:

> Next Wednesday will be Lent and so to please God and mortify my flesh, I resolve:
> 1. Not to eat between meals
> 2. Not to take water between meals
> 3. Dinner, everything but once
> 4. No butter, no fruit
> 5. To speak French [apparently a penance]
> 6. To give money to the poor

In 1876, at the age of 17, Kate expressed her patriotism in her diary during the beginning of the celebration of the Centennial Year of the Declaration of Independence:

> I am happy to say that our New Year's Eve was commenced in the most patriotic manner or if not in the most patriotic manner, at least with most patriotic feelings. Louise was wild with excitement. She decorated herself with five penny flags and danced violently before the dining room door. Lise and I rushed around the house lighting the gas for our illumination, whilst Hans was conducted to the balcony to drape our enormous "stars and stripes" over the balustrade.

In the spring of 1878, Kate ended her home schooling at the age of 19. She made her debut into Philadelphia society on January 1, 1879. Her "coming out" was the social event of the year and was attended by all the prominent people of Philadelphia. However, Kate humbly made only a brief reference to it in a letter to Bishop O'Connor. She wrote, "I attended a little party the other night where I made my debut." The good Bishop reminded her that she had a Christian responsibility to follow the good example of her parents who witnessed to Christ in the social setting of the rich where He was often ignored.

Redemptive Suffering

In 1879, Katharine's mother contracted malignant cancer and suffered intensely for the next three years. Katharine was her bedside nurse and did her best to relieve her pain. Thoughts of the religious life came to her constantly and forcibly. She even teased her mother, "You had better not go away from us, darling, or else I shall run off to a convent." Katharine also realized through her mother's sufferings the enormity of original sin through which suffering and death came into the world.

At one point, Katharine's mother offered her suffering to redeem any pain that her husband might suffer. She told him, "O Frank, how I pray that when your time comes, you will be spared all this and now I offer this pain I suffer, for you."

Mrs. Drexel died on January 29, 1883. Philadelphia poet Eleanor Donnelley wrote this eulogy in her memory:

> No golden shrine all gem-bespent
> Fame o'er your ashes rears.
> Behold the poor - your monument!
> Your epitaph - their tears!

The Vocational Seed Spouts

The seed of Katharine's vocation began to sprout from the time of her mother's death. She wanted to dedicate her life to God and resolved to do her part to relieve the suffering of others. After her mother's death, the family made a trip to the West. Katharine noted the abject and degrading state of the Native Americans who lived on reservations that were the result of broken promises from the United States government. Her awareness of this painful situation signaled the beginning of a lifetime of personal and financial commitment to support numerous missions and missionaries in the United States for the Catholic education of Native Americas and African-Americans. At the same time, Katharine was becoming increasingly convinced that God was calling her to give herself totally to Him. She felt attracted to the comtemplative life in order to contribute with prayer and penance to the expansion of the missions.

Throughout 1883 and 1884, Katharine struggled to discern her vocation. A man proposed to her but she "refused the offered heart." Four months after her mother's death, she wrote down the pros and cons of her entry to religious life. Each pro had its con. The pro of imitating Christ's self-sacrifice had its cons of family separation, homesickness and the repulsion of community life and its constant contact with "*old maidish dispositions.*" The pro of a whole-hearted gift of her life to God had its con of submission to a Superior "whom I felt to be stupid, and whose orders showed her thorough want of judgment." The pro of a higher place in Heaven had its con of uncertainty of bearing "the privations and poverty of religious life. I have never been deprived of luxuries." The pro of the attainment of perfection had its con of "weariness, disgust and a want of final perseverance which might lead me to leave the convent. And what then!!"

Katharine wrote her analysis to Bishop O'Connor. His advice was "Don't be in a hurry. Think, pray, wait and all will turn out for you peace and happiness." Two months later he wrote:

> Your vocation to *religion* is not pronounced, and with-
> out a very decided vocation, one in your position should
> not enter it.

Katharine's inclinations were not for the world but for religious life. During a European tour in November of 1883, she wrote to Bishop O'Connor from Venice:

> The outlook in the future to a life of perpetual celibacy
> *is contrary to my present inclinations to the religious
> life.* If, however, God calls me to remain in the world, to
> be exposed to its temptations, to be obliged to serve it, to
> remain in the world and yet not be of the world, to know
> how great is the beauty of God's House, and yet to have
> duties which constantly withdraw from it, to feel that
> God has given graces, which to quote your own words
> "*must* be used under direction lest they lead from the
> path of prudence" and yet to be deprived of daily direction
> such as those in religious receive, to be looked down
> upon as an old maid – if all this is for God's greater glory
> – I must drown inclination and say *Fiat*. Most likely I
> can, *with God's Grace*, do more for Him in the world.

Two months later, she wrote to him from San Remo about the emptiness of a worldly life:

> Like the little girl who wept when she found that her
> doll was stuffed with sawdust and her drum was hollow,
> I, too, have made a horrifying discovery and my
> discovery like hers is true. I have ripped both the doll
> and the drum open and the fact lies *plainly* and *in all its*
> glaring reality before me: *All, all, all* (there is no
> exception) is passing away and will pass away. European
> travel brings vividly before the mind how cities have risen
> and fallen, and risen and fallen; and the same of empires

and kingdoms and nations. And the billions and billions who lived their common every day life in these nations and kingdoms and empires and cities, where are they? The ashes of the kings and might of this earth are mingled with the dust of the meanest slave . . . . Of one thing alone we are *sure*. In God's own time – then shall come the Son of Man in great power and majesty to render to each according to his works.

The reward and punishment for these will *not* pass away, nor does *the* Day, Eternity, then opening before us. An *eternity* of happiness infinite or an eternity of misery infinite! . . .

What was the consequence of [the little girl] finding out that her doll was stuffed with sawdust? She says she does not wish to play with dolls any more. Once being fully convinced that dolls are not flesh and blood she asks herself seriously what is the good of fondling that which is in reality but a bag of ugly sawdust. Now, dear Father, that is my case. I am disgusted with the world. God in His mercy has opened my eyes to the fact of the vanitas vanitatis, [vanity of vanities], and as He has made me see the vile emptiness of this earth I look to Him, the God of Love, in hope. . . .

I hope that God may place me in a state of life where I can best know Him, love Him and serve Him for Whom alone I am created. I am ambitious. I desire to become the disciple of Our Lord Jesus Christ. And therefore, what course should I now adopt to become a disciple; please instruct me, dear Father.

"Dear Father" kept concluding in his letters through May of 1888 that Katharine's vocation was not to enter a religious order but "to be in the world, but not of it, and to labor there for your own salvation, and the salvation of others, just as you are now doing. Living as you do, and as you will continue to live, you will benefit not only Christ's poor, but by your example, the rich of this world also, who after all, are the poorest of the poor. You are doing more for the Indians now, than any religious, or even any religious community has ever done, or perhaps, ever could do for them in this country. I take all the responsibility for having 'kept you out of a convent.' "

Katharine found this direction hard to follow. She replied, "As far as I can read my heart, I am not happy in the world. There is a void in my heart that only God can fill. Can God obtain full possession of my heart while I live in the world?"

The Inheritance

On February 16, 1885, Katharine was nursing her sick father. While she was in the next room, she heard a noise and rushed in to find her father slumped in a chair. Francis Drexel was dead. Katharine and her sisters inherited the income from a Trust Estate that he established of 14 million dollars, a huge amount of money in 1885. The daughters followed their parents' example and supported various charities. Soon after, Katharine received a visit from Bishop Martin Marty, who served the Indians in the Dakota Territory and Father Joseph Stephan, Director of the Bureau of Catholic Indian Missions. They told her about their work and the needs of the Indians on the Rosebud Reservation. This was the beginning of Katharine's financial support of the needs of American Indians.

The Drexel sisters became very close and called themselves "The All Three." In the summer of 1886, they sailed to Europe. During their time in Europe, Katharine received frequent letters from Father Stephan concerning the plight of the Indians and his accounting of how he spent her donations. Bishop O'Connor also wrote to her concerning his dream to build and staff a mission school for the Indians. Katharine sought help from European monasteries to send priests to help them, but none would make such a commitment. So, she decided to ask the Pope. She pleaded with him for missionary priests for Bishop O'Connor's Indians. To her astonishment, he responded, "Why not, my child, yourself become a missionary?"

She responded, "Because, Holy Father, Sisters can be had for the missions, but no priests."

Years later, Katharine told her Sisters that once she left the Holy Father, she could not get away from the Vatican fast enough. When she got outside she sobbed and sobbed. She was initially frightened at the implications of the Pope's words. But slowly, after prayer and spiritual direction, she accepted his advise and gave up the idea of a contemplative vocation.

To the West

Upon their return from Europe, the Drexel sisters received letters from Bishop O'Connor and Father Stephan. They invited them to come and see for themselves the Indian missions that they were helping to support so that they could learn about the difficulties and successes. This trip would not be as easy as the European tour. The Indian missions had no luxury hotels or gourmet meals.

In the fall of 1887, they visited the Dakota Territory missions where schools and convents were being built through their generosity. They traveled by railroad and horse carriage. The next fall they visited other missions of the Indian Northwest. They learned that the missions did not need just money; they needed people who were willing to serve them. Many of the missionary orders were not able to make a permanent commitment to serve them and only stayed for short periods. What was needed was an order that would work exclusively with the Indians. Pope Leo XIII's question kept nagging at Katharine.

The Vocation Blossoms

Katharine and Bishop O'Connor, her spiritual director, had corresponded about her vocation for years. He insisted on her remaining in the world, a world that could not give peace to her heart. Finally, in November of 1888, she boldly wrote him, "Are you afraid to give me to Jesus Christ? It appears to me, Reverend Father, that I am not obliged to *submit* my judgment to yours, as I have been doing for two years, for I feel so sad in doing it because the world cannot give me peace, so restless because my heart is not rested in God."

He answered her immediately and, surprisingly, without any opposition. He wrote, "I had come to regard it as certain that Our Lord has chosen you for Himself, but, for reasons with which you are familiar, I was inclined to think He wished you to love and serve Him as His spouse, but in society. This letter of yours, and your bearing under the long and severe tests to which I subjected you, as well as your entire restoration to health, and the many spiritual dangers that surround you, make me withdraw all opposition to your entering religion."

Now the question became whether to enter an existing order or to found a new one. In December of 1888, Katharine wrote Bishop O'Connor, "I want a missionary order for Indians and Colored people." Several orders helped them but none of them exclusively. Two months later, Bishop O'Connor received an inspiration at Mass that Katharine should establish a new order to work exclusively for the Indian and Colored people. He wrote her:

> The more I have thought of your case the more convinced I become that God has called you to establish an order for the objects above mentioned. The need for it is patent to everybody. All the help the established orders can give, in the work, will be needed, but a strong order devoted to it exclusively is also needed. You have the means to make such an establishment. Your social position will draw to it subjects and friends without number. God has put in your heart a great love for the Indian and the Negroes. He has given you a taste and capacity for the sort of business which such a foundation would bring with it. All these things point more clearly, than an inspiration or a revelation could, to your duty in the premises.

However, Katharine wanted to receive daily Communion which was unusual at that time for active orders but was permitted in contemplative orders. She thought that perhaps a life of prayer, contemplation and daily communion would give more glory to God than an active life to save souls. Also, she lacked self-confidence in her ability and virtues to found and direct a new active religious order. She wrote, "I know the self-sacrifice necessary in the missionary life! I know the privations, the trials, the temptations, and I as myself, could I go through all these in a manner suitable for edifying the religious of my order?"

That same week, the answer from Bishop O'Connor came loud and clear:

> I was never so quietly sure of any vocation, not even of my own, as I am about yours. If you do not establish

the order in question, you will allow to pass an opportunity of doing immense service to the Church, which may not occur again.

Your objections are simply scruples.

Daily Communion can well and easily be made a rule of the new institute. It is simply a matter of history that every great need that arose in the Church, called into being a new order.

Even as foundress you will have your faults, but God not you, will do the work. He often makes use of very weak instruments. The question is not, will you be all that you should be, but does God will that you be His instrument?

I regard it as settled that you are to establish a new order. The Church has spoken to you through me, her unworthy organ, and you must hear her or take the consequences. Do you wish for a decree of a general council in this matter, or for a decision ex cathedra of the Pope?

Two weeks later, Bishop O'Connor wrote that he had met Archbishop John Ireland in Chicago and asked him his opinion of a new order. "Why," he said, "it is just the thing we needed. It is a great, an indispensable work. Miss Drexel is just the person to do it, and if she does not undertake it, it will remain undone."

That settled it. Katharine decided to found her own order. She wrote Bishop O'Connor in humility, "The Feast of St. Joseph brought me the grace to give the remainder of my life to the Indians and Colored, to enter fully and entirely into your views and those of Reverend Stephan as to what is best for the salvation of the souls of these people."

She overcame her self-doubts and her family's objections and entered the Sisters of Mercy Convent in Pittsburgh as a postulant on May 7, 1889 to begin her training in religious life. Her uncle Anthony thought that she was making the mistake of her life, yet he consented. So, Kate became Sister Katharine in honor of her patron, St. Catherine of Siena.

A Philadelphia newspaper wrote:

> [She has taken] her first step yesterday in the
> renunciation of the world, with all that it contains of family,
> brilliant associations, and great wealth. One of America's
> greatest heiresses [will be] laying aside all that so many
> thousands live for and adopting a new life as opposite as
> can be well imagined from that which she might be
> supposed to favor.

Kate, the former socialite, became Sister Katharine, the postulant, and humbly did her duties just as the other postulants. One of her companion postulants wrote, "With childlike simplicity [Sister Katharine] changed over from a life of luxury and ease to which she had been accustomed to the humble self-effacing life of our novitiate. When the little bell in the novitiate tinkled, calling us to the chapel, it was a regulation of the novitiate that the sewing room in which we had been recreating and mending our clothes was to be left in perfect order. Again and again I saw Sister Katharine, at the sound of that bell, jump up, run and get the pan and brush and be the one to get down on her knees and gather up the scraps that had fallen on the floor."

She was a delight to her companions, had a natural gaiety and sense of humor and used to teach them Indian dances. Her scrupulous mending of her clothes, darning of her stockings and even darning the napkin that she used at meals, evidenced her spirit of poverty. She wasted nothing.

Sister Katharine dreaded Bishop O'Connor's idea that she should be a foundress of a new religious order. She wrote him, "The undertaking you propose, Reverend Father, seems enormous, and I shall freely acknowledge that my heart goes down in sorrow when I think of it. To be the head of a new order! New orders always, I think, have to pass through the baptism of the Cross!"

Again Bishop O'Connor immediately replied:

> I have never for one instant doubted that the conclusion
> reached was in accord with the Divine Will. If you expect
> an angel to be sent to enlighten you in regard to this
> matter, you may be looking for a little too much.
>
> I am not surprised to find you dreading and shrinking
> somewhat from the responsibility of the undertaking. If
> you did not, I should feel very nervous about your

success. But you must remember that the work will be God's work, and that you are to be only a weak instrument in His hands. You should distrust yourself, but can you not, in a work of charity, confide in God?

Three weeks later he wrote her, "The highest ambition of "the girl of this period," and even of the great majority of girls is, to go on "a coon hunt" for a husband. This is all very well in its way, but what a poor pursuit it is, compared with the quest to which God has called you!"

Five months later, on November 7, 1889, Archbishop Ryan received Sister Katharine as a novice and the bride of Christ in a white wedding gown trimmed with orange blossoms, with diamond rings on her fingers and diamonds in her necklace.

A few days later, Archbishop Ryan addressed some the Bishops:

> Let us now come in the name of God and resolve to make reparation for [the injustices to the Colored People and Indians] of the past.
>
> On the threshold of the new century, I lately beheld a scene prophetic of this reparation. On Thursday last, in the quiet Convent chapel of the Sisters of Mercy in Pittsburgh, I could well imagine along each side of that chapel the representatives of the different races. On one side the Indians and Colored, on the other the white race that oppressed both. They, the oppressor and oppressed, gazed on each other with little feelings of fraternal love. And then I saw coming out from the ranks of the white race, a fair young virgin. Approaching midway between the contending lines, she knelt before the illumined altar of the God of all the races of men, and offered her great fortune, her life, her love, her hopes, that until the grave shall receive her, all she possesses now or shall possess in the future, may belong to God and to the Indian and Colored races. The hope is that other Christian maidens may unite with her and thus inaugurate the great work of reparation, and help to render it perpetual.

On May 27, 1890, Bishop O'Connor died. Sister Katharine was devastated. She had depended on him for spiritual direction, for the writing of a rule for the new order and for making it a reality. All of her self-doubts returned. But Archbishop Ryan visited her after the funeral and said, "If I share the burden with you, if I help you, can you go on?" She continued on.

Archbishop Ryan reconciled her vow of poverty and the possession of her fortune by saying, "You can retain the possession and the administration, but you have to promise in case of my requiring it, that you would renounce your possessions."

Sister Katharine's sorrow at the death of Bishop O'Connor was augmented by the tragic death of her newly married sister Elizabeth. She had returned to Philadelphia from her honeymoon in Europe and she went into premature labor. The baby was stillborn and Elizabeth died. The losses of her mother, father, Bishop O'Connor and her sister strengthened her ability to carry her cross.

Sister Katharine and her postulants began construction of a new motherhouse while they still lived in the convent in Pittsburgh and prepared for the foundation of her new missionary order. The objective of the congregation founded by Sister Katharine was to carry Christ present in the Eucharist to the Native Americans and African-Americans, particularly through Catholic education and social assistance.

Sister Katharine always found in the Eucharist the source of her love for the poor and the oppressed and the inspiration to combat the effects of racism. The Eucharist was at the heart of her spirituality. Her love and devotion to Jesus was expressed in the union of adoration of the Most Blessed Sacrament with active service for the good of others, giving of herself and everything she possessed.

"The spirit of the Eucharist consists in the donation of one's own being," she wrote. In order to point out the central nucleus of the charism of the congregation she founded, she wrote to her Sisters, "Get up after receiving Holy Communion and go find Him in the people. Everything you do for the people, you do for Him."

Archbishop Ryan and Cardinal James Gibbons, Archbishop of Baltimore, paid the new congregation a visit. The Cardinal said, "Your work is a truly apostolic one. Be apostles and carry the glad tidings of the Gospel to these neglected races, for 'beautiful are the feet that carry the Gospel to heathen lands.' " This was their Great Commission as apostles for social justice to the Native Americans and African-Americans.

On February 12, 1891, Sister Mary Katharine Drexel was professed as the first Sister of the new missionary congregation, the Sisters of the Blessed Sacrament for Indians and Negroes. Mother got approval to change the Vatican's translation of "Negroes" to "Colored People," a more universal term. Today they are known simply as the Sisters of the Blessed Sacrament. Sister Katharine became Mother Katharine and made her vows before Archbishop Ryan.

In addition to the normal vows of poverty, chastity and obedience, she added another. She vowed, "To be the mother and servant of the Indians and Negro races according to the rule of the Sisters of the Blessed Sacrament; and not undertake any work which would lead to the neglect or abandonment of the Indian and Colored races."

When Mother made her perpetual vows in 1895, she received a ring which she wore as a symbol of her perpetual espousal to Jesus. The ring was engraved with her motto, "My beloved to me and I to Him."

The Work Begins

The new order opened their novitiate at the Drexel summer home of St. Michel near Torresdale, Pennsylvania, while their motherhouse was being built in Cornwells Heights. Mother Katharine began with 10 novices and three postulants. Here they formed their strong foundation in the interior life before they began their active apostolate.

Bishops from New Orleans, the Oklahoma territory, North Carolina and Cheyenne came to the new community. They described their missionary work and needs and sought Mother's help. The mission fields of the West were lonely and dangerous without any resources. Bishop Maurice Burke of Cheyenne, Wyoming, wrote Mother:

> I am a bishop in name and title – Maurice Burke, Bishop of Cheyenne. I am here in a vast desert without inhabitants and without any means under Heaven to accomplish any work in the interests of the Church or of religion. If I had the zeal and the ability of St. Paul, I could accomplish nothing here. I am without people,

without priests, without any means whatever of living or
staying here.

In early 1891, shortly after the United States Army's massacre of the
Indians at Wounded Knee Creek, some young Sioux warriors on the
nearby Pine Ridge Reservation in South Dakota rose up in armed rebellion
against the injustices perpetrated against them. Their violence posed a
great danger to the Franciscan missionary sisters there who maintained
the Holy Rosary Mission built by Sister Drexel years before. When the
Drexel sisters first visited the reservation years before, they promised
Chief Red Cloud that they would build a school. They did so and the
Chief remembered. Franciscan Mother M. Kostka and her nuns stayed
at the Mission in spite of the danger, resting fully dressed in case their
home was set on fire. She wrote to Sister Drexel:

> The poor, wild, fearful, enraged Indians kept in their
> hostile lodge, only a quarter of an hour's ride distant from
> the Mission, for almost three weeks. No man, woman or
> child was to be seen, and all was as still as death. Yet
> everyone who approached the lodge in civilized dress
> was shot down. Every sunset the sky was dark with
> smoke from burning houses. Wherever one looked was
> fire, and nobody was in sight.

The Sisters prayed and Chief Red Cloud interceded. He and his followers
convinced the rebels of the goodness of the Sisters and told them that if
anyone harmed the Mission or the Sisters, they would go over to the
soldiers and fight against their own people. The Mission was saved while
most everything else in the area was destroyed.

Mother had been supporting St. Stephen Mission for the Indians in
Wyoming since 1885. However, soon after her profession in 1891, she
learned that the school had closed for lack of teachers. She made an
arduous journey by stagecoach with Bishop Burke to the Mission,
investigated the situation and purchased furniture and supplies. She had
hoped that this would be the Sisters' first mission. However, on her return
to Philadelphia, Archbishop Ryan prudently refused her permission to
staff the Mission.

Although there was an immediate need, the fledgling order had not developed a deep and mature interior life before it began its active life. Mother was the only professed member, the others were just postulants or novices. A disappointed Mother humbly and obediently submitted to the Archbishop's decision. In later years she wrote about the incident, "Oh how audacious I was in those days. Almighty God was certainly good to save us from such a mistake. I see now what a wild scheme it was. It would have been the ruination of our little Congregation."

On July 16, 1891, the cornerstone was laid for the new Motherhouse. Unfortunately, the ceremony was marred by a bomb scare. Some of the locals were prejudiced against Catholics and someone had said that all the Catholics on the platform would be blown to Hell. However, the work went on and in December of 1892, the Sisters moved in with 15 orphan children in the nearby Holy Providence School.

In 1893, two missionary Bishops visited Mother and implored her congregation to take over St. Catherine School in Santa Fe, New Mexico. The Drexel family had paid for the construction of the school but, like St. Stephan's in Wyoming, it closed for lack of teachers. Mother Katharine pleaded their case to Archbishop Ryan who once again refused. The next spring, the school was still closed for lack of teachers. Mother asked the Archbishop for permission to make a visitation as she had done at St. Stephan's in Wyoming.

Mother Katherine and Sister Mary Evangelist took the train to New Mexico and received an enthusiastic welcome from Archbishop Chapelle at the train station in Lamy. He shouted, "Thank God, my prayer is answered. You are coming to take St. Catherine's." The Sisters made an inventory and hired workmen to repair the building. When they returned to Philadelphia, Mother once again asked the Archbishop for permission to send her Sisters to St. Catherine's. He finally agreed to permit the new congregation to begin its first mission and take over the school.

The Missions

Over the next 42 years, Mother Katharine made many missionary journeys, established many missions, schools and convents and made many visitations to supervise them. She traveled by train, stagecoach, boat and car from one end of the country to the other in a flurry of apostolic activity. In most cases in the early days of her missions, Mother herself went to help the mission get set up and welcomed the sisters when they arrived. She had to deal with architects, contractors, lawyers and local church authorities. She had to be familiar with all of the details of the mission and plan its implementation. She also helped to clean and furnish the buildings. It took all of her talents in cooperation with God's graces to do what seemed the impossible.

Mother believed that the best help for Native Americans and African - Americans was a Christian education that taught the whole person, mind and spirit. She could not change a racist society but she did what she could do within its limitations. She taught the victims of discrimination that they were children of God, equal in dignity to all. That education entered into their homes and later into society.

Discrimination, racism, and segregation through so-called "separate but equal" public facilities remained as the law of the land of the United States until the Supreme Court reversed itself in 1954 in the case of *Brown v. Board of Education of Topeka*. Finally, after 335 years of living in the United States, racial discrimination against African-Americans was declared illegal. Mother Katharine's schools, teachings and example helped to lead the way to de-segregation and the Civil Rights Movement that followed it.

St. Catherine's School, Santa Fe, New Mexico. In 1894, Mother sent nine Sisters, with Mother Evangelist as Superior, to staff their first mission. On June 13, 1894, the new congregation had its first departure service for the new missionaries to St. Catherine's School. They were off to the city of Santa Fe (Holy Faith) to continue the mission of evangelization that the Spanish had begun in the 16th century.

St. Francis de Sales High School, Rock Castle, Virginia. In the fall of 1899, Mother opened a new high school for girls, St. Francis de Sales High School. It sat on 600 beautiful acres on a hill overlooking meadows and the James River. Like the groundbreaking for the Motherhouse, this opening was marred by arson that destroyed the new barn. However, the school opened and served as an industrial and normal school to educate poor African-American girls. It was a twin school to a nearby school established for boys by Mother's sister, Louise Morrell.

In addition to teaching, the Sisters made home visitations to help their families with food, clothing and firewood. The school became a cultural center with concerts and lectures. Mission stations were established where the Sisters taught catechism. This school became the model for the others to follow.

St. Michael's Mission, Arizona. In 1896, Mother Katharine donated the money to purchase about 200 acres of land near Gallup, New Mexico, at the edge of a Navajo Indian reservation. The Franciscan Fathers staffed the Mission. It was a difficult mission as the Indians distrusted the whites. Later, Mother visited the Mission, named it St. Michael's, bought additional land and built a new school and convent.

The Spanish first evangelized Navajo country in 1744 and two missions were established in 1748. They were burned two years later in a revolt that drove out the missionaries. This is how one Navajo leader told the story of his people and of their history with the whites:

> About two hundred years ago, the Spanish came to our country and said they were our boss; in 1846 the United States took our land from the Mexicans and told us we belonged to them. Why these nations, who had so much land of their own, had to fight about our land and take it way from us is hard for us to understand. When the United States' soldiers came, they said we would have to stop fighting. Most of our people did not believe we had to obey these strangers so kept on doing the same as they did before.

Eventually, the soldiers rounded up all of the Navajos and confined them to a fort for four years until a treaty in 1868 gave them a reservation in Arizona and New Mexico where they became sheepherders and craftspeople. By the end of the 19th century, there was no Catholic mission and there were no Catholic Navajos. Mother's Mission, staffed by her Sisters and Franciscan priests, gave witness of true poverty and self-sacrificing Catholicism. The Navajos admired this especially since the missionaries made the great effort to learn the Navajo language. Finally, they now trusted these whites and began to send their children to them to be educated.

Mother expressed her goal for St. Michael's, as with all of her Indian missions, in a letter:

We both burn with a desire to bring the full-bloods, what is left of them, somehow to the Church, to educate them so that they may not be cheated out of their land by the teeming population of whites, so that they, too, may be fit to intermarry with good Catholic whites, and not the worst white element. Thus they may be saved unto generation and generation, soul and body.

Immaculate Mother Academy and Industrial School, Nashville, Tennessee. In 1904, Mother Katharine agreed to purchase a house in Nashville for a school for poor African-American girls. When the owner of the house and his neighbors learned of this plan, they objected. The owner wrote to the newspaper and offered to rescind the deal.

Mother answered his letter, "The Sisters of the Blessed Sacrament, who have purchased the property, are religious, of the same race as yourself. We will always endeavor in every way to be neighborly to any white neighbors in the vicinity; we have every reason to hope we may receive from our white neighbors the cordial courtesy for which Southern people are so justly noted."

The school opened and flourished. Mother continued to overcome opposition and built and staffed more schools in Atlanta and Macon, Georgia; St. Louis, Missouri; Cincinnati, Ohio and Harlem, New York.

Xavier University, New Orleans, Louisiana. Mother Katherine had supported Archbishop Francis Janssens of New Orleans ever since his visit as her first supplicant in 1891. Over the years, through the Drexel Trust Fund, she had helped him build and support churches, schools and missions for the poor African-Americans of Louisiana. There was a great need to educate them because Louisiana provided no teachers to educate them and there were no African- American teachers for them.

New Orleans sits at the mouth of the Mississippi River and was the major southern commercial port and cultural center. The French explorer La Salle discovered it on April 9, 1692. He claimed the territory for his king, Louis XIV, and named it after him, Louisiana. The French settled New Orleans in 1717. By the late 19th century, the majority of African-American Catholics in the United States lived in New Orleans. Discriminatory segregation between whites and African-Americans was the way of life. Each race had supposedly separate but equal accommodations for travel, lodging, housing, restaurants, recreational facilities and schools. In fact, the buildings and equipment and supplies of the African-American schools were deplorable.

In 1913, New Orleans Archbishop James Blenk asked Mother to realize his dream to establish a high school and a teacher's college for African-Americans on the same site. He hoped that the high school graduates would form the student body for the college and those graduates could then teach the poor African-Americans at the elementary school level.

In 1915, Archbishop Blenk purchased the vacant buildings of the closed Southern University outside New Orleans. There, in spite of racial bigotry Mother Katherine established Xavier Academy High School. She sent her Sisters to staff their largest mission with integrated white and African-American lay teachers. Soon the new Blessed Sacrament parish was established at the site. The school grew very quickly with large enrollments.

In 1916, a 12th grade was established. In 1917, a two-year normal school was established and soon its graduates staffed the rural schools. In 1925, Xavier was established as a College of Liberal Arts and Sciences and conferred its first degrees in 1928. Xavier was the only predominantly African-American Catholic institution of higher learning in the United States. Archbishop Blenk's dream was finally realized.

Mother Katharine established Xavier University because at the time no Catholic university of the South was prepared to accept African-American students. Xavier, like Mother's other foundations, offered the opportunity to cement the greatest cohesion possible among students. All of them were considered by her to be children of God, independent of their race or color. In addition, she had the practical objective to give love and enterprising activity that in turn would favor the rise of united and balanced families to insure the spread and consolidation of the Catholic faith.

Louisiana Schools. Within a few short years, Mother Katharine established six parish schools in New Orleans and schools in six other rural towns. Then she journeyed throughout southern Louisiana and saw the poverty and deplorable state of education there. In the mid 1920s, she paid for the erection of 24 new rural schools that were supervised by Xavier University with teachers paid by the Drexel Trust Fund.

Speaking Engagements. Mother witnessed much racial hatred, bigotry and discrimination against African-Americans. In one such incident in Beaumont, Texas, her Sisters went to attend Mass at their parish church and were confronted with a sign, "We want an end to services here. We will not stand idly by, while White priests consort with nigger wenches in the face of our families. Suppress it in one week or flogging and tar and feathers will follow."

She resolved to speak publicly for the African-Americans who had no voice. She spoke directly to Catholics about their own prejudice against African-Americans. She pleaded not for money for them but for simple justice that they be treated equally. She implored the newspapers to be more objective and not to slant the news against African-Americans.

The Holy Rule

All religious congregations must have a Holy Rule to guide the lives of its members. The Rule must be approved by the Church. Early in 1907, Mother Drexel made an eight day retreat to discern the provisions of the Rule of the congregation that she founded. She wrote the Rule and had it approved by all of the Sisters and Archbishop Ryan. Then she sent it to Rome for the Church's approval.

Rome sent the Rule back and requested more information. When Mother Drexel was about to send everything back to Rome, she received a visit from Mother Cabrini, Foundress of the Sisters of the Sacred Heart. She recently had her Rule approved by Rome and advised Mother Drexel to deliver her Rule in person.

Mother Cabrini said, "You see, it is like this. You get a lot of mail every day. Some of it you must take care of immediately. Other items are important but you put them on the shelf to take care of tomorrow. Then tomorrow, something else demanding attention comes in and you leave the other letter still on the shelf. Before you know it there are a lot of other items before it. It is like that in Rome. Things get shelved even though they are important. If you want to get your Rule approved, you go yourself to Rome and take it with you."

Mother Drexel took Mother Cabrini's advice and left for Rome. She had a private audience with Pope Pius X. He was very interested in herwork and had a special concern for the needs of the Native American and African-American populations. He blessed Mother, the congregation and the people that they served. Soon after, he approved her Rule.

The Contemplative Life

In the fall of 1935, after a series of visitations, Mother Katharine suffered from a cerebral hemorrhage in St. Louis. She was advised to change her lifestyle, end her visitations and curtail her activities. With great reluctance, she agreed and returned to the Motherhouse in Cornwells Heights, Pennsylvania. She said, "Nobody is necessary for God's work. God can do the work without any of His creatures." Her sister Louise wrote, "Truly the zeal of God's house has consumed Mother. It is well nigh impossible in the span of our life to cover such a vast extent of ground and influence so many lives."Mother had to live with the knowledge that her life was very precarious and that she could die at any time. She wrote, "My heart action both regarding disturbances in rhythm and inefficiency of the myocardiac muscle renders me subject to a condition either of a stroke of paralysis which would incapacitate me, or of instant death. This is the answer the doctor gave me when I asked for the absolute truth about my condition."

Mother was confined for her last 20 years to two rooms on the second floor of the Motherhouse. She lived a life of prayer, penance and writing in her wheelchair. She prayed at daily Mass and daily two complete Rosaries of 30 mysteries, many Stations of the Cross, hours of meditation and countless litanies and ejaculations. Her wheelchair and writing evidenced her penitential poverty. The wheelchair was a makeshift thing consisting of a pupil's desk fastened to wheels. She wrote letters giving guidelines for her Sisters on scraps of paper with pencils that she sharpened down to the erasers.

By God's providence, Mother Katharine had become the contemplative nun that she always wanted to be. She prayed in the chapel for hours, interceding for the Order and its needs and the needs of those who they served. She prayed for peace throughout World War II. She wrote on June 28, 1944:

> My soul is sorrowful at what is going on now in the bombed cites of Calais, of Normandy, and the suffering and anguish of France and Italy. Oh, if we here in our convent motherhouse were to suffer as they. But here in the United States we have been spared miraculously.
> But our youth are being killed by the thousands, and

fathers, mothers, wives, etc, are in anguish of soul. Jesus
had to grieve over the sins of the whole world and it is
sin which has wrought this world war.

Mother suffered from physical ailments. She lived like this for the next 15 years. For the last five years of her life, she was confined to her bed. On the morning of March 3, 1955, she suddenly opened her eyes, looked straight ahead, closed them again, gave a sigh and breathed her last at the age of 96.

Her body lay in state at the Motherhouse for two days. Hundreds came to mourn her loss. One of them was a former student in Rock Castle who said, "We came to look upon a saint. She surely was a saint to live the way she did."

Mother Katharine's friend, Helen Grace Smith, stood by her coffin and said, "Her love of personal poverty made her oblivious to comfort of any kind. She went long distances, in all kinds of conveyances, and often walking when there was no other way, and she went simple, silent and unknown."

Bishop Joseph McShea, Auxiliary Bishop of Philadelphia, preached at the funeral that was attended by 250 Bishops, priests and brothers. He said, "The beloved soul of Mother Katharine was activated, inspired and impelled by an insatiable love of God and by complete subjection to His adorable Will. Hers was not a humanitarianism that stops where true love should begin. She was not a mere social reformer, educator or philanthropist striving to better the condition of her fellow man while permitting him to ignore God." Mother was a true missionary with a contemplative heart and true love of God and neighbor.

Six pallbearers carried out her coffin. Fittingly, two were white, two were African-American and two were Native Americans. Her coffin was interred in a crypt underneath the chapel at the Motherhouse in Bensalem, Pennsylvania.

Virtues

Katharine Drexel's holiness was grounded in her practice of the virtues. She had a firm faith that she instilled in others by education. Her hope endured in spite of many disappointments and opposition. Her love fordevotion which alone can banish the coldness of our time. The renewal which I seek and which we all seek is a work of love and can be accomplished by love alone.

Mother Drexel strictly obeyed her vow of poverty. She traveled by train in the least expensive seats and often carried her food with her. She mended her clothes and repaired her shoes until they were useless. She used scraps of paper and pencils worn to the erasers to write. She lived her last years in a cheap makeshift wheelchair fashioned from a student's school desk.

Fruits

Mother Drexel's long life was framed by the Civil War and the Korean War. It included the Industrial Revolution, the Centennial Year of the Declaration of Independence and the Atomic Age. Prejudice, bigotry and governmental inertia precluded the Native Americans and African-Americans from fully entering the mainstream of United States' society with equal rights and equal opportunity. The doors to the mainstream begin to open with educational opportunity and that's where Mother Drexel began.

Jesus said, "When much has been given a man, much will be required of him. More will be asked of a man to whom more has been entrusted." (Lk. 12:48). Mother Drexel had been given much, much was required of her, more was asked of her and she gave it all.

Cardinal Dennis Dougherty wrote, "If she had never done anything else than set such an example to a frivolous, self-seeking world, she should be regarded as a benefactress of the human race. She gave her immense fortune to her work. She did still more by giving herself to it. . . Whilst others persecute and revile Indians and Negroes as if they are mere hewers of wood and drawers of water, rather than God's children for whom our Savior's Blood was shed, she, a refined lady of culture, takes them to her heart and makes their cause her own."

A senior at St. Francis de Sales High School wrote a poem:

> … A woman walked on the bayou
> A woman walked in the fields
> A woman prayed for the souls of black folk
> A woman wept for the minds of black folk
> A woman – in cotton fields.

> "Sweet Lord, here is land for a harvest,
> Dear God, here are souls for Thee."
> "Sweet Savior," she whispered, "please answer
> If the work of these fields be for me."
> The answer was given, "Go child."
> She went - . . . .

In her lifetime, Mother spent millions of dollars from the income of the Drexel Trust Fund and used it to establish 60 institutions to care for the education of 25,000 Native Americans and African-Americans. She started with 13 Sisters who grew to 503 at the time of her death. She founded 49 convents for her Sisters, set up training courses for catechists and teachers, established 12 schools for Native Americans and nearly 100 schools in rural areas and inner cities of the South to educate African-Americans. She founded Xavier University, the first Catholic university predominantly for African-Americans in the Western Hemisphere. The schools and the Sisters who staffed them influenced generations of students, their parents and their communities.

Soon after Mother Drexel's death, the American Civil Rights Movement began to bring equal justice under the law to all. She was a true American. Her roots begin in early American history and she implemented the American democratic principles of equal rights and opportunities for all regardless of race, color, religion or national origin. She helped to forge the way for the Civil Rights Bill of 1964 and the Voting Rights Bill of 1965.

Saint

In 1974, 14 year-old Robert Gutherman was deaf in his right ear from a bone-dissolving infection. Two of his three ear bones were eaten away. The doctors had given up hope. His mother resigned herself to his permanent deafness. However, she prayed for an end to his terrible pain and suffering from the infection. She called the Sisters of the Blessed Sacrament at their Motherhouse near the Gutherman's home in Bensalem, Pennsylvania.

The Sisters recommended that they all pray for Mother Drexel's intercession. One night, Robert also prayed to Mother Drexel while he was alone in his hospital bed. When he awoke in the morning, the pain was gone and his hearing was restored to normal. His doctor said that this was impossible but he examined him and discovered that the two dissolved ear bones had re-grown. The Church adjudged the healing as a miracle. As a result, Mother Drexel was beatified and declared "Blessed" by Pope John Paul II on November 20, 1988.

In 1992, Amy Wall, also of Bensalem, was born with nerve deafness. Her mother heard about the miracle of Robert Gutherman and asked her family and friends to pray for Mother Drexel's intercession. They touched a relic of Mother Drexel to Amy's ears and prayed. Later, Amy's pre-school teacher noticed a change in her hearing. She was tested and had normal hearing in both ears. The Church adjudged the healing as a miracle. As a result, Mother Drexel was canonized and declared "Saint" by Pope John Paul II on October 1, 2000. Her Feast Day is March 3, the day of her death.

In his canonization Mass homily, the Holy Father said:

> Mother Katharine Drexel was born into wealth in Philadelphia. But from her parents she learned that her family possessions were not for them alone but were meant to be shared with the less fortunate.
>
> Later, she understood that more was needed. With great courage and confidence in God's grace, she chose to give not just her fortune but her whole life totally to the Lord. May her example help young people in particular to appreciate that no greater treasure can be found in this world than in following Christ with an undivided heart and in using generously the gifts we have received for the service of others and for the building of a more just and peaceful world. . . .
>
> Her apostolate bore fruit in the establishment of many schools for Native Americans and African-Americans, and served to raise awareness of the continuing need, even in our own day, to fight racism in all its manifestations.

When the Mass was over, a reporter asked one of the Navajos from Arizona, why Mother Drexel had become a saint. He simply said, "When nobody else did, she loved us."

Opening Prayer for the Mass in Commemoration of
Saint Katharine Drexel

Ever-loving God,
You called Saint Katharine Drexel
to teach the message of the gospel
and to bring the life of the Eucharist
to the African-American and Native American peoples.
By her prayers and example,
enable us to work for justice
among the poor and the oppressed,
and keep us undivided in love
in the eucharistic community of your Church.
Grant this through our Lord Jesus Christ, your Son,
who lives and reigns with you and the Holy Spirit,
one God for ever and ever.

Shrine:

Sisters of the Blessed Sacrament
1663 Bristol Pike
Bensalem, PA 19020
Telephone: 215-244-9900
Website: www.katharinedrexel.org
The Motherhouse is the shrine and home of the body of Mother
Drexel. It is located in a tomb one floor below the chapel above it.

22. The New Helpless – The Innocent Unborn

In 1973, the United States Supreme Court ruled that the unborn were not "persons" entitled to the protection of life guaranteed by the United States Constitution. The decision reminds us of the Dredd Scott decision of the United States Supreme Court in 1857 that ruled that African-American slaves were also not entitled to the protection of the Constitution. In 1973, in the case of *Roe v. Wade*, the court ruled that the states could not prohibit abortion. Since then, over 30 million innocent unborn children have been killed by abortion in the United States.

Pope John Paul II called the culture of the third millennium, a Culture of Death. It is a culture that legalizes and supports abortion, infanticide, embryonic experimentation, cloning and the death penalty – all of which result in death.

In *The Gospel of Life,* Pope John Paul II characterized the morals of our culture as "freedom of choice" and "ethical relativism." He said, "[I]ndividuals claim for themselves in the moral sphere the most complete freedom of choice and demand that the State should not adopt or impose any ethical position but limit itself to guaranteeing maximum space for the freedom of each individual, with the sole limitation of not infringing on the freedom and rights of any other citizen. . . . [I]n carrying out one's duties the only moral criterion should be what is laid down by the law itself. Individual responsibility is thus turned over to the civil law, with a renouncing of personal conscience, at least in the public sphere."

"At the basis of all these tendencies," he said, "lies the ethical relativism which characterizes much of present-day culture. . . . But it is precisely the issue of respect for life which shows what misunderstandings and contradictions, accompanied by terrible practical consequences, are concealed in this position." (Pope John Paul II, Encyclical Letter, *The Gospel of Life,* Nos. 69-70).

Pope John Paul II described the Culture of Death in a Message for the World Day of the Sick on February 11, 2003 in Washington, D.C. at the Basilica of the National Shrine of the Immaculate Conception. He said:

A model of society appears to be emerging in which the powerful predominate, setting aside and even eliminating the powerless: I am thinking here of unborn children, helpless victims of abortion; the elderly and incurable ill, subjected at times to euthanasia; and the many other people relegated to the margins of society by consumerism and materialism. Nor can I fail to mention the unnecessary recourse to the death penalty. . . . This model of society bears the stamp of the Culture of Death, and is therefore in opposition to the Gospel message. Faced with this worrying fact, how can we fail to include the defense of the Culture of Life among our pastoral priorities?

Pope John Paul II said in his encyclical, *The Gospel of Life*, "Nothing and no one can in any way permit the killing of an innocent human being, whether a fetus or an embryo, an infant or an old person. . . . The use of human embryos or fetuses as an object of experimentation constitutes a crime against their dignity as human beings who have a right to the same respect owed to a child once born, just as to every person." (Pope John Paul II, Encyclical Letter, *The Gospel of Life*, No. 63).

On July 23, 2001, Pope John Paul II urged United States President George W. Bush to reject medical research on human embryos. He said, "A free and virtuous society, which America aspires to be, must reject practices that devalue and violate human life at any stage from conception until natural death. In defending the right to life, in law and through a vibrant Culture of Life," the Holy Father continued, "America can show the world the path to a truly human future, in which man remains the master, not the product, of his technology."

He then referred to fundamental human rights, such as the right to life itself, and spoke about the "tragic coarsening of consciences" that makes possible the evils of abortion, euthanasia, infanticide and, more recently, "proposals for the creation for research purposes of human embryos, destined to destruction in the process."

Our Lady of Guadalupe and St. Juan Diego inculturated the Gospel into 16th century Mexico. They brought the Gospel message in terms that the natives could understand with Our Lady's pictographic image and with Juan's explanation of it and the apparitions and messages of Our Lady.

In the culture of the third millennium, they intercede as the Protectress of the Unborn and the Model for the Lay Apostolate.

Our Lady of Guadalupe, Protectress of the Unborn

One day when Pope John Paul II visited the Basilica of Our Lady of Guadalupe in Mexico City, he prayed to her, "Grant to our homes the grace of loving and respecting life in its beginnings, with the same love with which you conceived in your womb the life of the Son of God." When he dedicated a chapel to Our Lady of Guadalupe on May 12, 1992 at St. Peter's Basilica in Rome, he prayed that she would "always defend the gift of life."

On January 23, 1999, Pope John Paul II concelebrated Mass at the Basilica of Our Lady of Guadalupe with 500 Bishops and 5,000 priests. He virtually declared the end of the Culture of Death and preached, "The Church must proclaim the Gospel of Life and speak out with prophetic force against the Culture of Death. This is our cry: life with dignity for all. . . . The time has come to banish once and for all from the Continent every attack against life. . . . As a matter of urgency, we must stir up a new springtime of holiness on the Continent so that action and contemplation will go hand in hand."

Our Lady of Guadalupe said to Juan Diego, "I will give all my protection to the people. I am the merciful mother of all mankind. . . . Am I not your fountain of life?" She came to Tepeyac to replace Tonantzin, the false mother goddess that was worshiped there. Our Lady of Guadalupe is a mother who protects her children, both born and unborn, from death.

The promise of the *Memorare* prayer to Mary is, "Never was it known that anyone who fled to your protection was left unaided." As Our Lady of Guadalupe ended human sacrifice in Mexico, so she will also end human sacrifice by abortion. She acts as a mother who protects her unborn child from death. For these reasons, Our Lady of Guadalupe is now known as the "Patroness and Protectress of the Unborn."

By this title, we place under her patronage and protection all unborn children. We beg her protection of the mothers of the unborn and the children within their wombs. We ask her to help these mothers to bring their children to birth and to save the souls of those who have been killed by abortion. Three major pro-life apostolates in the United States, Human Life International, Priests for Life and the Missionary Image of Our Lady of Guadalupe entrusted their apostolates to the patronage of Our Lady of Guadalupe.

The late Cardinal John O'Connor of New York said, "We commend the Pro-Life Movement of the Archdiocese of New York to the protection and guidance of Our Lady of Guadalupe. . . . Our Lady of Guadalupe pray for America, pray for the Unborn."

Pope John Paul II concluded his encyclical *The Gospel of Life* with this prayer that entrusts the cause of life to Mary:

O Mary,
bright dawn of the new world, Mother of the living,
to you do we entrust the *cause of life:*
Look down, O Mother
upon the vast numbers
of babies not allowed to be born,
of the poor whose lives are made difficult,
of men and women
who are victims of brutal violence,
of the elderly and the sick killed
by indifference or out of misguided mercy.
Grant that all who believe in your Son
may *proclaim the Gospel of life*
with honesty and love
to the people of our time. . . . Amen.

Saint Juan Diego, Model for the Lay Apostolate

An apostle is one who is sent to a nation as a messenger for God. Saint Juan Diego was a layman who was the apostle to Mexico and as such is the Model for the Lay Apostolate. He was sent by the Queen of Apostles as a messenger to manifest her Son to the people.

Juan was a model lay apostle who foreshadowed those described in *The Decree on the Apostolate of the Laity* of the Second Vatican Council. Juan may become known as one of the great saints in the history of the Church. He should be recognized as something of a Patriarch, like Abraham or Moses. He didn't lead thousands to the Promised Land but he led millions to the Promised One through the intercession of Our Lady of Guadalupe.

Pope John Paul II said at Juan's beatification ceremony:

> Similar to ancient Biblical personages who were collective representations of all the people, we could say that Juan Diego represents all the indigenous peoples who accepted the Gospel of Jesus, thanks to the maternal aid of Mary, who is always inseparable from the manifestation of her Son and the spread of the Church, as was her presence among the Apostles on the day of Pentecost.
>
> The recognition of the veneration that has been given for centuries to the layman, Juan Diego, assumes a particular importance. It is a strong call to all the lay faithful of the nation to assume all their responsibilities in the transmission of the Gospel Message and in the witness of a living and operative faith. . . .
>
> The lay faithful share in the prophetic, priestly and royal role of Christ (cf. Documents of Vatican II, *Lumen Gentium*, No. 31), but they carry out this vocation in the ordinary situations of daily life. Their natural and immediate field of action extends to all the areas of human coexistence and to everything that constitutes culture in the widest and fullest sense of the term.

On November 13, 2005, Pope Benedict XVI recalled that the Second Vatican Council "paid great attention to the role of the lay faithful," defining "their vocation and mission, rooted in Baptism and Confirmation, and oriented to seeking the Kingdom of God by engaging in temporal affairs and by ordering them according to the plan of God." (cf. Documents of Vatican II, *Lumen Gentium*, No. 31)

Juan Diego is the model for the lay apostolate and, like him, all of the lay faithful are called to imbue every area of social life with the spirit of the Gospel and to be witnesses in words and deeds of his virtues of humility, obedience, charity, trust and patience in our own time and place.

"The mission of the Church pertains to the salvation of men, which is to be achieved by belief in Christ and by His grace. The apostolate of the Church and of all its members is primarily designed to manifest Christ's message by words and deeds and to communicate His grace to the world."

(Documents of Vatican II, *Decree on the Apostolate of the Laity,* ch. 2, No. 6). The Queen of the Apostles, Our Lady of Guadalupe, and her apostle Juan Diego carried out this mission to the greatest degree known in the history of the world.

"Whether the lay apostolate is exercised by the faithful as individuals or as members of organizations, it should be incorporated into the apostolate of the whole Church according to a right system of relationships. Indeed, union with those whom the Holy Spirit has assigned to rule His Church (cf. Acts 20.28) is an essential element of the Christian apostolate." (Documents of Vatican II, *Decree on the Apostolate of the Laity* ch. 5, No. 23).

Juan Diego received the mission from Our Lady of Guadalupe who called him and sent him to the Bishop. He was chosen as an individual, but he exercised his role in union with the whole Church through his Bishop just as the Council requested over 400 years later. The experience of Juan Diego shows that the inspirational grace for a great work may first come to a layperson who then cooperates with the hierarchy. Because he did so, he is truly worthy to be "The Model for the Lay Apostolate."

Pope John Paul II's response to the Culture of Death is hope for a Culture of Life and a Civilization of Love in a New Evangelization with protection of the lives of the innocent unborn. The Culture of Life needs a saint for them. Perhaps Servant of God Dorothy Day, a laywoman, will be canonized some day.

23. Servant of God Dorothy Day and Unborn Children

Born	November 8, 1897 in Brooklyn, New York
Catholic Convert	Baptized December 28, 1927
Died	November 29, 1980, in New York, New York Co-founder with Peter Maurin of the Catholic Worker Movement

"I wish every woman who has ever suffered an abortion would come to know Dorothy Day. Her story was so typical. Made pregnant by a man who insisted she have an abortion, who then abandoned her anyway, she suffered terribly for what she had done, and later pleaded with others not to do the same. But later, too, after becoming a Catholic, she learned the love and mercy of the Lord, and knew she never had to worry about His forgiveness. [This is why I have never condemned a woman who has had an abortion; I weep with her and ask her to remember Dorothy Day's sorrow but to know always God's loving mercy and forgiveness.] She had died before I became Archbishop of New York, or I would have called on her immediately upon my arrival. Few people have had such an impact on my life, even though we never met."
New York Cardinal John O'Connor.

The young woman hobbled down the darkened stairwell of the Upper East Side flat in New York City. Her steps were unsteady. Her left arm held the banister tightly. Her right arm clutched her abdomen. It was burning in pain. She walked out onto the street alone in the dark. It was in September of 1919. Dorothy Day had just aborted her baby.

Dorothy Day co-founded the Catholic Worker Movement in 1933 with Peter Maurin. She is a model pro-life lay witness and intercessor. She advocated the philosophy of Personalism, later taught by Pope John Paul II, that God endows every human being with equal dignity and rights to life, work, social justice and freedom of religion. She was chosen as the 20th century's most outstanding lay Catholic. Cardinal John O'Connor of New York introduced the cause for her canonization and said, "It is with great joy that I announce the approval of the Holy See for the Archdiocese of New York to open the Cause for the Beatification and Canonization of Dorothy Day. With this approval comes the title Servant of God. What a gift to the Church in New York and to the Church Universal this is!"

Dorothy Day died at age 83 on November 29, 1980. This chapter substantially contains her actual words as edited and sometimes paraphrased by the author. The information concerning her abortion was obtained from her biographers and her autobiographical novel, *The Eleventh Virgin.* Dorothy herself never publicly wrote or spoke about her abortion.

Lionel, my boyfriend, promised to pick me up at the flat after the abortion was over. I waited in pain from nine a.m. to ten p.m. but he never came. When I got home to his apartment I found only a note. He said he had left for a new job and, regarding my abortion, that I "was only one of God knows how many millions of women who go through the same thing. Don't build up any hopes. It is best, in fact, that you forget me."

I wrote about this experience in my autobiographical novel, *The Eleventh Virgin.* In my youth I had thought that the greatest gift that life could offer would be a faith in God and a hereafter. But then there were too many people passing through my life, – too many activities – too much pleasure (not happiness). The life of the flesh called to me as a good and wholesome life, regardless of God's laws. What was good and what was evil? It is easy enough to stifle conscience for a time. The satisfied flesh has its own law. How much time I wasted during those years! I had fallen a long way from my youthful ideals. When I was fifteen I wrote, "I am working always, always on guard, praying without ceasing to overcome all physical sensations and be purely spiritual."

But these "physical sensations" allured me. I lived a social-activist Bohemian lifestyle in Greenwich Village, New York City. I think back and remember myself, hurrying along from party to party, and all the friends, and the drinking, and the talk, and the crushes, and falling in love. I fell in love with a newspaperman named Lionel Moise. I got pregnant. He said that if I had the baby, he would leave me. I wanted the baby but I wanted Lionel more. So I had the abortion and I lost them both.

I later wrote in my autobiography, *The Long Loneliness*, "For a long time [after my abortion] I had thought I could not bear a child, and the longing in my heart for a baby had been growing."

In 1924, I started a "live-in" relationship with Forster Batterham, an atheist and an anarchist. He believed in nothing except personal freedom to do as you please. We took up residence in a beach bungalow on Staten Island, New York. We foreshadowed the hippies of the 1960s and lived a carefree lifestyle living off the land and sea – gardening, fishing and clamming. I thought that we would be contributing to the misery of the world if we failed to rejoice in the sun, the moon and the stars, in the rivers which surrounded the island on which we lived and in the cool breezes of the bay. Like Dostoevsky, I began to believe that the world would be saved by beauty. It was this beautiful, natural world that slowly led me back to God. "How can there be no God," I asked Forster, "when there are all these beautiful things?"

However, I felt that my home was not a home without a child. For a long time I had thought that I could not have another child. No matter how much one is loved or one loves, that love is lonely without a child. It is incomplete. Soon I became pregnant again. I saw this as a miracle from God because I thought that He had left me barren after the abortion. I wrote in a letter to a friend, "I always rather expected an ugly grotesque thing which only I could love; expecting perhaps to see my sins in the child."

On the contrary, I gave birth to a beautiful daughter, Tamar Teresa, on March 3, 1927. I remembered that the labor pains swept over me like waves in the beautiful rhythm of the sea. When I became bored and impatient with the steady restlessness of those waves of pain, I thought of all the other and more futile kinds of pain I would rather not have had. Toothaches, earaches, and broken arms. I had had them all. And this was a much more satisfactory and accomplishing pain, I comforted myself.

I thought about famous men who wrote about childbirth such as Tolstoy and O'Neill and I thought, "What do they know about it, the idiots." It gave me pleasure to imagine one of them in the throes of childbirth. How they would groan and holler and rebel. And wouldn't they make everybody else miserable around them. And there I was, conducting a neat and tidy job.

The waves of pain became tidal waves. Earthquake and fire swept my body. Through the rush and roar of the cataclysm that was all about me, I heard the murmur of the doctor and the answered murmur of the nurse at my head. In a white blaze of thankfulness I heard faint about the clamor in my ears, a peculiar squawk. They handed my baby to me. I placed her on my full breast where she mouthed around, too lazy to tug for food. I thought, "What do you want, little bird? That it should run into your mouth, I suppose. But no, you must work for your provender already!" No matter how cynically or casually the worldly may treat the birth of a child, it remains spiritually and physically a tremendous event. God pity the woman who does not feel the fear, the awe, and the joy of bringing a child into the world.

I was filled with awe of my baby's new life and in gratitude to God I wanted her to be baptized in the Catholic Church. I did not want my child to flounder as I had often floundered. I wanted to believe, and I wanted my child to believe, and if belonging to the Church would give her so inestimable a grace as faith in God, and the companionable love of the saints then the thing to do was to have her baptized a Catholic. This was the final straw for Forster who wanted nothing to do with any commitments or what he termed as my "absorption in the supernatural."

I knew that I was going to have my child baptized a Catholic, cost what it may. I knew I was not going to have her floundering as I had done, doubting and hesitating, undisciplined and amoral. I felt it was the greatest thing I could do for my child.

So Tamar was baptized in June. For myself, I prayed for the gift of faith. I was sure, yet not sure. I postponed the day of decision. To become a Catholic meant for me to give up a mate with whom I was much in love. It got to the point where it was the simple question of whether I chose God or man. I chose God and I lost Forster. I was baptized on the Feast of The Holy Innocents, December 28, 1927. It was something I had to do. I was tired of following the devices and desires of my own heart, of doing what I wanted to do, what my desires told me to do, which

285

always seemed to lead me astray. The cost was the loss of the man I loved, but it paid for the salvation of my child and myself.

I painfully described this loss in *The Long Loneliness*: "For a woman who had known the joys of marriage, yes, it was hard. It was years before I awakened without that longing for a face pressed against my breast, an arm around my shoulder. The sense of loss was there. It was a price I had paid. I was Abraham who had sacrificed Isaac. And yet I had Isaac, I had Tamar."

I always had a great regret for my abortion. In fact, I tried to cover it up and to destroy as many copies of *The Eleventh Virgin* as I could find. But my priest chided me and said, "You can't have much faith in God if you're taking the life given to you and using it that way. God is the one who forgives us if we ask, and it sounds like you don't even want forgiveness – just to get rid of the books." I never forgot what the priest pointed out – the vanity or pride at work in my heart. Since that time, I wasn't as worried as I had been. If you believe in the mission of Jesus Christ, then you're bound to try to let go of your past, in the sense that you are entitled to His forgiveness. To keep regretting what was, is to deny God's grace.

After my conversion, I struggled to support my child as a single parent working as a free-lance writer. In December 1932, I was in Washington D.C. covering the Hunger March of the Unemployed. Watching the ragged men marching moved my sense of social justice and I was inspired to go to the Basilica of the National Shrine of the Immaculate Conception to pray. I cried out to God in anguish that some way would open up for me to use what talents I possessed for my fellow workers, for the poor.

When I returned to New York, I found waiting for me an unkempt man with fire in his eyes. Immediately, he began preaching to me in a thick French accent his grand vision for social justice. His name was Peter Maurin and together we founded the Catholic Worker Movement.

We opened houses of hospitality for the poor, the hungry, the homeless, and for abused women and pregnant mothers. We practiced the spiritual and corporal works of mercy. One day 30-year old Elizabeth came to us at the end of her pregnancy. Her husband was a drug addict. It was New Year's Eve, the eve of the Feast of the Holy Family. He came to our house drugged and sat at supper asleep while his wife fed him.

I called the ambulance, but he refused their help. He muttered, "She's my wife. She has to stick to me. She has to take care of me." *Oh*, I thought, *the distortion of the idea of the Holy Family. She has to take care of him and she about to bear his child*! But we had a little bed ready for the baby, and a box of pretty garments, and she was happy as she looked at them, and there was even gaiety in our midst as we sat around the fire and had a cup of tea in the holiday spirit.

I'll never forget the time that I had to literally stand up against birth control. My sister Della had worked for Margaret Sanger, foundress of Planned Parenthood. When Della exhorted me that I shouldn't encourage my daughter Tamar to have so many children, I stood up firmly and walked out of the house whereupon Della ran after me weeping, saying, "Don't leave me, don't leave me. We just won't talk about it again." To me, birth control and abortion are genocide. I say, make room for children, don't do away with them. I learned that prevention of conception when the act that one is performing is for the purpose of fusing the two lives more closely and so enrich them that another life springs forth and the aborting of a life conceived, are sins that are great frustrations in the natural and spiritual order.

The Sexual Revolution is a complete rebellion against authority, natural and supernatural, even against the body and its needs, its natural functions of child bearing. This is not reverence for life, it is a great denial and more resembles Nihilism than the revolution that they think they are furthering.

Once I asked a man why he signed a petition for the Rosenbergs, who had been convicted of treason in the 1950s. "It is because I am against capital punishment," he said. In other words, he, as the rest of us, is in favor of life – life until natural death.

I was happy that I could be with my mother the last few weeks of her life and for the last ten days at her bedside daily and hourly. Sometimes I thought that it was like being present at a birth to sit by a dying person and see their intentness on what is happening to them. It almost seems that one is absorbed in a struggle, a fearful, grim, physical struggle, to breathe, to swallow, to live. And so, I kept thinking to myself, how necessary it is for one of their loved ones to be beside them, to pray for them, to offer up prayers for them unceasingly, as well as to do all those little offices one can.

When my daughter Tamar was a little tiny girl, she said to me, "When I get to be a great big woman and you are a little tiny girl, I'll take care of you." I thought of that when I had to feed my mother by the spoonful and urged her to eat her custard. Shortly before she died I told her, "We can no more imagine life beyond the grave than a blind man can imagine colors." How good God was to me, to let me be there. I was there, holding her hand, and she just turned her head and sighed. That was her last breath, that little sigh; and her hand was warm in mine for a long time after.

Dorothy Day died at the age of 83 on November 29, 1980. Long before her death, many regarded her as a saint. She brusquely responded, "Don't call me a saint. I don't want to be dismissed so easily."

When he placed her cause before the Vatican Congregation for the Causes of Saints, New York Cardinal John O'Connor said, "Dorothy Day is a saint – not a 'gingerbread' saint or a 'holy card' saint, but a modern-day devoted daughter of the Church." Her story is a sign of the mercy of God for the millions of women who've had abortions. "Mercy," he said, "in that a woman who sinned so gravely could find such unity with God upon conversion." She confirmed, and anticipated the teachings of Pope John Paul II. The Cardinal, who was a former military chaplain, confirmed that her radical social teaching "is in complete fidelity to the Church." He even found her pacifism saintly. "Like so many other saints of days gone by," he said, "she urged people to live on earth the life they would one day lead in Heaven, a life of peace and harmony."

24. The New Immigration

Migrant farm workers are among the new immigrants. Unlike former immigrants, however, many of them are "illegal" or "undocumented" since they arrived in the United States without a visa. They move from farm to farm and pick various crops as they ripen at different times of the year. In the 1960s, Cesar Chavez brought their plight in California to national attention. He was a union organizer and a former migrant worker himself. He said, "The love for justice that is in us is not only the best part of our being but it is also the most true to our nature."

These migrant workers were Mexican-Americans who lived in tin shanties or their cars and trucks. They ate whatever they could get their hands on and worked in the scorching sun for hours on end picking unsafe pesticide-laden fruits and vegetables in the San Joaquin Valley for low, piecework wages. Like the earlier immigrants, they had no unemployment insurance, no medical insurance, no worker's compensation and no benefits. They called it, *En El Labor*.

Chavez appealed for justice for them. He said:

Today, thousands of migrant farm workers live under savage conditions – beneath trees and amid garbage and human excrement – near fields that use the most modern farm technology and pesticides – all unsafe and unhealthy working conditions. Vicious rats gnaw on them as they sleep. They walk miles to buy food at inflated prices. And they carry in water from irrigation pumps. Almost 800,000 of their under-aged children work across America. Migrant workers are not agricultural implements. They are not beasts of burden to be used up and thrown away. They are human beings with inherent dignity as children of God and have natural rights to good living and working conditions and fair pay!

Chavez used the methods of the great Indian leader, Mahatma Gandhi. Chavez used peaceful marches and boycotts to raise public awareness of the workers' plight, all in the hopes of gaining better conditions for them. He gave the Hispanic people a sense of *coraje* – righteous anger – and urged them to unite in a union. This resulted in the formation of the United Farm Workers. It led a national grape boycott against grapes so that the migrant laborers would receive better pay and better living and working conditions.

Dorothy Day supported Chavez and was jailed in 1973 at the age of 75 for picketing with him and the United Farm Workers in California. When she was in jail, she wrote a prayer in the front of her Bible to Pope John XXIII:

> Dear Pope John – please, yourself a *campesino*, watch over the United Farm Workers. Raise up more and more leader-servants throughout the country to stand with Cesar Chavez in this nonviolent struggle with Mammon, in all the rural districts of North and South, in cotton fields, beet fields, potato fields, in our orchards and vineyards, our orange groves – wherever men, women, and children work on the land. Help make a new order wherein justice flourishes, and, as Peter Maurin, himself a peasant, said so simply, "where it is easier to be good."

However, the struggle goes on and we await Dorothy's "new order wherein justice flourishes." Many of the new immigrants await this new order in the small town of Immokolee in southwest Florida.

"Immokolee" means "my home" in the native Seminole Indian language. Today it is the home of many Mexican migrant farm laborers. Immokolee is the center of the southern Florida migrant labor industry. The workers live in ramshackle mobile homes in trailer parks that house multiple families and individuals who share the rent and divide the trailer into multiple living quarters. Immokolee is also the home of Our Lady of Guadalupe Church. This church services the migrant laborers and helps to feed and clothe them.

The migrant laborers' day begins at dawn at 5 a.m. when they meet at the town square to board the buses that take them to the tomato fields. The youngest and strongest men (no women are wanted) compete in a survival of the fittest to get on the busses for a day's work. Their day continues as they pick tomatoes from dawn to dusk for the same wages that were paid 40 years ago. Their maximum annual wage is $7500. There has been no cost of living increase for migrant laborers and they are not paid the minimum wage, but by the weight of the crops that they pick. They suffer from unjust wages and unjust living and working conditions. Their day ends in squalid exhaustion.

Some of the migrant laborers suffer from slavery. Several people were convicted of conspiracy for involuntary servitude in southern Florida. The farm owners insulate themselves from criminal liability and hire labor bosses as subcontractors to find and hire migrant laborers for them. These labor bosses often physically force the migrant laborers to remain on the farm and keep them as their own slaves for the owners until they pay off exhorbitant debts for smuggling them into the United States or for getting them employment.

In several modern cases, a dozen Florida farm labor bosses, smugglers and their associates have been sent to prison for enslaving and exploiting migrant laborers. Most of the victims were Mexicans who are susceptible to mistreatment because they lack proper work authorization and are reluctant to speak out.

"They're not on the radar. They don't have status. Oftentimes, they're not familiar with the rights they do have," said an FBI agent. "They're fearful of the repercussions if they're found."

Renegade labor bosses use against them the Mexican workers' illegal immigration status and their fears. Some threaten or commit violence. Others charge outrageous amounts for food, shelter and loans.

All these factors combine to create in South Florida, what a Justice Department official calls "ground zero for modern slavery." An agent with the United States Border Patrol said, "Most of the time, these workers are housed miles from civilization, with no telephones or cars. They're controllable. There's no escape. If you do escape, what are you gonna do? Whoever's got you, they'll find you. And Heaven help you when they do."

The treatment of migrant laborers is not merely a political matter of deciding the best immigration policy for foreign laborers. It is a moral matter of deciding to do the right thing for other human beings who have the same dignity as us as children of God.

Foreigners have a natural right to migrate, especially for the basic human needs of food, clothing and shelter. At the same time, the United States has a right to its security and to reasonably regulate the flow of immigration. These two rights often come in conflict when determining immigration policy. In the current condition of the world, in which poverty and persecution are rampant, the presumption is that persons must migrate in order to support and protect themselves and their families and that nations such as the United States who are able to receive them, should do so whenever possible.

The Church has always contemplated the image of Christ in immigrants. He said, "I was a stranger and you made me welcome." (Mt. 25:35). Jesus Himself was an immigrant who was born in a manger and fled with his Mother and foster father into Egypt, where they were foreigners.

The United States has experienced many immigrations, as waves of men and women came to its various regions at different times in the hope of a better future. Over seventy five percent of the saints of the states were immigrants. This phenomenon continues today.

Immigrants often bring with them a cultural heritage of faith and family values. We should foster a welcoming attitude to them among the local population, in the belief that a mutual openness will bring enrichment to all. In this process, immigrants should take the necessary steps towards social inclusion, such as learning the English language and complying with our laws.

The Church in America must be a vigilant advocate, defending against any unjust restriction the natural right of individual persons to move freely within their own nation and from one nation to another. Attention must be called to the rights of migrants and their families and to respect for their human dignity, even in cases of non-legal immigration. (See *Strangers No Longer: Together on the Journey of Hope,* Pastoral Letter of the Catholic Bishops of Mexico and the United States, January 22, 2003.)

Pope John Paul II called us to be in solidarity with the Mexican undocumented immigrants and their families whose entry to the United States was non-legal. They are our brothers and sisters in Christ with Our Lady of Guadalupe as our mutual Mother. Hopefully, the needs of these new immigrants will be met through the intercession of Our Lady of Guadalupe and Saints John Neumann and Mother Cabrini, the missionaries to the earlier immigrants.

Part Four:

The New Evangelization of America

25. Our Lady of Guadalupe, Patroness, Queen, Mother and Evangelizer of America

Patroness of the States

The image of Our Lady of Guadalupe is the representation of the Immaculate Conception and, as such, it is the representation of the Patroness of the United States who is the Immaculate Conception.

Our Lady of Guadalupe identified herself as "the *perfect* and perpetual Virgin Mary." When Juan Diego unfurled his tilma in front of Bishop Zumarraga, the Bishop exclaimed, "It is the Immaculate One!" The Immaculate Conception is the Patroness of the United States of America as proclaimed by Pope Pius IX in 1847 who granted the request of the American Bishops gathered for the Sixth Provincial Council of Baltimore. In 1959, the United States Bishops consecrated the country to the Immaculate Conception and renewed this consecration in 2006.

The Immaculate Conception Church in Allentown, Pennsylvania was dedicated on October 5, 1974 in honor of Our Lady of Guadalupe. On that occasion, Bishop Sidney Metzger said, "It is eminently fitting that Our Lady of Guadalupe is welcomed here because it is accepted as certain and evident that her painting represents the Immaculate Conception. This interpretation was authorized by Pope Benedict XIV who in a Papal Brief in 1754 does not hesitate to call Our Lady the Blessed Virgin Immaculate of Guadalupe."

The United States Bishops entrusted the New Evangelization in the United States to Our Lady of Guadalupe. In 1992, the United States observed the five hundredth anniversary of the evangelization of the Americas begun by Christopher Columbus in 1492. The American Bishops entrusted this observance to Our Lady of Guadalupe. They said in their pastoral letter *Heritage and Hope: Evangelization in America,* "We entrust our observance of the quincentennial year, our commitment to giving birth with new fervor to the life of the Gospel in our hemisphere, to Our Lady of Guadalupe, Patroness of the Americas. She truly was the first Christ-bearer; by her maternal intercession, may her faithful sons and daughters be renewed and discover afresh the joy and splendor and promise of being bearers of the good news." A shrine to Our Lady of Guadalupe is located in La Crosse, Wisconsin.

Mother and Evangelizer of America

Pope John Paul II had a great devotion to Our Lady of Guadalupe. In January of 1979, he made his first pilgrimage to Mexico and consecrated his papacy to her. He stressed her evangelistic role at St. Peter's Basilica in Rome on the four hundred and fiftieth anniversary of the apparitions. On December 12, 1981, he talked about Our Lady leading us to Christ from the Basilica Shrine in Mexico City as a center "from which the light of the Gospel of Christ will shine out over the whole world by means of the miraculous image of His Mother."

On the same day, Cardinal Casaroli, the Papal Legate, was present at the Basilica Shrine in Mexico representing the Pope. During his homily he said, "From that humble height [Tepeyac Hill] the Virgin's eye turned to the immense expanses of the Americas, from the impassable peaks to the deep valleys, from the wind-swept plateaus to the boundless plains, as far as the extreme end of the continent, where the two oceans that surround it unite in a stormy embrace. It was as if the Mother's gentle smile illuminated them all with love and hope. Just as the sun, reflecting its brightness in the rivers and lakes, brings forth, as it were, new suns, so the Virgin's smile, beaming from Tepeyac Hill, seemed to be reflected in every part of this continent." He prayed to her, "O our Merciful Mother! From this house of yours and from all your sanctuaries scattered all over the Americas and throughout the world, lend your ears and your help to those who invoke you. O Mother of God and our Mother: give us peace! Amen."

Cardinal Casaroli also dedicated a statue of Pope John Paul II located on the Basilica grounds. He said, "Today we inaugurate this monument, which will perpetuate in your midst, in the Marian center of Mexico and of the Americas, his mild and beloved fatherly figure. Perhaps you do not need this, you who have carved his effigy in your hearts; but the monument is addressed to the future generations which will come here, so that they will remember that Pope John Paul II came here one day, a pilgrim like them, to lay his supplications and his hopes at the feet of Our Lady of Guadalupe."

One day, when Pope John Paul II paused before a replica of the tilma he said, "I feel drawn to this picture of Our Lady of Guadalupe because her face is full of kindness and simplicity... it calls me."

He responded to this call and on May 6, 1990, he made another pilgrimage to the Basilica Shrine. There he proclaimed Juan Diego as "Blessed." On this occasion he said, "The Virgin chose him from among the most humble as the one to receive that loving and gracious manifestation of hers which is the Guadalupe apparition. Her maternal face and her blessed image which she left us as a priceless gift is a permanent remembrance of this."

On May 12, 1992, Pope John Paul II dedicated a chapel to Our Lady of Guadalupe in St. Peter's Basilica in Rome below the main altar and near the tomb of St. Peter. He referred to Our Lady as the "Star of Evangelization and consequently the symbol of unity. . . ." He prayed, "Most Holy Virgin of Guadalupe, . . . always defend the gift of life, make truth and justice reign; promote industriousness and the Christian sharing of resources. May there be a joyous fulfillment of the civilization of love in the great family of the children of God. Amen."

The year 2003 marked Pope John Paul II's 25th anniversary as Pope. He credited Our Lady of Guadalupe as his guide. He said, "Ever since I went on pilgrimage for the first time to the splendid Shrine of Guadalupe on January 29, 1979, she has guided my steps in these almost twenty five years of service as Bishop of Rome and universal pastor of the Church. I wish to invoke her, the sure way to encounter Christ, and who was the first evangelizer of America, as the 'Star of Evangelization,' entrusting to her the ecclesial work of all her sons and daughters of America."

In 1983, in an address in Haiti, Pope John Paul II called for a "New Evangelization, one that is new in its fervor, new in its methods, and new in its expression." This call is for all of those who are baptized, not just for missionaries.

In his Apostolic Exhortation, *On the Christian Laity* in 1988 he said, "Each Christian's words and life must make this proclamation resound: God loves you, Christ came for you, Christ is for you 'the Way, the Truth, and the Life!' (Jn. 14:6)." (Pope John Paul II, Apostolic Exhortation, *Christifidelis Laici (On the Christian Laity)*, No. 34). The laity can participate in this role by intentionally living their faith through their daily duties in the world with Christian values as a sign of contradiction to worldly values. We must bring the good news of the Gospel into our culture through our words and actions. This is known as inculturation.

On December 12, 1998, the Feast Day of Our Lady of Guadalupe, Pope John Paul II called her the "Mother and Evangelizer of America" at the historical First Synod of all of the Bishops of America in Rome. He announced a new mission "to undertake the New Evangelization of the American continent." He saw America as one continent "from Alaska to Tierra del Fuego, from the Pacific to the Atlantic. . . ., a continent called in its various sectors to integration and solidarity."

He entrusted to her, as the Star of the New Evangelization, the "future path of the Church on the great continent of America." He referred to America in the singular to emphasize the call to all Americans to unity and solidarity.

In 1999, Pope John Paul II made his fourth pilgrimage to Mexico and consecrated the entire Continent to Our Lady of Guadalupe. He was invited to come to the Basilica to deliver his Summary of the American Bishops' Synod. He signed the Summary, his Apostolic Exhortation, *The Church in America*, and symbolically laid it at the feet of Our Lady of Guadalupe.

The Pope wrote, "In this moment of her history, the Church in America is called to respond with loving generosity to the fundamental task of evangelization. (No.1). . . . I announced the theme of the Special Assembly for America of the Synod in these words: Encounter with the Living Jesus Christ: The Way to Conversion, Communion and Solidarity in America. Put this way, the theme makes clear the centrality of the person of the Risen Christ, present in the life of the Church and calling people to conversion, communion and solidarity. The starting-point of such a program of evangelization is in fact the encounter with the Lord. Given by Christ in the Paschal Mystery, the Holy Spirit guides us towards those pastoral goals which the Church in America must attain in the third Christian millennium." (No. 3).

The Holy Father referred to America as one continent and said that Americans are called to unity. "Open to the unity which comes from true communion with the Risen Lord, the particular Churches, and all who belong to them, will discover through their own spiritual experience that the encounter with the Living Jesus Christ is the path to conversion, communion and solidarity. To the extent that these goals are reached, there will emerge an ever increasing dedication to the New Evangelization of America." (No. 7). . . . He continued:

> From the beginning invoked as 'Our Lady of Guadalupe', Mary, by her motherly and merciful figure, was a great sign of the closeness of the Father and of Jesus Christ, with whom she invites us to enter into communion.
>
> The appearance of Mary to the native Juan Diego on the hill of Tepeyac in 1531 had a decisive effect on evangelization. Its influence greatly overflows the boundaries of Mexico, spreading to the whole Continent. America, which historically has been, and still is, a melting-pot of peoples, has recognized in the mestiza face of the Virgin of Tepeyac, 'in Blessed Mary of Guadalupe, an impressive example of a perfectly inculturated evangelization'. Consequently, not only in Central and South America, but in North America as well, the Virgin of Guadalupe is venerated as Queen of all America.
>
> With the passage of time, pastors and faithful alike have grown increasingly conscious of the role of the Virgin Mary in the evangelization of America. In the prayer composed for the Special Assembly for America of the Synod of Bishops, Holy Mary of Guadalupe is invoked as 'Patroness of all America and Star of the first and new evangelization'. In view of this, I welcome with joy the proposal of the Synod Fathers that the feast of Our Lady of Guadalupe, Mother and Evangelizer of America,

be celebrated throughout the continent on December 12.
(No. 11).

The Holy Father's Exhortation concludes with a prophecy and a prayer.
"In America, the mestiza face of the Virgin of Guadalupe was from the
start a symbol of the inculturation of the Gospel, of which she has been
the lodestar and the guide. Through her powerful intercession, the Gospel
will penetrate the hearts of the men and women of America and permeate
their cultures, transforming them from within. (No. 70). . . . I therefore
invite all the Catholics of America to take an active part in the evangelizing
initiatives which the Holy Spirit is stirring in every part of this immense
continent, so full of resources and hopes for the future. . . . Our Lady of
Guadalupe, Mother of America, pray for us!" (No. 76).

The next day, he concluded his homily at the Basilica of Our Lady of
Guadalupe with a prayer, "Oh, Sweet Lady of Tepeyac, Mother of
Guadalupe! We present to you this countless multitude of faithful who
pray to God in America. You who have come into their hearts visit and
comfort all homes, parishes and dioceses of all the Continent."

Queen of America

Pope Pius XII proclaimed Our Lady's Queenship in 1954 in his encyclical
Ad Caeli Reginam (*To the Queen of Heaven*). He said, "Mary has
been made Queen of Heaven and earth by God, exalted above all the
choirs of angels and all the saints. She is to be called Queen not only
because of her divine motherhood, but also because she, by the will of
God, had an outstanding part in the work of our eternal salvation." She
was given the power by her Son "of bestowing upon us the fruits of the
redemption."

As the Second Vatican Council tells us, "Taken up to Heaven Our
Lady did not lay aside her saving role, but by her manifold acts of
intercession continues to win for us gifts of eternal salvation. (Vatican
Council II, *Dogmatic Constitution on the Church*, No. 62). So Our
Lady is busy working for us as the Mediatrix of All Graces, bestowing
upon us the fruits of the redemption and winning for us gifts of eternal
salvation. As our Queen and Mother, she helps to convert us, guide us,
heal us, protect us and save us.

Pope Pius XII decreed that the Feast of her Queenship be celebrated on May 31st (now August 22nd). He established this day as the day on which the consecration of mankind to her Immaculate Heart is to be renewed. In a 1955 radio message to Fatima he said, "Jesus is King throughout all eternity by nature and by right of conquest. Through Him, with Him and subordinate to Him, Mary is Queen by grace, by divine relationship, by right of conquest, and by singular election." He prophesied, "We are certain that as long as Our Lady of Guadalupe is recognized as Queen and as Mother, the Americas and Mexico will be safe."

Our Lady's Queenship reflects the characteristics of the Old Testament queens of Judah. The queen was not the king's wife but his mother. She occupied the throne at the right side of her son, had great influence upon him and a right to intervene in the king's affairs. (See 1 Kgs. 2:19).

On the Feast Day of Our Lady of Guadalupe, December 12, 1981, Pope John Paul II prayed to her, "Since you are the Empress of the Americas, protect all the nations of the American continent and the ones that brought faith and love for you there."

On another occasion he said, "Christians look with trust to Mary Queen and this exalts their filial abandonment to her, who is Mother in the order of grace. Mary's glorious state brings about a continuous and caring closeness. She is a queen who gives all that she possesses participating above all in the life and love of Christ."

In 1999 he said, "The Virgin of Guadalupe is venerated as Queen of all America." (Pope John Paul II, Apostolic Exhortation, *The Church in America,* No. 11). He consecrated the entire continent to her as our Queen and Mother. He also referred to her as the Mother of Hope.

Mother of Hope

In contrast to the Culture of Death with its loss of hope, Pope John Paul II called Our Lady of Guadalupe the "Mother of Hope." He did this at the historical First Synod of all of the Bishops of America in Rome in December 1998 that closed on the Feast Day of Our Lady of Guadalupe. "Now is the time," he said, "of the New Evangelization to lead the People of God in America to cross the threshold of the third millennium with renewed hope."

"It is my heartfelt hope that she, whose intercession was responsible for strengthening the faith of the first disciples (cf. Jn. 2:11), will by her maternal intercession guide the Church in America, obtaining the outpouring of the Holy Spirit, as she once did for the early Church (cf. Acts 1:14), so that the new evangelization may yield a splendid flowering of Christian life." ((Pope John Paul II, Apostolic Exhortation, *The Church in America*, No. 11).

Mary is the Mother of Hope. She is the Mother of Jesus Christ who is our hope as the conqueror of sin and death. As a people of hope, we are not afraid but look forward to the victory of good over evil; peace over war; truth over lies; equality over discrimination; love over hate and life over death. We look forward to eternal salvation and an existence full of happiness in God.

Hope is the confident expectation of divine blessing. (*Catechism of the Catholic Church*, No. 1818). Our Lady of Guadalupe told St. Juan Diego that she is the Mother "of all those who have confidence in me." Through her, we should have confidence in divine blessings – confidence that her intercession will bring a Culture of Life and a Civilization of Love in America in solidarity with the innocent unborn, the sick, the dying, the poor, the marginalized and the new immigrants. May there be saints for them! That is hope, the hope of Mother Cabrini who called the United States, "this vast field of Christian hope."

Shrine:

Shrine of Our Lady of Guadalupe
5250 Justin Road
LaCrosse, WI 54601
Website: www.guadalupeshrine.org

26. Our Lady of America, Hope for the States

When the Blessed Virgin Mary appeared in Mexico she revealed her title as "The Perfect Virgin, Holy Mary of Guadalupe." When Bishop Zumarraga first saw her miraculous image on St. Juan Diego's cloak he said, "It is the Immaculate One!" Similarly, the Blessed Virgin Mary appeared in the United States and revealed her title as "Our Lady of America, The Immaculate Virgin", another representation of the Immaculate Conception, the Patroness of the United States.

She appeared to a young nun in the United States in several apparitions during the latter half of the 20th century. The nun's name was Sister Mary Ephrem (Mildred Neuzil). She was born in Brooklyn, New York, on August 2, 1916. In 1929, she entered the Sisters of the Precious Blood at Rome City, Indiana. In 1959, she became a Contemplative of the Indwelling Trinity in Fostoria, Ohio. In 1938, she began to have mystical experiences that continued until her death in her convent on January 10, 2000 at the age of 83.

Our Lady revealed her title, her image and messages. Sister Mildred's spiritual director was Bishop Paul F. Leibold. He later became the Archbishop of Cincinnati, Ohio. Bishop Leibold had a medal struck of the image and, on January 25, 1963, he gave his Imprimatur for them. He also approved the printing of the messages and had two large plaques depicting Our Lady of America made and displayed, one in the Cincinnati Catholic Chancery.

In the course of approving the printing of the revelations to Sister Mary Ephrem, Bishop Leibold considered the Blessed Virgin Mary under the title, "Our Lady of America", as basically referring to her patronage over the United States of America and distinct from her title, "Empress of The

Americas", basically referring to her patronage over all of the nations of America as Our Lady of Guadalupe, as declared by Pope Pius XII in 1945.

On September 26, 1956, then the Feast of the North American Martyrs, the Blessed Virgin Mary appeared to Sister in a veil, robe and mantle of pure white as "Our Lady of America." She requested that Americans honor her by the purity of their lives. Our Lady promised that greater miracles than those granted at Lourdes and Fatima would be granted in the United States if the people responded to her requests.

Later that day, Our Lady came again and repeated the call to her children in America to dedicate their lives to her purity. She said,

> My child, I entrust you with this message that you must make known to my children in America. I wish it to be the country dedicated to my purity. The wonders I will work will be the wonders of the soul. They must have faith and believe firmly in my love for them. I desire that they be the children of my Pure Heart. I desire, through my children in America, to further the cause of faith and purity among peoples and nations. Let them come with confidence and simplicity, and I, their Mother, will teach them to become pure like to my Heart that their own hearts may be more pleasing to the Heart of my Son.

Sister Mildred said that Our Lady called herself "Our Lady of America" in response to the love and desire that reached out for this special title in the hearts of her children in America. This title is a sign of Our Lady's pleasure in the devotion of her children of America towards her, and this visit is a response to the longing, conscious or unconscious, in the hearts of her children in America.

Our Lady's Desire for the National Shrine

On November 15, 1956, Our Lady of America requested that a statue be made according to her likeness and that it be solemnly carried in procession and placed in the Basilica of the National Shrine of the Immaculate Conception in Washington, D.C. She wishes to be honored there in a special way as "Our Lady of America, the Immaculate Virgin."

Our Lady promised that the placement of her statue in the National Shrine would be a safeguard for our country, and the placement of her picture or statue in the home would be a safeguard for the family. She also promised that the medal would be a safeguard against evil for those who wear it with great faith and devotion.

Warning and Grace for the States

In April of 1957, Our Lady said, "Unless my children reform their lives, they will suffer great persecution. If man himself will not take upon himself the penance necessary to atone for his sins and those of others, God in His justice will have to send upon him the punishment necessary to atone for his transgressions."

Our Lady called on America to be a nation dedicated to her purity and to lead the world, by her special mandate, to true peace, to a reform of life so necessary to avoid the chastisement threatened by sin. She called for the renewal of the family and of religious life, giving strong exhortations to parents for spiritual leadership with their children and equally strong exhortations to priests and religious to live their consecrated lives in prayer and penance for sin, leading the faithful toward holiness by the example of their own lives. She revealed that the youth of America are challenged to be the leaders of this movement of renewal on the face of the earth and that they must be prepared for it by instilling in them the knowledge and study of the Divine Indwelling so that the Divine Presence becomes an intimate and necessary part of their life and daily living. Those who are willing wholeheartedly to follow her in her great battle against evil will bear the special title of "Torchbearers of the Queen," bearing the torch of Divine Love that will conquer hate.

On November 22, 1980, Our Lady said:

> Beloved daughter, the United States is a small one among nations, yet has it not been said that 'a little child shall lead them'? It is the United States that is to lead the world to peace, the peace of Christ, the peace that He brought with Him from Heaven in His birth as man in the little town of Bethlehem. . . .Dear child, unless the United States accepts and carries out faithfully the mandate given to it by Heaven to lead the world to

peace, there will come upon it and all nations a great havoc of war and incredible suffering. If, however, the United States is faithful to this mandate from Heaven and yet fails in the pursuit of peace because the rest of the world will not accept or co-operate, then the United States will not be burdened with the punishment about to fall.

On May 30, in 2006, the Franciscan Friars of The Immaculate displayed a statue of Our Lady of America at Our Lady of The Angels Monastery in Hanceville, Alabama. The Monastery was founded by Mother Angelica.

Bishop Richard Garcia of Sacramento said, "To have the enthronement of Our Lady of America statue is a timely testimony and reminder to us all of the blessing Our Lady is for all of us who live in the United States of America. Our Lady guides and protects us in this critical time of our history when we need to value even more closely what she as a mother has taught us: to hold Christ in the center of our lives; to value the family and its unity; to do the will of the Father and to evangelize by pointing others to Christ."

On November 13, 2006, a new statue of Our Lady of America was publicly displayed for the first time at the United States Conference of Catholic Bishops in their Concelebrated Mass Room in Baltimore, Maryland. (See page 292).

Raymond L. Burke, Archbishop of Saint Louis, requested the display of this statue at this conference for the benefit of the Bishops. On November 15th, 2006, Archbishop Burke blessed this new statue. This blessing occurred precisely on the 50th Anniversary of the request that Our Lady of America made on November 15, 1956, to be placed and honored in the Basilica of the National Shrine of the Immaculate Conception in Washington, D.C.

Archbishop Burke, a world renowned canon lawyer, stated that the devotion to Our Lady of America was canonically approved. In a letter dated May 31, 2007, he reviewed the prior history and then state of the devotion as well as the earlier actions of Archbishop Leibold approving the devotion. Archbishop Burke wrote, "What can be concluded canonically is that the devotion was both approved by Archbishop Leibold and, what is more, was actively promoted by him. In addition, over the years, other Bishops have approved the devotion and have participated in public devotion to the Mother of God, under the title of Our Lady of America."

The Immaculate Virgin

What did Our Lady of America mean when she referred to herself as the "Immaculate Virgin?" Pope Benedict XVI explained this title in a homily:

> What does "Mary, the Immaculate" mean? Does this title have something to tell us? The liturgy illuminates the content of these words for us in two great images.
>
> First of all comes the marvelous narrative of the annunciation of the Messiah's coming to Mary, the Virgin of Nazareth. The Angel's greeting is interwoven with threads from the Old Testament, especially from the Prophet Zephaniah. He shows that Mary, the humble provincial woman who comes from a priestly race and bears within her the great priestly patrimony of Israel, is "the holy remnant" of Israel to which the prophets referred in all the periods of trial and darkness. . . .
>
> In the humility of the house in Nazareth lived holy Israel, the pure remnant. God saved and saves his people. From the felled tree trunk Israel's history shone out anew, becoming a living force that guides and pervades the world. Mary is holy Israel: She says "yes" to the Lord, she puts herself totally at his disposal and thus becomes the living temple of God.
>
> The second image is much more difficult and obscure. This metaphor from the Book of Genesis speaks to us from a great historical distance and can only be explained with difficulty; only in the course of history has it been possible to develop a deeper understanding of what it refers to.
>
> It was foretold that the struggle between humanity and the serpent, that is, between man and the forces of evil and death, would continue throughout history. It was also foretold, however, that the "offspring" of a woman would one day triumph and would crush the head of the serpent to death; it was foretold that the offspring of the woman - and in this offspring the woman and the mother herself

- would be victorious and that thus, through man, God would triumph. . . .

What picture does this passage show us? The human being does not trust God. Tempted by the serpent, he harbors the suspicion that in the end, God takes something away from his life, that God is a rival who curtails our freedom and that we will be fully human only when we have cast him aside; in brief, that only in this way can we fully achieve our freedom. . . .

He himself wants to obtain from the tree of knowledge the power to shape the world, to make himself a god, raising himself to God's level, and to overcome death and darkness with his own efforts. He does not want to rely on love that to him seems untrustworthy; he relies solely on his own knowledge since it confers power upon him. Rather than on love, he sets his sights on power, with which he desires to take his own life autonomously in hand. And in doing so, he trusts in deceit rather than in truth and thereby sinks with his life into emptiness, into death. . . .

We live in the right way if we live in accordance with the truth of our being, and that is, in accordance with God's will. For God's will is not a law for the human being imposed from the outside and that constrains him, but the intrinsic measure of his nature, a measure that is engraved within him and makes him the image of God, hence, a free creature.

If we live in opposition to love and against the truth - in opposition to God - then we destroy one another and destroy the world. Then we do not find life but act in the interests of death. All this is recounted with immortal images in the history of the original fall of man and the expulsion of man from the earthly Paradise.

Dear brothers and sisters, if we sincerely reflect about ourselves and our history, we have to say that with this narrative is described not only the history of the beginning but the history of all times, and that we all carry within us a drop of the poison of that way of thinking, illustrated by the images in the Book of Genesis.

We call this drop of poison "original sin." Precisely on the feast of the Immaculate Conception, we have a lurking suspicion that a person who does not sin must really be basically boring and that something is missing from his life: the dramatic dimension of being autonomous; that the freedom to say no, to descend into the shadows of sin and to want to do things on one's own is part of being truly human; that only then can we make the most of all the vastness and depth of our being men and women, of being truly ourselves; that we should put this freedom to the test, even in opposition to God, in order to become, in reality, fully ourselves. . . .

If we look, however, at the world that surrounds us we can see that this is not so; in other words, that evil is always poisonous, does not uplift human beings but degrades and humiliates them. It does not make them any the greater, purer or wealthier, but harms and belittles them.

This is something we should indeed learn on the day of the Immaculate Conception: The person who abandons himself totally in God's hands does not become God's puppet, a boring "yes man"; he does not lose his freedom. Only the person who entrusts himself totally to God finds true freedom, the great, creative immensity of the freedom of good. . . .

The closer a person is to God, the closer he is to people. We see this in Mary. The fact that she is totally with God is the reason why she is so close to human beings. For this reason she can be the Mother of every consolation and every help, a Mother whom anyone can dare to address in any kind of need in weakness and in sin, for she has understanding for everything and is for everyone the open power of creative goodness. . . . As a merciful Mother, Mary is the anticipated figure and everlasting portrait of the Son. Thus, we see that the image of the Sorrowful Virgin, of the Mother who shares her suffering and her love, is also a true image of the Immaculate Conception. Her heart was enlarged by being and feeling together with God. In her, God's goodness came very close to us.

Mary thus stands before us as a sign of comfort, encouragement and hope. She turns to us, saying: "Have the courage to dare with God! Try it! Do not be afraid of him! Have the courage to risk with faith! Have the courage to risk with goodness! Have the courage to risk with a pure heart! Commit yourselves to God, then you will see that it is precisely by doing so that your life will become broad and light, not boring but filled with infinite surprises, for God's infinite goodness is never depleted!"

Let us thank the Lord for the great sign of his goodness which he has given us in Mary, his Mother and the Mother of the Church. Let us pray to him to put Mary on our path like a light that also helps us to become a light and to carry this light into the nights of history. Amen.

(Pope Benedict XVI, Papal Homily on the 40th Anniversary of Close of Vatican II, December 14, 2005).

On October 5, 1956, Sister Mildred felt a sudden urge to write a prayer to Mary. Although she did not hear any words, the thoughts came into her mind with such profundity; she could not stop until the beautiful Prayer to the Immaculate Conception was finished. This is the prayer:

Prayer to the Immaculate Conception

O Immaculate Mother, Queen of our Country, open our hearts, our homes, and our Land to the coming of Jesus, your Divine Son. With Him, reign over us, O Heavenly Lady, so pure and so bright with the radiance of God's light shining in and about you. Be our Leader against the powers of evil set upon wresting the world of souls, redeemed at such a great cost by the sufferings of your Son and of yourself, in union with Him, from that same Savior, Who loves us with infinite charity.

We gather about you, O chaste and holy Mother, Virgin Immaculate, Patroness of our beloved Land, determined to fight under your banner of holy purity against the wickedness that would make all the world an abyss of evil, without God and without your loving maternal care.

We consecrate our hearts, our homes, our Land to your Most Pure Heart, O great Queen, that the kingdom of your Son, our Redeemer and our God, may be firmly established in us.

We ask no special sign of you, sweet Mother, for we believe in your great love for us, and we place in you our entire confidence. We promise to honor you by faith, love, and the purity of our lives according to your desire.

Reign over us, then, O Virgin Immaculate, with your Son Jesus Christ. May His Divine Heart and your most chaste Heart be ever enthroned and glorified among us. Use us, your children of America, as your instruments in bringing peace among men and nations. Work your miracles of grace in us, so that we may be a glory to the Blessed Trinity, Who created, redeemed, and sanctifies us.

May your valiant Spouse, St. Joseph, with the holy Angels and Saints, assist you and us in "renewing the face of the earth." Then when our work is over, come, Holy Immaculate Mother, and as our Victorious Queen, lead us to the eternal kingdom, where your Son reigns forever as King. Amen.

Statue of Our Lady of America
For more information visit:
www.jkmi.com

Recommended General Reading

Brière, Fr. Emile-Marie, *Under Mary's Mantle*, (Combermere, Canada 2000)

Carroll, Warren H., *Our Lady of Guadalupe and the Conquest of Darkness*, (Front Royal, VA 1983)

Carroll, Warren H., *The Cleaving of Christendom*, (Front Royal, VA 2000)

Fisher, James T., *Communion of Immigrants*, (New York, NY 2000)

Habig, Rev. M.A., O.F.M., *Saints of the Americas*, (Huntington, IN 1974)

Johnson, Paul, *A History of Christianity*, (New York, NY 1976)

Johnson, Paul, *A History of the American People*, (New York, NY 1997)

Tylenda, Joseph N. editor, *Portraits in American Sanctity*, (Chicago, IL 1982)

Recommended Reading on Saints

Juan Diego
Lynch, Dan, *Our Lady of Guadalupe, Hope for the World*, (St. Albans, VT 2005)

Isaac Jogues, René Goupil and Jean de la Lande
Talbot, Francis, S.J., *Saint Among Savages,* (San Francisco, CA 1935, reprinted 2002)

Elizabeth Ann Seton
Dirvin, Joseph I., C.M., *Mrs. Seton, Foundress of the American Sisters of Charity,* (Emmitsburg, MD 1962; reprinted 1993)

Frances Xavier Cabrini
Di Donato, Pietro, *Immigrant Saint* (New York, NY 1960)

Rose Philippine Duchesne
Callan, Louise, *Rose Philippine Duchesne: Frontier Missionary of the Sacred Heart,* (Westminster, MD 1965; reprinted Society of the Sacred Heart United States Province 2002)

Theodore Guerin
Mitchell, Penny Blaker, *Mother Theodore Guerin: A Woman for Our Time,* (Saint Mary-of-the-Woods, Indiana 1998)

John Neumann
Curley, Michael J. C.S.S.R. *Bishop John Neumann C.SS.R..,* (Philadelphia, PA 1952)

Katherine Drexel
Duffy, Sister Consuela, S.B.S., *Katharine Drexel: A Biography,* (Bensalem, PA 1966)

Damien de Veuster
Farrow, John, *Damien the Leper,* (New York, NY 1937; reprinted 1998)

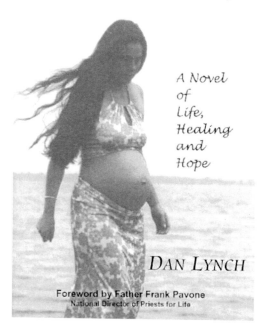

See the next page for a preview.

Order from page 327.

WE NEVER BONDED!

I looked down on my mother as she lay in a coma on her deathbed. I gently lifted my hand to her forehead and felt her taut and cool skin. I stroked her hair like she might have stroked mine while I slept as an infant. I heard the wissssh, whoosh *of her ventilator and smelled the distinctive antiseptic scent of her hospital room. Then I held her limp hand and said, "Hi Mom, it's me, Teresita. I'm home!" I began talking to her as if she were perfectly well and understood everything I was saying.*

I summoned all my courage and apologized for the past. "I'm sorry that I ran away. Please forgive me. I forgive you . . . I'm sorry that we never bonded with each other, and I'm sorry I never bonded with my son. . . . I had an abortion, Mom. . . ."

"The apple doesn't fall very far from the tree, does it? But it's never too late. You know, without that bond Mom—the special grace instilled in us mothers by God—there wouldn't be any continuation of the human race."

"It seems unnatural that the child should re-establish the bond with the mother, but that's what you and I need to do. We need to make peace with each other. We need to love one another. So as your daughter who really loves you, I'd like to restore the bond that we should have had all along."

I held her hand in both of mine and said, "I love you, Mom. Life is full of second chances. We can make up for our bad choices by making good ones. Let's make up for our estrangement by bonding NOW."

As I said this, she squeezed my hands. She had heard me, and she was responding to my love . . . at last. We were no longer estranged. I felt great relief . . . and then my tears began to flow.

One

R*aaah, erraaaaaaaaah!* The raucous and healthy cry of a newborn baby broke the expectant silence of the farmhouse bedroom. With joyful relief, the young mother laid back on the birthing bed. Her rugged husband smiled down on her and their new child with pride and tenderness. I quickly dried the little one off and asked, "What have we got here?"

"A girl!" the father yelled tearfully. I suctioned the baby's mouth and gently placed her near her mother's exposed breast. Her father cut the umbilical cord while caressing the baby's head. He was an experienced Vermont farmer who had helped birth many calves. Now he had assisted in delivering his own child. The mother gently guided the baby's searching mouth to her nipple and stared deeply into her eyes. Instant love!

It was early in the morning one day in August 2000, and I was a midwife performing my first delivery. While performing my professional duties, I couldn't help but notice the warm and wondrous intimacy that radiated from the little family as they celebrated this new life in the safety and comfort of their own home.

Soon feeling like a bit of an intruder, I limped off toward the bathroom to wash up. As I bent over the sink and looked into the mirror, I saw a young-looking, 32-year old woman. I looked tired from the long night birth vigil. My shoulder-length black hair, a bit disheveled, framed the cocoa brown face and bright blue eyes of a fourth generation Latina.

Reflected in the background of the mirror I could still see the young mother nursing her newborn. I always marveled at the sight of a nursing mother and child as they locked eyes with each other. I was reminded of the fact that humans were the only species in the animal kingdom that were designed so that mother and child could gaze at each other during the intimate act of nursing. I envied the bond being established between this mother and daughter – one which I had never known.

I took a deep breath, and I collected myself. Despite a tinge of regret because my own mother had never established such a bond with me, a soft smile formed on my lips. I was genuinely happy for this mother and child. But as the warm tap water rushed over my hands, I experienced the flash of a recurring memory—a silent scream that rose like mist from my earliest awareness. . . .

I am floating freely under water . . . like an underwater ballerina or a weightless astronaut. I bounce off the trampoline-like walls that closely surround me, somersaulting effortlessly. Then I rest and feel happy. But I sense another presence, someone very close.

Is someone else with me? It's dark . . . I can't see. I have this strong feeling that I'm not alone. But I'm not frightened. It seems that I have a companion—a friend nearby. I feel peace.

Suddenly, it seems like my water sanctuary is invaded. I sense aggression. I feel a cold fear. I get agitated. It seems as if something is searching for me. The water gets rough. I am in a vortex of chaos. My body is agitated like a washcloth in a washing machine on spin cycle. Instinctively, I try to swim away. But I can't.

I feel an incredible torrent of fluid rushing around me. It feels like I'm white-water rafting out of control. I'm terrified. I don't know what's happening to me.

I want to communicate my terror, but I can't. I scream but it's a silent scream—nobody can hear me. I am completely helpless. I can't help myself, and I can't help my friend. The sense of my friend's presence diminishes. Then there is only emptiness, a void. But it's quiet again. I feel sad that I was unable to help. I try to get to safety but my left leg is wrapped around my neck and I feel a newly experienced sensation—excruciating pain!

I still felt some pain in my left hip as I stood before that Vermont farmer's mirror years later. And I could still feel that emotional terror and the excruciating pain of my earliest memory that became a recurring nightmare for me. The cause of it remained unknown to me until I was 16 years old. It was then that my mother solved the mystery, but discovering the truth at last was both a relief and a painful shock.

I stared at myself in that mirror for what seemed like an eternity, facing my reflection with trepidation but also with courage. I resolved to head home to my own family, get some sleep, and finally finish writing the story of this memory. I had been at it on and off for over 12 years. Painful as it was, I felt morally obligated to provide hope for others. If even one person could learn from my choices and their consequences, I reasoned, the effort would be well worth it.

I left the smiling couple with their firstborn child and drove to my home in Burlington, Vermont. My husband, Miguel, and my two children, Lupe (pronounced Loo-pay) and Mickey happily greeted me. We lived in a large old farmhouse which we made into separate quarters for ourselves, my mother-in-law, and my retired father. We were one big and happy family now — but it wasn't always that way. Miguel watched the children while I took a nap. An hour later, I got up, refreshed, and sat right down at my computer, determined to finish my story.

On the advice of a lawyer who was representing me in a medical malpractice case, I began the process of putting my memories on paper in January of 1988. I was then 20 years old and living in Miami, Florida. He told me to write the whole story down, detailing my pain and suffering, so that I'd be prepared to answer the defense lawyers' questions in the pretrial depositions. I told him that I wasn't much of a writer, but I was willing to try in the hope that it would help our case and just maybe prevent someone else from going through the suffering that I had. Getting started was always difficult for me, and once I did start, I found it hard to keep at it for very long.

Then in the summer of 2000, something happened to move me to action. It was the national *Encuentro*—Meeting 2000. These Catholic meetings had always been exclusively for Latinos. But the Church decided to use the Latino leadership to open the *Encuentro* in 2000 to all races for the first time.

In his *Encuentro* homily, Boston's Cardinal Law confessed the errors of Church members in failing to recognize the equality of all men and women before God. The theme of the meeting was "The Many Faces in God's House," and in a beautiful tapestry of brown, white, black, red and yellow faces, the diverse children of God came together to tell their stories. I decided that it was now or never for me to show my face in God's House. At last, I was finally able to say, "This is *my* story."

You have just read the first chapter of Dan Lynch's novel, *Teresita's Choices*. To order this book and other Dan Lynch Productions, turn to page 327.

See the next page for a preview.
Order from page 327.

Foreword

The days of legalized abortion in America are numbered. This is true for many reasons, not the least of which is the story you will read in this book. It is a story of a mother concerned for the children, of a Virgin who accepts pregnancy and gives birth to God, of a woman who brings hope and ends bloodshed. It is a story of a Church responding to the call to give witness to the truth and preserve the very existence of civilization.

Abortion is not only a sin against life; it is a sin against hope. When the Aztecs practiced human sacrifice, they did so because they despaired of God's love. They thought they had to preserve themselves against the wrath of the gods. Into that world came the Virgin Mary of Guadalupe. She did not speak of a God who wanted to destroy, but rather of One who wanted to save and who, in fact, had become one of us in her womb. Despair turned to hope when the Aztecs realized that God was on their side.

Our Lady of Guadalupe continues to turn despair into hope in the hearts of all those who are afraid to welcome new life. She instructs them that God and His people are on their side. She helps them to see that the child is not the enemy, and that we find our deepest fulfillment precisely when we give ourselves away to others.

This book will instruct, encourage and inspire a wide variety of people in the Church and outside the Church. You may be a pro-life activist looking for signs of progress. You may be a priest seeking new ways to call your people to deeper faith. You may be a son or daughter of the Virgin Mary eager to find new ways to honor her. You may be someone considering abortion or wounded by it, and looking for hope. You may be away from the Church looking for a way back, or someone without any background in Catholicism but interested in finding out more. Whoever you are, give this book some of your time, and it will repay you abundantly.

Fr. Frank Pavone
National Director Priests for Life

Part One

The First Evangelization

1. The Aztec Culture of Death

Imagine yourself as an Indian prisoner of the Aztecs in 16th century Mexico. You and your fellow prisoners have been slowly moving like cattle since dawn in one of four single-file lines, each of which stretches up to five miles long. The four lines lead to the four sides of a pyramid temple 130 feet high.

You hear the incessant beat of big snake-skinned drums. As you approach the temple base, you raise your eyes towards the top. You see 114 bloodstained steps and bloodied dead bodies cascading down them towards you. At the top, you see Aztec priests with never-cut long hair, matted in dried blood, clenching knives in their bloodstained hands.

You see them arch the backs of your fellow prisoners over four small stone altars, slice open their chests and rip out their still-beating hearts. One person is killed every fifteen seconds. The stench of death is unbearable.

You hear the jaguars in the zoo roaring in anticipation of eating whatever body parts are not eaten by the Aztecs themselves. You see the bloodied hearts burnt in human sacrifice in front of the Aztec idols. You await your fate without hope. Soon it will be your turn to be killed.

Satan had much influence over the Aztecs in 16th century Mexico. Before the Spanish Conquest, the Aztec natives practiced human sacrifice on the greatest scale in the history of the world. In 1487, Tlacaellel, the 89-year old Aztec leader of human sacrifice, dedicated a new temple pyramid in the center of Tenochtitlan, now Mexico City. The temple was dedicated to the false god, Huitzilopochtli, called the "Lover of Hearts and Drinker of Blood." More than 80,000 men were sacrificed over a period of four days and four nights in a horrific satanic ritual with the copious flow of blood and piles of dead bodies.

The Aztec Empire extended from the Gulf of Mexico to the Pacific Ocean and south to Guatemala. Their capital of Tenochtitlan was one of the largest and most beautiful cities in the entire world. The Aztecs had advanced far in mathematics, astronomy and architecture, but they had not advanced in virtue. This was because they still practiced the horror of human sacrifice to their grotesque stone idols. Huitzilopochtli, god of war, was their principal false god. Coatlicue was their Earth Mother goddess. Around the neck of this horrific idol was a necklace of hands and hearts. The Aztec priests ripped out the hearts of their victims, threw them into the vase at the top of the idol's skull and ate the other body parts.

The Aztecs had a pantheon of false gods and a complicated mythology. They also worshiped heavenly bodies as gods such as Tonatiuh, god of the sun, Tezcatlipoca, "the god of Hell and Darkness" and Quetzalcoatl, the feathered serpent, god of agriculture. Pyramids were built in their honor in the huge plaza at the center of Tenochtitlan. The priests placated the gods by offering them human victims in an idolatrous attempt to attract benign forces such as the sun and rain; to bring victories in war and to avoid disasters. They believed that these sacrifices were indispensable for the life of the world and the continuance of the rising of the sun. At least 50,000 victims were sacrificed to these idols each year. One out of every five children was sacrificed. It was a world without hope.

Prior to these abominations, God had planted seeds of the gospel in Mexico. In the late 10th century, a good priest-king lived in Tula named Ce Acatl Topiltzin Quetzalcoatl. He should not be confused with Quetzalcoatl the false god. He was considered a great teacher and benefactor of his people. He taught that the true God was of light, not darkness and that He wanted men to live and not to be slain in His name.

Quetzalcoatl taught that human sacrifice was wrong. Because of this he was exiled and sailed to the East, but he prophesied that he would return on April 22, 1519 and usher in a new age.

Later, in the late 15th century, Netzahualcoyotl, King of Texcoco, followed the beliefs of Quetzalcoatl. He reasoned that there had to be only one Supreme God. He built temples to the one true God whom he called "The God Through Whom We Live." He offered sacrifices of flowers and incense at these temples and not bloody sacrifice. He also taught his people to long for Quetzalcoatl's return. Shortly before he died, he made a great speech and prophesied, "How deeply I regret that I am not able to understand the will of the great God, but I believe the time will come when He will be known and adored by all the inhabitants of this land." That time soon came through the discovery of Christopher Columbus.

You have just read the first chapter of Dan Lynch's book, *Our Lady of Guadalupe, Hope for the World.* To order this book and other Dan Lynch Productions, turn to page 327.

Our Lady of Guadalupe, Hope for the World. This **book** will instruct, encourage and inspire a wide variety of people in the Church and outside the Church. It explains the history of the miraculous image of Our Lady of Guadalupe and its continued relevance for our own day.

Foreword by Father Frank Pavone, National Director, Priests for Life.

Our Lady of Guadalupe, Mother of Hope! In this **video**, see and hear from Guadalupe experts and the Pope in Mexico with the Mother of Hope.

Reviews by producers Ted Flynn, Tom Petrisko, Drew Mariani and Ignatius Press say: "Stirring, gripping, comprehensive with moving testimonies!"

Our Lady of America, Our Hope for the States. The devotion to Our Lady of America is the only canonically approved devotion that is based upon apparitions of Our Lady in the United States. This is the ONLY BOOK OF ITS KIND!

Teresita's Choices. If you want to know the truth about the consequences of real choices for pre-marital sex and abortion, you should read this **book**!

If you want to know the truth about the consequences of respect for life and the dignity of all human beings of all races from conception until natural death, you should read this book.